£9·95

D1421928

*Gendered jobs and
social change*

Gendered jobs and social change

Rosemary Crompton and Kay Sanderson

London
UNWIN HYMAN
Boston   Sydney   Wellington

Published by the Academic Division of
Unwin Hyman Ltd
15/17 Broadwick Street, London W1V 1FP, UK

Unwin Hyman Inc.,
8 Winchester Place, Winchester, Mass. 01890, USA

Allen & Unwin (Australia) Ltd,
8 Napier Street, North Sydney, NSW 2060, Australia

Allen & Unwin (New Zealand) Ltd in association with the
Port Nicholson Press Ltd,
Compusales Building, 75 Ghuznee Street, Wellington 1, New Zealand

First published in 1990

British Library Cataloguing in Publication Data

Crompton, Rosemary
Gendered jobs and social change
1. Sex-typed occupations
I. Title   II. Sanderson, Kay
306.36

ISBN 0-04-445597-6
ISBN 0-04-445596-8

Library of Congress Cataloging in Publication Data

Data applied for

Typeset in 10/11 point Bembo by Fotographics (Bedford) Ltd
and printed in Great Britain by Billing and Sons, London and Worcester

Contents

List of figures

List of tables

Acknowledgements

The empirical research reported in this book has been carried out over several years and received funding from a number of sources. The initial work on professional qualifications amongst women was assisted by a number of small grants from the Equal Opportunities Commission, the University of East Anglia, and the Economic and Social Research Council (G00232169). In 1985, a further ESRC grant was made available under the Social Change and Economic Life Initiative (G13250008). The Joseph Rowntree Memorial Trust also made an award for the study of 'Women professionals and part-time work'. We are grateful to all of these bodies, and further to the University of East Anglia which gave the study leave without which this book could not have been written. Kay Sanderson worked at UEA as a research officer for nearly four years between 1984 and 1988. From June 1988 she has been working with the Norwich Women's Enterprise and Employment Training Unit. Rosemary Crompton, therefore, has been responsible for the writing of this book.

We would like to thank all of those women and men who co-operated with the empirical research. There are too many to mention as individuals but, should any of them chance to read this book, we hope they will be satisfied with the representation of the information and opinions they shared with us. Other members of the SCEL Initiative also made available their help and advice and we would like to thank John Lovering and, in particular, Kate Purcell for help and support. Alison Scott, Alan Warde, and Kate Purcell read the first draft of the manuscript and I am grateful for their comments. Finally, Hazel Taylor processed both draft and final manuscript, and her interest, speed and accuracy have been much appreciated.

Rosemary Crompton
University of East Anglia 1989

1 Men's work, women's work: some theoretical issues

Introduction

One of the characteristics of industrial capitalist society is that most production for the market is organized away from the domestic unit. In the western world a sexual division of labour gradually achieved predominance during the eighteenth, nineteenth and twentieth centuries when men in households went 'out to work', whilst women assumed the major responsibility for production of non-marketed goods and services within the household (Mann, 1986). Young, unmarried women might go 'out to work' before taking on full household responsibilites, and the never-married might remain in paid employment for an extended period. They would, however, be considered unfortunate – as indeed they often were. The wages available to women would not, on the whole, enable them to be self-supporting, and women lacking male protection or inherited wealth have been driven to circumstances ranging from genteel poverty to prostitution.

Since the Second World War, however, the employment statistics of industrial societies have all shown an increase in the proportion of married women going 'out to work' (OECD, 1985). Much of this book develops a sociological account of the postwar increase in paid employment amongst women in Britain. The rate of women's employment has been increasing within a social context that has included the growth of 'neo' or 'second-wave' feminism and the extension of legal 'citizenship' rights for women, and an academic context that has included a sustained, self-consciously feminist, critique of 'malestream' sociology – particularly in the area of social stratification.

Social stratification describes the division of societies into hierarchical groups or strata. Stratification theory seeks to explore the principles upon which these divisions rest. Following Weber, a distinction is frequently drawn between stratification deriving from differences in social honour, or status, and that deriving from different life chances in the market, or class (Gerth and Mills, 1948). Thus class and stratification are closely linked, but not identical, concepts. However, it is a common practice to describe elements within a hierarchical ordering as classes, signifying the division of a population into unequally rewarded groups. In contemporary societies, the occupational structure is frequently employed to perform this exercise – as in, for example, the Registrar General's class scheme, or the ABCD categories of psephologists and market research agencies. 'Class' has also been used as an abstract concept to describe a social force which has the capacity to transform society, a perspective most closely associated with Marx's analysis of capitalism (Marx and Engels, 1962). However, because class in Marx's work also gives an account of exploitation, the concept obviously has considerable significance for explanations of material inequalities as well.

The concept of class, therefore has a variety of meanings. No single one of these may be designated as 'correct' (or 'incorrect'); rather, they are more or less appropriate to the task at hand. However, it will be argued that a failure to specify the particular meaning of class under discussion has been a major source of confusion in arguments concerning the relationship between gender and class.

One of the aims of this chapter, therefore, is to clear away some of the undergrowth surrounding the issue of gender and class, which has become rather entangled. This is not, however, simply in the interests of tidiness or sociological good housekeeping. It will be suggested that the debates in question reflect underlying theoretical tensions and issues in the social sciences which have yet to be resolved. These relate first, to the dichotomy of 'structure' versus 'action', which has been extensively discussed in contemporary sociology as the 'duality' of social structures (Giddens, 1984); and second, a continuing tension between 'material' and 'normative' (or 'idealist') explanations in sociology (Mann, 1979). Furthermore, it will be argued that particular developments within an important empirical tradition in sociological class analysis – the construction of theoretical schemes which section the division of labour into classes – have been counter-productive as far as our understanding of gender is concerned.

This chapter will also briefly discuss the concept of patriarchy, which has been widely canvassed as an explanation of the prevailing division of labour between men and women. Finally, the methodological implications of this discussion of class, gender and patriarchy will be examined.

Gender and Class Theory

As indicated above, the concept of class has a number of different meanings in sociology. Its relationship to gender will initially be discussed in respect of two related uses; first, the idea of classes as social forces having an impact upon historical development, and second, the idea of class as an ensemble of positions or places – that is, the 'class structure'. The idea of classes as social forces is associated, above all, with a Marxist perspective: 'the history of all hitherto existing society is the history of class struggles' (*The Communist Manifesto*). Classes and class conflicts are seen as the driving force of history. The bourgeoisie had assumed a revolutionary role in the transition from feudalism to capitalism, and the proletariat was emerging as the revolutionary class of capitalist society. Although Marx never provided a satisfactory definition of precisely what he meant by 'class' (or to put it another way, he never operationalized the concept), it cannot be seriously argued that class was not central to Marx's work as a whole.

However, it is not only Marxists who have seen classes as important social forces in historical change and development. Although Weber clearly disputes the *inevitability* of class action, he does not question that it may occur: ' "classes" are not communities; they merely represent possible, and frequent, bases for communal action.' (Gerth and Mills, 1948, p. 181). Similarly, an influential theorist who has worked within what may be broadly described as a neo-Weberian class framework suggests that ' "communal" and "corporate" social interactions of a class or status kind constitute more or less systematic properties of total societies' (Lockwood, 1986, p. 11).

Although there are considerable differences between Marxist and Weberian class theorists, and they should not be minimized, both groups would agree that industrial societies are characterized by the emergence of collectivities – classes – structured in economic/production relationships, which have the potential to generate considerable conflict and may be the cause of far-reaching changes.

At the level of these abstract collectivities, class theories are gender blind. Marxists would argue, for example, that capitalism is indifferent to the kind of labour it exploits, and can co-opt whatever extra-economic oppressions (such as gender) as are historically and culturally available. Indeed, bourgeois ideology, given its emphasis on the rights of the individual, runs counter to structured social discrimination deriving from specific characteristics such as sex (Eisenstein, 1981). Wood has summarized the situation recently as one of a paradoxical combination of 'structural indifference to, indeed pressure against, this extra-economic inequality, and a kind of systemic opportunism which allows capitalism to make use of it' (1988, p. 8). Lockwood's defence of stratification theory against feminist critics develops a parallel argument. He asks whether societies 'can be differentiated according to the predominance of gender relations, that is, structures of social action comparable to those within the range of class polarization and status-group consolidation' (1986, p. 12), and concludes that 'outside the pages of Lysistrata', they cannot be. Women, as women, have not organized themselves *systematically* in opposition to men except in relatively short-term, issue-centred campaigns such as the suffrage movement.

Thus gender blindness is not a substantive criticism of either Marxist or Weberian class theory in the abstract. Although it is true that capitalism has built upon and may in some circumstances reinforce the oppression of women (Lown, 1983), it is also the case that a society lacking gender oppression could still be capitalist – there is no specific structural necessity for gender oppression in capitalism. Sex has not, historically, constituted the basis of a structure of social action similar to that of a class or status group, although this should not be allowed to obscure the fact that men have combined to exclude women, and women to resist these practices (Walby, 1988). It is true that neither Marxist nor Weberian class theory throws much light on the explanation of gender oppression, but this was not what either of them was designed to achieve.

However, the political focus of second-wave feminism in the 1960s – captured in the statement 'the personal is the political' – created a milieu in which the failure of abstract class theory to explain the oppression of women was perceived as a manifestation of a more general intellectual sexism. Thus considerable effort was devoted both to attempts to extend class theory in order to explain the oppression of women – as in, for example, the domestic labour debate (Seccombe, 1974), and to develop class-independent explanations of gender oppression focusing on the concept of patriarchy. These arguments contributed to a long-running dispute about the ultimate determinants of gender inequality – that is, 'class first' versus 'patriarchy first' arguments.

There are good political reasons for engaging in this debate which may be briefly summarized: is women's oppression explained by their specific relationship to the predominant mode of production? In which case women should associate themselves with other oppressed groups (classes) to work for the revolutionary transformation of the mode of production (society) itself. Or is the primary axis of exploitation in society that of men over women, in which case it is men who are the 'main enemy' (Delphy, 1977) as far as women are concerned? Although these are political questions, they are not irrelevant to sociology. However, they are not central to the sociological, in contrast to the political, enterprise.[1] As both Wood and Lockwood have argued, albeit from rather different perspectives, class theory is about *class*, not gender. The gender-blindness of abstract class theory, it may be argued, is not fatal to the theoretical approach of either Marx or Weber. Some contemporary analyses which use 'class' as an analytical concept (for example, Lash and Urry, 1987) may be similarly defended. However, this is not the case as far as empirical class schemes, whether derived from Marxist and/or Weberian approaches, are concerned.

Two examples will be examined: Wright's neo-Marxist social class scheme, and Goldthorpe's neo-Weberian occupational class classification. Both authors are explicit that their class schemes are theoretical rather than descriptive – in contrast to the occupational aggregations of the Registrar General or consumer researchers. The 'theoretical' emphasis of both authors is reflected in the fact that they each use their class schemes in order to carry out theoretical work (as they define it). Wright is concerned to explore the validity of Marx's theory of society and historical change. As a self-identified Marxist, his approach is a sympathetic one, and his class scheme has been developed with explicit reference to Marxist class theory (Wright 1980, 1985; Wright and Martin, 1987). Goldthorpe, in contrast, has not been concerned to demonstrate the validity of Marx's class theory but rather, following Popper, to subject propositions derived from it to the test of falsification (Goldthorpe, 1988). Such testing requires an empirical measure of social class. In Goldthorpe's case, however, the theory informing the construction of the scheme is closer to that of Weber than to Marx.

Wright's initial strategy in the drawing of a Marxist class map transposed relationships identified at the system level on to the division of labour in a straightforward manner. Individuals were identified as 'bourgeois', 'managers', 'proletariat', 'small employers', 'semi-autonomous employees' and 'petty bourgeois'.[2] These individuals are located in groups ('classes') according to their relationship to property and the forces of production.

This approach to the empirical generation of classes does not differ, in essence, from that of Goldthorpe's neo-Weberian class scheme. Goldthorpe writes: 'one could say that class analysis begins with a structure of positions, associated with a specific historical form of the division of labour' (1983, p. 467). This division of labour is constituted, first, by basic employment relationships and second, by 'varying employment functions and conditions of employment which differentiate categories of employee' (ibid.). This approach generates a seven-fold occupational class schema which collapses into 'service', 'intermediate', and 'working' classes. In respect of 'employment functions and conditions of employment', occupations are allocated to a class using Lockwood's concepts of 'work' and 'market' situation. Goldthorpe's class categories, like Wright's, are gender-blind, and within this framework, as Lockwood has argued, 'it is the position of an occupation within some hierarchy of authority that is decisive for its status and not the sex of the person who happens to be in it' (Lockwood, 1986, p. 21).

Thus the central focus of both Wright's and Goldthorpe's operationalization of social class is paid employment. Although neither scheme simply replicates the occupational hierarchy, there are nevertheless close parallels between them and occupational classifications (for example, that of the Registrar General).

In a capitalist market society, relations of production, and the operation of market forces, will both be significant elements in the structuring of occupations. However, the division of labour in the public sphere as a *whole* is composed of a myriad of inputs of which capitalist relations of production and market forces are only two, albeit important, factors. The impact of both market forces and production relationships will be mediated by other factors which may not be strictly 'economic', and amongst the most important of these will be gender. The sexual division of labour, in both the 'public' and 'private' spheres, is probably the most universal form of the division of labour, although its precise nature is subject to considerable variation (Stacey, 1981).

A broad distinction between men's work in the public sphere and women's work in the private has already been drawn, and public sphere work is further divided by gender. Occupational segregation reflects this division of labour; men are concentrated into 'men's' occupations, women, into 'women's'. Gender affects not only what kinds of jobs people do, but also the kinds of rewards accruing to the occupation in question. Lockwood is in a strict sense correct when he argues that it is the position of an occupation, rather than the sex of the individual, which is the determinant of the status of the incumbent, but the status of the *occupation* will often have been decisively influenced by gender. This is noticeable, for example, in respect of a number of 'caring' professions which developed initially as all-female occupations – for example, nursing, speech therapy, physiotherapy, etc. The levels of qualification and length of training required for such occupations are equivalent to non sex-stereotyped and/or 'male' occupations such as pharmacy or dentistry, which are ranked higher. Another example would be secretarial work, which developed within clerical work as a female speciality associated with shorthand and typing. This work has since its emergence had lower returns, and poorer prospects, than clerical work in general.

These criticisms raise more general questions about the empirical investigation of 'social class' using theoretical schema derived from the division of labour. Gender is not the only other factor, in addition to class relationships, structuring the division of labour in any particular society. As well as market and production relations, there are individual attributes such as ethnicity or age, and societal factors, including the presence or absence of natural resources and variations in climate; political factors such as state support for key industries and expenditure on welfare services, as well as the strength – or otherwise – of trade unions and occupational associations. In short, however, social class has been defined theoretically (that is, with reference to production, ownership, and/or market forces), it is not possible, empirically, to study the 'classes' so defined in isolation from the other factors which structure the occupational division of labour as a whole.

This argument has been demonstrated empirically in a recent study which has analysed data from a randomly selected national sample of 1770 men and women using the class schemes of Wright, Goldthorpe, and the Registrar General (Marshall *et al.*, 1988). Individuals were classified according to Wright's scheme on the basis of a battery of questions devised to identify their location within the social relations of production. However, Marshall *et al.* found that factors irrelevant to Wright's definition of class had the effect of persistently confounding attempts to measure it. His measure of work autonomy, for example, produced van drivers, caretakers and hospital orderlies, who were categorized as 'semi-autonomous' workers, 'intermediate' between the proletariat and the petty bourgeoisie (Marshall *et al.*, pp. 52, 53). This occurred because the degree of an individual's work autonomy is a function of both locale and the hours during which the work is performed, as well as the worker's relationship to capital. Wright (1985) also suggests that the probable work trajectories of the incumbent will have to be added to structural location as a determinant of an individual's 'class position' – and, as Marshall *et al.* argue, the trajectory will clearly be affected by non-class factors such as gender, and ethnic origin. Wright's treatment of the location of women within the class structure is cavalier but consistent. His approach is methodologically individualistic; 'class consciousness', for example, is identified as 'a particular aspect of the concrete subjectivity of human individuals' (Wright, 1985, p. 243). Thus for

practical purposes, individuals have a 'class situation' when they are
engaged in some kind of production relations (or are 'economically
active'), and the same criteria are used to locate women in the 'class
structure' as men. In a recent discussion of class identity amongst
women, Wright develops his original approach and draws a
distinction between 'direct' class relations embodied in employment,
property ownership, and so on, and those which are 'mediated'
through other relationships – as in, for example, the conjugal unit
(Wright, 1989). This strategy is to be welcomed as an attempt to
incorporate the domestic sphere into the project of class analysis, but
does not deal with the fundamental problem which the impact of
gender on the occupational structure presents for class schemes
grounded in the occupational division of labour.

Goldthorpe's scheme was judged by Marshall *et al.* to be superior
to that of Wright as an empirical measure in that it did not create the
occupational anomalies which produced implausibly high numbers
of managers and supervisors within the class structure (Marshall *et
al.*, p. 94; see also Wright and Martin, 1987). However, they are
critical of Goldthorpe's exclusion of women from empirical class
analysis. The rationale of their criticism has parallels with the
argument being developed here. Their comparison of individual male
and female (relative) rates of social mobility within the (occupational)
class structure demonstrated that men's opportunities were far
superior to women's. This was because men's upward mobility was
(and is) facilitated by women's lack of, or downward, mobility. As
they argue, in this instance, 'Classes and class phenomena are
conditioned by the peculiar pattern of women's participation
(however intermittent) in the market for paid labour . . . class
structures, and the market processes behind them are . . . "gendered" '
(Marshall *et al.*, 1988, pp. 73, 83).

This recent research, therefore, provides a clear demonstration of
the impossibility of measuring class in isolation from other factors
structuring the division of labour. Marshall *et al.* make it clear that,
in their view, gender should be included within the framework of
class analysis: 'People are distributed to places through time according
to processes that are powerfully shaped by gender. The structuring
of opportunities . . . is . . . a legitimate part of the subject matter for
a class analysis' (ibid., p. 84).

However, as we have seen, other factors also enter into this
'structuring of opportunities': race, region and nationality to name
but a few. If gender is 'allowable', why not these other factors?

In Goldthorpe's work, the problem of gender is not separable from
that of the proper unit of class analysis – that is, whether it should be

the individual or the household. In practice, Wright's class analysis is individualistic and straightforward – individuals are aggregated into classes on the basis of their common class properties. For Goldthorpe, however, patterns of social mobility are crucial in determining whether classes have emerged:

> For any [such] structure of positions, the empirical question can [then] be raised of how far classes have formed within it, in the sense of specific social collectivities; that is, collectivities that are identifiable through the degree of continuity which, in consequence of patterns of class mobility and immobility, their members have been associated with particular sets of positions over time. (Goldthorpe, 1983, p. 467)

The class location of the family is clearly central to whether mobility (or lack of it) can be said to have occurred. Two related problems, as far as the class position of women is concerned, are immediately apparent. First, is it legitimate to assume that members of the same conjugal unit share the same 'life-chances'? (Delphy and Leonard, 1986). Second, where more than one member of the unit is economically active, which individual's class situation should determine that of the conjugal unit? Goldthorpe has provoked a lively debate by arguing that, where a male 'head of household' is present, his 'class situation' should determine that of the household (Goldthorpe, 1983, 1984; Heath and Britten, 1984; Stanworth, 1984).

The solution advanced by Marshall *et al.* to this problem is essentially a practical one. They argue that different class measures are appropriate for different 'levels' of analysis – the individual in the labour market, as well as the household:

> Social classes comprise neither families nor individuals but individuals in families. It is for this reason, therefore, that the study of class is properly conducted at different levels of analysis. In this way the collective effects of women's limited access to economic and political power on the reproduction of positions within the structure can be explained, as well as the complex determination of life-chances accruing to individuals in conjugal units. (Marshall *et al.*, 1988, p. 85)

A similar strategy is advocated by another team of empirical researchers who use Wright's class scheme. Duke and Edgell (1987) propose that individual-level investigations into production-based behaviour and attitudes should include both men and women as individuals, whilst empirical studies of consumption behaviour and attitudes should use a measure of 'household class', which is a product of the class situation of (male and female) household members. In short, different class measures are appropriate to different research situations.

It is entirely reasonable that empirical research into occupational class should treat the problem as one concerning the validity of the research instrument; that is, its appropriateness to the problem in question. However, there are underlying issues which are left unresolved. The theoretical class schemes of both Wright and Goldthorpe have been devised in order to produce, as a consequence of their application to the division of labour in the public sphere, *classes*. Both Goldthorpe and Wright are methodological individualists, but each would claim to have identified not mere statistical aggregates, but classes. As such, these classes have collective interests. As we have seen, Wright derives individual consciousness from supposed interests in a straightforward manner. As Goldthorpe would wish to avoid imputations of 'historicism'[3] (that is, the suggestion that there is any law-like order in class development) he is more cautious. Nevertheless, in respect of the 'service class', for example, he argues that its members will seek to 'use the superior resources that they possess in order to *preserve* their positions of relative social power and advantage' (Goldthorpe, 1982, p. 180, emphasis in original).

The thorny – and perennial – question of the nature and existence of class consciousness has often been used to criticize the kind of class analysis which has been developed by Wright and Goldthorpe. For example, Hindess (1987) has used the apparent failure of classes to develop an appropriate 'consciousness' (as well as the failure of class analysis satisfactorily to accommodate the 'woman question'), as evidence to support his more general critique of class theorizing. He argues that class theory cannot escape the problem of reductionism: the assumption that, in the last instance, social phenomena (in this case, the position of women), may somehow be 'reduced to' classes. Class analysis *asserts* the existence of a link between structural location and class interests, rather than demonstrating its existence. As we have seen, in the arguments of Wright and Goldthorpe, structural location is given by placement within a class scheme.[4] The classes so defined do not, argues Hindess, in themselves have any mechanisms for formulating and reaching decisions, therefore they cannot be said to 'act'. Thus any reference to classes as actors is 'allegorical at best', and:

> To the extent that such spurious actors and their supposed interests are called upon to perform an explanatory role, they thoroughly obscure investigation of the conditions in question and political decisions as to what can be done to change them. (Hindess, 1987, p. 124)

A parallel, although not identical, argument is developed by Holmwood and Stewart (1983). They argue that stratification theory separates the different factors affecting structural location, and then develops different explanations for different types of factor. This, they suggest, is an expression of the *failure* of the original theory (or theories). For example the theory of 'empty places', or a structure of 'class positions' as developed by Wright fails as a theory of social experience and consciousness. Structural location (class position), it has often been argued, fails to result in the development of class consciousness because of the contradictions of experience – class experience, for instance, might be 'overlaid' by gender (or other cultural norms and values such as those of religion). Holmwood and Stewart, however, regard the persistence of such 'contradictions' as examples of the explanatory failure of the existing class theory, and call for the development of a new theory in social science which does not separate structural position from the individual's experience of it.

Although these critiques might initially appear persuasive, and would strike a responsive chord in any investigator sensitive to the complexities raised by the question of women and class analysis, they do not take us very far. The integrated theory which Holmwood and Stewart call for has yet to be developed, and the logic of Hindess's position leads to a perspective on history and politics which is both random and contingent: 'Not only is there no absolute determination, there are no determinate conditions, possibilities, relations, limits, pressures. Anything – or nothing – goes' (Wood, 1986, p. 85).

In the absence of a theoretical resolution, some progress may nevertheless be achieved through a brief exploration of sociological discussions of class action, and the relationship between 'structure' and 'action' more generally.

In a class society, class is assumed to provide a basis for action. The assumption is made that society has an impact on behaviour, as in the familiar sociological model of structure → consciousness → action. As we have seen, the supposed failure of class identity (and thus consciousness) to develop has been used in arguments against the significance of class as an explanatory concept, and to dispute the existence of a class structure as such. In particular, Marxist theories have been subjected to extensive sociological criticism on the grounds that a perspective which perceives human consciousness as somehow determined by structural position leaves out of account any role for the human actor, and sensuous human beings are reduced to the mere 'bearers' of structural capacities. Thus the action frame of reference has been developed, which stresses the significance of the *individual's* interpretation of his or her structural location.[5] Within this perspective, class is regarded as only one of the factors which an individual might (or might not) incorporate in developing his or her identity and consciousness (Pahl and Wallace, 1988).

The action frame of reference questioned the extent to which humans were and are 'structural dopes' but did not fundamentally question that a structure existed. However, from the late 1960s onwards, there developed within sociology an emphasis on the phenomenological tradition in social theory which, in its emphasis on the centrality of the subject (or actor) virtually denied the existence of the object (or structure). In this version of sociology, classes disappeared altogether. These arguments reflected the relative failure to resolve fundamental dualisms in the social sciences, manifest in the persisting tension between those who would take a broadly positivist approach to the social sciences (and adopt a natural science model of sociology), and the interpretative or hermeneutic approach, which would draw a radical distinction between the social and natural sciences. It is a dangerous matter for a sociologist to raise these methodological problems. In so doing, he or she runs the risk of being deflected, by intractable philosophical questions, away from empirical research which might enhance our sociological understanding.[6]

It will be argued, therefore, that the problems of dualism may be avoided at the empirical level by taking on board Gidden's suggestion that dualism is reconceptualized as duality – the duality of structure. As a first step, one may add a feedback loop to the sociological model introduced earlier, that is, → *structure* → *consciousness* → *action*. More formally, this process has been described as 'structuration'.

Giddens' (1984) account of structuration revolves around a well-known statement by Marx' which, suitably amended, reads as:

> Men and women make their own history, but they do not make it under circumstances chosen by themselves, but under circumstances directly encountered, given, and transmitted from the past. (K. Marx: Eighteenth Brumaire of Napoleon Bonaparte)

This 'duality' of the structure is defined by Giddens as follows:

> Structure [is] the medium and outcome of the conduct it recursively organises; the structural properties of social systems do not exist outside of action but are chronically implicated in its production and reproduction. (Giddens, 1984, p. 374)

That is, what people do always presupposes some kind of pre-existing structure (rules of behaviour, resources, etc.), but in what they do, people simultaneously create the structure anew. This appreciation of the duality of structure is a first step towards the recognition of the fact that the dualisms and theoretical dichotomies which pervade social science are not, in the last instance, particularly helpful. Empirical sociology has to recognize that both structure and action are bound together and investigations focusing upon only one or the other are likely to be deficient. [7]

The close association in sociology between the structure/action dichotomy and debates about social class is not difficult to comprehend. As we have seen, structural location (or 'class position') is held to explain action and, indeed, there are many common-sense manifestations of this basic sociological insight. (Occupational class has been empirically associated with actions as various as voting behaviour (Heath *et al.*, 1985); child-rearing patterns (Newsom and Newsom, 1963); language use (Bernstein, 1971) and so on.) It has not been an object of the argument developed here to deny the utility of occupational class as an explanatory variable in investigations of this kind. However, the claim that these kinds of measures may satisfactorily resolve major issues in class analysis or theory (for example, the question of proletarianization) is more difficult to justify for, as we have seen, it is not possible to identify classes within the division of labour which are uncontaminated by other, non-class, factors (Crompton, 1988a). Moreover, it may be suggested that the sustained defence of the *theoretical* validity of such class schemes has been a factor inhibiting the investigation of the impact which the changing pattern of women's employment since the Second World War has had on the occupational class structure. If occupational class is to be a useful instrument in social policy, for example, the structure of women's employment should be incorporated within this measure.

The dualism of structure versus action discussed above is rooted in philosophical differences which have been present since the initial development of the social sciences. There is, also, a different but related contrast which is found between both different social science disciplines and within sociology itself. This is the distinction between the 'economic' and the 'normative' (or cultural). It is a commonplace of first year sociology courses that 'modern' societies are characterized by a separation between 'the economy' and other aspects of society, but this statement should always be accompanied by the reminder that, despite this apparent separation, the actual interpenetration of different spheres of human activity is still extensive. 'Class thinking', as we have seen, tends to emphasize the significance of economic factors in the structuring of occupations – whether deriving from the political economy of Marx or the marginalist economics of Weber. The emphasis on 'interests' in explanations of class action will also tend to reinforce this aspect. However, as has been stressed in this chapter, the division of labour (and thus occupational classes) is structured not just by economic interests, whether of the class or the individual, but also by social and cultural factors.

This book, therefore, will explore the division of labour between men and women within the occupational structure. This empirical structure comprises resources (the kinds of jobs available) and rules. These rules may be related to 'rationally' justified prescriptions such as those relating to required qualifications. They may also derive from what Lockwood, following Parsons, has described as non-rational beliefs; that is 'conformity to rules or norms that [are regarded] as obligatory because they embody some ultimate end or value' (Lockwood, 1982, p. 441). These could include conventions relating to 'men's jobs' and 'women's jobs', as well as religious and/or moral prescriptions. To the extent that humans abide by the rules, and use the resources, then these practices reproduce the division of labour more or less in its own image. However, such simple reproduction hardly ever occurs, even from one generation to the next. For the occupational structure is simultaneously transformed by people even as they reproduce it. The class struggle may be seen as having a significant impact here, even if it falls short of revolutionary transformation. Capital is shaping the occupational structure through the development of new technologies, through new methods of work organisation and by extending into new markets; even as it does so, organizations of employees, through the trade union movement for example, are also seeking to impose their own standards and requirements. Occupational groups which achieve a monopoly of a vital skill may decisively shape not only the reproduction of their own particular tasks, but also those of occupations associated with them. Gender relations, and their associated practices, as we have seen, are also crucial elements shaping this structure.

Such an approach would still leave a central place for theories of class and status, for the practices which reproduce and transform the structure are not random. Thus the notion of class interests, for example, might be used in order to suggest the likely stratagems of particular groups within the structure, and the historical balance of class forces may suggest why strategies developed within one particular context might not be appropriate in a different one. To recognize that the structure is fluid and dynamic is not to collapse into an atheoretical eclecticism, but should provide the resources for further theoretical development.

Although, therefore, the feminist critique of class and stratification theorizing has forced a substantial reassessment of some basic concepts, there is no reason why they should be abandoned in their entirety. As we have seen, the relative weakness of class and stratification theory in respect of gender relationships was initially perceived as an expression of 'patriarchal' attitudes within 'malestream' sociology. It is to an examination of the concept of patriarchy that we now turn.

Patriarchy

The domination of women by men has been extensively documented. It has become commonplace to describe this domination as 'patriarchy', a term which, strictly speaking, describes the 'rule of the father'. As Mann (1986) has argued, as a generalization it holds remarkably well as a description of much of recorded history. To embark upon a systematic discussion of the history and meaning of the concept is beyond the scope of this book but, nevertheless, it is important that the general perspective being used here should be made explicit.

In feminist debate, much discussion has taken the form of arguments over the ideological, as contrasted with the material, bases of patriarchy. Mitchell (1975) has used psychoanalytic concepts in combination with those of structuralist anthropology to argue that patriarchal ideology is deeply rooted in human culture. It is a relatively autonomous system which articulates with the capitalist mode of production but is not necessary to it; indeed, patriarchy is increasingly redundant, given capitalist production relations.

In contrast, other feminists have argued that patriarchy has a primarily material base. One strand of this argument has been briefly identified in a previous section of this chapter – the Marxist 'domestic labour debate'. Another is the socialist feminist project of the identification of a material system of patriarchy which combines with the capitalist system. Hartmann's (1981) initial statement of 'dual systems' theory has been extremely influential in setting the terms of the debate: 'Capitalist development creates the places for a hierarchy of workers, but traditional Marxist categories cannot tell us who will fill which places. Gender and racial hierarchies determine who fills the empty places.' This insight has been systematically explored by a number of authors (Cockburn, 1986; Game and Pringle, 1984), but the discussion here will focus primarily upon a recent attempt by Walby to theorize a system of patriarchy through the analysis of the patriarchal mode of production.

Walby (1986) gives a general definition of patriarchy as 'a system of interrelated social structures through which men exploit women'. The patriarchal 'mode of production' is located in the household: 'The producing class is composed of housewives or domestic labourers, while the non-producing and exploiting class is composed of husbands' (Walby, 1986, pp. 52-3).

The wife replenishes the labour power of her husband but has no control over what she produces, that is, her husband's labour power. When the patriarchal mode of production is in articulation with the capitalist mode: 'The primary mechanism which ensures that women will serve their husbands is their exclusion from paid work on the same terms as men' (ibid., p. 54).

In capitalism, there is a 'tension between the interests of capital and patriarchy in the allocation of women's labour time' (p. 68) – that is 'capital' and 'patriarchs' are in competition for the labour of women. Thus the patriarchal division of labour in the household is cross-cut by patriarchal relations in paid work, the patriarchal state, and male violence.

Walby's argument is supported by a series of industrial and occupational case studies which document the systematic exclusion in Britain of women both from access to 'better' jobs, and from full participation in the labour market. This discussion is valuable because of its emphasis on the non-domestic constraints which have been placed on women – all too often, problems faced by women in employment have been perceived as originating solely in the domestic sphere. However, it may be argued that Walby has not established the theoretical basis of a *system* of patriarchy.

The patriarchal mode of production is central to Walby's theoretical claims. However, when this 'mode' is further examined, a number of weaknesses are evident. In the first place, the argument is grounded in typicality rather than a systemic regularity. Within Walby's formulation, the typical male and female division of labour within the household could be reversed and the 'househusband' would then become the exploited domestic labourer, engaged in the replenishment of his wife's labour power – in essence, the contrast lies between 'market' and 'non-market' *workers*, rather than male and female. This criticism may be made again, to her description of the operation of this mode of production:

> The portion allocated to the wife's use on herself is *typically* less than the part of the wage allocated for the use of the husband on himself. In addition, the housewife *typically* works longer hours than the man. (Walby, 1986, p. 53, our emphasis).

However, what if the wife was allocated more to herself, and worked shorter hours, than her husband? Would she still be exploited? The position of other household members, such as children, is also far from clear. At any one time, only a minority of households can be implicated in the patriarchal mode of production, a heterosexual household where both are employed and domestic labour is shared presumably would not be, nor would a household consisting of a retired couple.

If the theoretical coherence of the patriarchal mode of production cannot be sustained, then neither can Walby's claims to have established a theory of patriarchy as such. To establish that men may gain various advantages from their relationships with women restates what is already known, rather than demonstrates the existence of a 'system' of patriarchy.

This recent, and ambitious attempt to identify a theory of patriarchy has, therefore, despite its many other insights, not been successful. In any case, it might be suggested that efforts to establish the theoretical basis of a system of patriarchy are in constant danger of raising problems of what Connell (1985) has described as 'categoricalism'. That is, if patriarchy is demonstrated to have a theoretical status of a system analogous to class exploitation, then presumably as a category men oppress women as a category and the future outlook seems bleak.

In summary, therefore, there would seem to be little objection to the use of the concept of patriarchy to describe the organization of power relations between men and women which prevailed until modern times: 'Gender, though fundamental to stratification, was asymmetric: men could act, women could not. Exceptions can be found – but how many sociological generalizations spread out over 4000 years of global history can do even half as well?' (Mann, 1986, p. 43). Patriarchy may still be used in a more general way to describe the oppression of women – although Mann, for example, would argue that this description is misleading given the transformation of male and female statuses which have taken place over the last two centuries. Despite these formal changes in status, many feminist writers have nevertheless argued that a system of patriarchy is identifiable today. It is true that the relationships between men and women show many instances of oppression but, nevertheless, efforts to establish the existence of a system of patriarchy have not been particularly successful, despite these empirical regularities.[8]

In this book, patriarchy will not be regarded as a universal system, but as a particular aspect of gender relations. Gender relations are universal. Rules governing the relations between the sexes, and the relative status of men and women, are an invariable feature of human societies. However, there is a lack of uniformity in the content of these rules and, indeed, their variation has been one of the grounds upon which the inappropriateness of a general concept of patriarchy has been argued (Beechey, 1979). Recent anthropological literature has suggested that there are no behaviours and/or meanings that are universally and cross-culturally associated with either masculinity or femininity (MacCormack and Strathern, 1980). Nevertheless, as far as those individuals engaged in the relationships are concerned, the rules governing gender relationships may take on the character of absolutes. In such cases, they may appear as social structures irreducible to individual action, and beyond the capacity of the individual to transform. [9]

This view of gender relations as relatively impervious to change was apparent in early writings within 'second-wave' feminism which laid much emphasis upon sex-role theory. Gender differences were seen as originating in, and being maintained by, practices which determined appropriate roles for men and women (Friedan, 1975; Oakley, 1972). At one level, this is self-evidently the case. Girl and boy babies are treated differently, schools and peer groups reinforce appropriate 'masculine' and 'feminine' behaviour, and the world of work provides 'masculine' and 'feminine' occupations. Sex role theory, however, like role theory in general, is fundamentally static. That is, it provides no explanation of *why* sex roles should take the shape they do in the first place, nor of why and how they are changed and modified.

However, it is possible to move towards an explanation of such change without abandoning these basic perceptions. One such recent attempt is to be found in the work of Connell. He identifies three interrelated structures of gender relations: first, the overall division of labour; second, power – in particular, the general connection of authority with masculinity; and third, 'cathexis' – that is, 'the construction of emotionally charged social relations with "objects" [that is, other people] in the real world' (1987, p. 112). [10] The 'gender order' describes a historically constructed pattern of power relations between men and women, together with definitions of femininity and masculinity, at the level of a society; the concept of 'gender regime' describes these patterns at the level of the institution.

The duality of the structure is central to Connell's theoretical conceptualization; indeed, the concept of 'structuration' is central to his approach. He argues that the structure (in this case, the gender order) is not only a constraint but an object of practice. The gender order (or gender regime) is *institutionalized* through practice, which can be cyclical or divergent. (The occupational structure is clearly a major locus of the gender order.) Gender relations are stable to the extent that groups constituted in the network of gender relations have interests in the conditions for cyclical rather than divergent practice (Connell, 1987, p. 141). There are obvious functional elements in this account of gender relations. That is, particular types of arrangements are viewed as having a disposition to perpetuate particular kinds of gender relations. Although functionalist explanations have been extensively criticized, they nevertheless remain an indispensable strategy for social analysis. It is surely indisputable, for example, that some categories of gender relations are functional for the maintenance of particular institutional orders, such as the rules governing women, and sexual behaviour more generally, in theocratic societies.

If the analysis of the gender order is to be theoretical as well as descriptive, it is important that the likely points of change in the gender order (or the origins of divergent practices) are capable of being specified. In the next chapter, a model of occupational segregation will be developed which will attempt to capture both the fluidity of the structure as well as suggesting these likely points of change. First, however, the methodological issues which arise out of the discussion so far will be examined.

A note on method

The arguments of this chapter may be briefly summarized: 'classical' class analysis (for instance, as in the work of Marx and Weber), was not formulated to give an account of gender relationships. The fact that it fails to do so, therefore, does not constitute a sufficient argument for the rejection of class theory as such. However, contemporary attempts to operationize class theories through the application of class schema to structures of employment are fatally flawed – not least because (amongst other things) these structures are 'gendered'. The attempts to argue that the postwar growth of women's employment is not relevant to the structure of classes produced by these schemes has almost certainly obstructed the development of a fruitful dialogue between feminists and 'mainstream' class theorists. In particular, feminists have emphasized the extent to which the division of labour in the public sphere is structured by socio-cultural factors, even in a capitalist market society.

'Patriarchy' has been developed as an alternative to 'class' to explain the location of women in the division of labour in the public sphere. Perhaps because of an established tradition of class theorizing, attempts have been made to develop a theory of patriarchy analogous to class. It is argued that patriarchy is a particular aspect of gender relations, which may not necessarily be patriarchal. The absence of a single theory of gender relations, therefore, means that their manifestation in particular industries and occupations will vary. In order to understand and explain these variations, comparative work is required. Most of the comparative work in this book will be within a single country (Britain) but in the final chapter, comparisons will be drawn with the experience of women's employment in other nation states. This general approach to the topic has particular implications for research methods.

It has been argued that the exploration of the changing pattern of women's paid employment is most fruitfully to be approached through making explicit the duality of the occupational structure (and indeed, of the division of labour in general). As Giddens has argued, the structural properties of social systems are simultaneously the medium and outcome of social acts (1981, p. 19). Thus the occupational structure is at the same time a social 'product' as it sets limits on, and creates opportunities for, the people with (and without) 'jobs' who are producing it. In order to explain this process, rather than simply to describe the outcome (as in occupational classifications), a distinctive strategy is required of empirical research.

In the first place, a holistic approach, rather than what Gellner (1985) has described as the 'granular metaphysic', should inform the approach to reality. In empirical research, this is best achieved via the method of the case study, which has been described as 'a way of organising social data so as to preserve the unitary character of the social object being studied' (Goode and Hatt quoted in Mitchell, 1983). Methodological holism, however, runs the risk of getting bogged down in what Gellner calls, in an illuminating metaphor,

> a world of the tropical jungle, in whose thick undergrowth everything is so tangled with everything else that you can never isolate any one single thing, or can do it only by the ruthless use of a machete which kills that which it separates. (Gellner, 1985, p. 33).

It should be stressed, therefore, that the adoption of the case study method is not being used as a justification for an atheoretical description which 'takes everything into account'. This line of argument is usefully clarified in Mitchell's (1983) discussion of the epistomological basis of case study research.

Case studies are often regarded as qualitative, in contrast to the quantitive research methods associated with, say, large-scale survey work. The quantitive/qualitative distinction is rather misleading and is *not* being pursued here; case studies can be, and often are, quantitive. However, one consequence of the pervasiveness of this quantitive/ qualitative characterization is that case studies are often seen by (quantitive) sociologists as suitable only for suggesting hypotheses or interpretations for future investigation by quantitive survey methods. A variant of this position is also found in the suggestion that case studies may be used to illustrate social processes which have been, supposedly, more definitively established through large-scale survey methods – as in, for example, the use of the 'juicy quote' in the final report. When case studies are used in this way, the primary requirement is that they should be somehow 'typical' of the phenomenon in question. Indeed, the question of whether the case study is a 'good' one or not rests upon whether it is 'typical', and the underlying procedures used to judge a case study are similar to those used to evaluate quantitative survey research.

However, argues Mitchell, case study research should not necessarily be judged on its typicality but, rather, 'on the validity of the analysis rather than the representativeness of the events' in question (1983, p. 190). Because case studies *are* holistic, they facilitate theoretical/logical thinking, that is, causal explanations. Case studies, therefore, are valuable not just to the extent that they represent typicality (or the apt illustration); but rather, because they present material from which theoretical principles may be inferred. Central to Mitchell's argument is the distinction (taken from Znaniecki) between enumerative (or statistical) and analytical induction or inference. In a sample survey, the logic of extrapolation from the sample to the universe involves two inferences: a statistical inference, which makes a statement about the confidence with which we might expect to find the characteristics of the sample reproduced in the population, and a logical or scientific inference 'which makes a statement about the confidence we may have that the theoretically necessary or logical connection among the features observed in the sample also pertain to the parent population' (1983, p. 207); as when, for example, the analytical properties of individuals located in occupational class schemes result (or do not result) in the global property of class consciousness. Case studies, however, incorporate only logical or scientific inference and stand or fall on this account: 'The validity of the extrapolation [i.e. from the case study] depends not on the typicality or representativeness of the case but upon the cogency of the theoretical reasoning' (ibid.).

Case studies, therefore, are analytical rather than illustrative if they are embedded in an appropriate theoretical framework. Their utility rests upon their capacity to explain, rather than their typicality. A similar reasoning informs the work of Bertaux and Bertaux-Wiame (1981), who have described as the 'saturation of knowledge' the process through which empirical researchers acquire the knowledge of social relations which bestows a confidence in the validity of the case study. That is, investigation may reasonably cease when the causal explanation of a particular phenomenon is felt to be complete. The case studies developed in this book, therefore, are not presented as merely typical (although they may well be), but rather, as theoretical illustrations of the complex processes which sustain the gender distribution of labour in the 'public' sphere of paid employment.

Notes

1   It is not being suggested that a clear line can be drawn between the objects of 'political' and 'sociological' investigation. Nor is it being argued that sociology is somehow independent of politics. It should be possible, however, to maintain a distinction between 'doing sociology' and 'doing politics'.

2   Wright (1980). Wright (1985) subsequently developed his Marxist theory in a way that increased considerably the number of class categories. The strategy of transposing classifications to individuals, however, has remained exactly the same.

3   See the exchange between Goldthorpe and Peacock in Hirsch and Goldthorpe (eds), (1978), pp. 214–16.

4   Strictly speaking Goldthorpe's insistence on the family as the class 'unit' renders families, rather than classes, as the basic 'actors'. However, this strategy assumes that the 'class situation' of family members really is comparable, and that the family form is both stable and ubiquitous.

5   The work of Goldthorpe and Lockwood was extremely influential in the development of the 'action' perspective in the 1960s and 1970s. In industrial sociology, it initiated an extensive debate around the notion of the role of 'orientations' to work in the explanation of workplace behaviour. (See Goldthorpe, 1966; Goldthorpe et al., 1968.)

6   A number of sophisticated solutions have been offered, for example Popper's (1972) prescriptions for social science investigation, and 'realist' philosophies, which seek to delineate the underlying (real) mechanisms having causal powers to affect the world (Keat and Urry, 1975).

7   A parallel argument is developed by Mann in his discussion 'Idealism and materialism in sociological theory' (1979). He argues that the dualism of 'ideas' versus 'material reality' is unacceptable, and indeed has 'obstructed scholarship'. '[The] argument is not over the relations of "ideas" to "reality" or "practice" but that between "ideas-and-practice-combined" in two different spheres of society, the economic

and the ideological . . . Once arrived at this position . . . we are out of the dualist terrain'(p. 99).

8 In opposition to this kind of argument, it may be suggested that the day-to-day experience of being female is sufficient to demonstrate the existence of such a 'system' – should one therefore be too concerned about a relative failure to theorize, given its everyday reality? (Dworkin, 1981). It should be made explicit here, therefore, that it is not the empirical reality of male oppression which is being disputed, but rather, its theoretical significance.

9 These kinds of impersonal social constraints have been interestingly discussed by Lockwood in his elaboration of the Durkheimian concept of fatalism (Lockwood, 1982). He explores the origins of this 'moral despotism' through the structure of religious beliefs. Many of the rules concerning the relations between the sexes, of course, are rooted in religious prescriptions. Purcell (1986) has also developed the concept of fatalism in her discussion of women and their attitude to employment.

10 Note that this three-fold location of gender relations in fact corresponds quite closely to Walby's (1986) identification of patriarchy at and in work, the State, and male violence. Another multi-factor approach to the analysis of gender is to be found in J. Scott (1986), which is discussed further in the final chapter.

2 Occupational segregation

Introduction

The persistence of occupational segregation has been used to explain the fact that the average earnings of women are considerably below those of men despite equal pay legislation. Median hourly earnings for manual men in 1985 were 350.2p, for non-manual men, 523.7p. The corresponding figures for women were 244.1p and 323.1p. (Source: Annual Abstract of Statistics, 1987). However, since equal pay legislation in 1975, men and women no longer receive different rates of pay for the *same* job. The income differential is explained, therefore, by the fact that men and women are *not* employed in the same jobs, and women's jobs are low paid.

Aggregate level data suggest considerable continuity. In a review of segregation in Britain published in 1979, Hakim concluded:

> The data show that there has been a certain amount of change, notably in the reduction of exclusive or almost exclusive occupations for men and women, and that horizontal segregation has declined to some extent. On the other hand, the data also suggest a trend towards greater vertical segregation within broad categories of work. Thus the overall picture is one of continuity within change. (Hakim, 1979, p. 43). [Horizontal segregation refers to different types of occupation, vertical segregation to hierarchical distinctions within the same occupational category.]

More recent empirical updates (Hakim, 1981, Mallier and Rosser, 1985) suggest that, at the aggregate level, the broad description of 'continuity within change' is still appropriate. Using a standardized index of occupational segregation (calculated as the difference between the level of over-representation in typically female jobs and of the level of under-representation in typically male jobs), Hakim shows that this index declined steadily between 1901 and 1971, with a sharp fall (reflecting the impact of legislation) between 1971 and 1977. However, between 1977 and 1979 the trend was reversed. This reversal of trend in respect of horizontal segregation, she argues, reflects the impact of the recession. In the late 1970s women's jobs were lost at a faster rate than were men's. Mallier and Rosser also report some convergence in respect of horizontal segregation. Comparing the 1971 and 1981 national census figures, in 79 per cent of all occupations, the proportion of females was found to have increased. Nevertheless, they conclude that 'when the occupational structure of the labour force as a whole is considered, the changes in segregation have only been marginal'. That this is so is in part due to the fact that, whereas horizontal segregation may have declined long-term, vertical segregation has become more apparent. Here, however (although an accurate measure is difficult to apply), there may be some signs of change. A major area of job gain for women has been in low-level white collar and clerical work, a trend which has intensified vertical segregation. However, Hakim's data suggest that women made substantial gains in their share of higher-grade white-collar work in the 1970s (1981, p. 525). Nevertheless, census data confirms that in 1981 the majority of women (80 per cent) were in occupations where 50 per cent or more of those employed in the occupation are women. 'Women's work' includes unskilled work in manufacturing, routine clerical and sales employment, and all kinds of public sphere caring and provisioning – cooking, cleaning, nursing, etc.

It may be argued, however, that aggregate level analyses of long-term trends in occupational segregation are of restricted value to the understanding of the processes which sustain gendered patterns of employment. In the first place, aggregate measures may give a misleading picture of what is occurring at the individual or company level (Bielby and Baron, 1984); analyses in this area are particularly prone to ecological reasoning as Hakim (1981) suggests. To take an extreme example: the provision of separate facilities for men and women in Islamic countries would generate a relatively high proportion of women in the professions in the richer Islamic nation states. Thus an increase in the number and proportion of women in professional and managerial jobs at the level of the industry or occupation (and an apparent decline in the extent of segregation) could co-exist with rigorous segregation at the workplace. Aggregate or 'macro' measures of segregation trends are also problematic given transformations of occupational content over time (as well as changes in both the number and gender of those employed in the occupation in question). Thus longitudinal comparisons are difficult. A good example is provided here by the single most populous occupation for women, which is often cited as the major example of occupational 'feminization': clerical work. In 1911, 21 per cent of clerks were women; by 1981, 74 per cent of 'clerical and related' workers were female. However, breaking the clerical category down by industry and occupation (and maintaining longitudinal comparisons), reveals a rather different picture from a straightforward process of feminization (Crompton, 1988b). The feminization of the occupation as a whole has occurred as a consequence of a number of different processes, including the development of all-female clerical occupations such as shorthand and typing, and the expansion of all-female industrial sub-categories such as clerks in education. Although technical change may have facilitated the penetration (at the more junior levels) of such previously all-male bastions as the finance sector, men have remained a majority of clerks in industries such as mining and the railways. Thus the feminization of clerical work has been achieved via a massive technological and industrial restructuring of the occupation, and to compare 'clerks' in 1931 with 'clerks' in 1981 is frankly misleading.

This lack of stability of occupational content and meaning is exacerbated, as far as aggregate level measures are concerned, by the fact that occupations are not, in any case, equivalents. Differentiated occupations emerge out of the division of labour that characterizes the development of complex societies. In the first chapter, it has been stressed that although, in a capitalist market society, economic factors might predominate, cultural factors will also shape these divisions. Labour may be both *socially* divided according to particular tasks or craft specialities, as well as *technically* divided into fragmented tasks within the labour process itself (Braverman, 1974). Thus an occupational title may describe an area of expertise, a subdivided, routine task, a supervisory/managerial role, or some combination of these. Individual occupations may be a consequence of the division of productive tasks in the public sphere, as described above, or they may emerge as a coalition of tasks from the 'subjective economy' or 'private sphere'.[1] Occupations vary in the extent to which the boundaries of their operations, and their content, are clearly defined. At one extreme are the professions, where content is specified by a closely-monitored programme of education and training, and boundaries may even be fixed by the state. At the other are general categories such as 'labourer' or 'manager'. As a result of these variations, 'occupations' have very different consequences for their occupants. Some occupations represent staging-posts in a career trajectory, others are final destinations, some will lead nowhere at all. What is ostensibly the same occupation may have a very different outcome depending on the gender of the occupant – as in the example of women and clerical work (Stewart, Prandy and Blackburn, 1980). The occupational structure, therefore, describes an agglomeration of different types of occupation; it is a crudely-stitched patchwork rather than a whole cloth. Standardized segregation indices, however, treat each occupation as an equal 'unit' and the contribution of a high status or a low status, a large or a small, 'occupation' to the index will be exactly the same.

The kinds of problems summarized above are familiar to those working with aggregate measures, and a number of strategies have been evolved to deal with them. It is not being suggested that they should lead to the rejection or abandonment of the attempt to chart occupational segregation at the 'macro' level, but caution should be exercised in interpreting the trends they reveal. Nevertheless, aggregate measures do demonstrate conclusively the persisting differentiation amongst the jobs that men and women do, and in the next section some of the explanations which have been offered for this phenomenon will be examined.

Theories of Occupational Segregation

Theories of occupational segregation are particular instances of more general theories which seek to explain the location of individuals in the positional structure. This admittedly clumsy phrase may be used in a relatively narrow fashion (for example, to describe the structure of paid employment) or more broadly, to encompass the location of individuals in respect of wealth, standing, opportunities and so on in the structure of society as a whole. The explanation and under-standing of the genesis and maintenance of structured social inequality may be approached from a variety of standpoints which draw upon different strands within social theory. Thus the signifi-cance of (rational) individual preferences might be emphasized (as in rational choice theories (Banton, 1983)), or that of external con-straints (as in Marxist and neo–Marxist theories (Braverman, 1974)), or of some kind of over-arching value system (as in normative functionalism (Davis and Moore, 1964)). (This listing of theoretical inputs is intended to be illustrative, rather than comprehensive.) Corresponding to this theoretical diversity, neo-classical economic theories of supply and demand, Marxist and Marxist-derived theories of capitalist exploitation and labour market segmentation, as well as the descriptive accounts of cultural anthropology have all been employed in attempts to explain the 'woman question'.

The causes of occupational segregation are often described as resting in the nature of the female labour supply. Supply side explanations focus on the particular *qualities* of female labour. They may be divided into first, normative explanations which emphasize socio-cultural features of female roles (particularly in the domestic sphere) and second, economistic explanations which see the quality of female labour as determined by the outcome of rational decision-taking by the individual and within the domestic unit.

Socio-cultural explanations of occupational segregation have much in common with sex-role theories of gender inequality. They point to the fact that women's paid work closely parallels women's work in the household – cooking, cleaning, caring for small children and the sick, etc. – in short, nurturing and supportive. In this view, work is seen not just as a source of income, but also as a primary source of social identity. Gender is usually the first source of social identity learned by children, and the individual's social respectability and sense of self-respect depends on behaving in a manner appropriate to the gender in question (Matthaei, 1982). Clearly, occupations such as nursing and primary school teaching, and working in old people's homes and in the school meals service, *are* congruent with feminine stereotypes. However, to make the perfectly valid empirical point that women's public sphere activities are reflective of their domestic roles and feminine identities does not take us very far. Tasks in the *household*, it may be argued, are potentially diverse and no insight is given as to *why* particular tasks should be defined as 'male' or 'female'. In short, unelaborated sex role explanations describe, rather than explain the gendered division of labour.

Neo-classical economic theories also view occupational segregation as a consequence of the quality of the different 'offerings' of men and women in the labour market. However, the concentration of women into particular occupations is seen as resulting from the relative failure of women to invest in their 'human capital': to gain formal, work-related qualifications, have long, unbroken service records, and so on (Chiplin and Sloane, 1982). Neo-classical theories have been elaborated by the 'new home economics', where the division of labour between men and women (where the woman takes the responsibility for domestic tasks and thus acquires negligible 'human capital') is seen as an outcome of rational decision-taking by individuals within the family unit (Mincer and Polachek, 1974; Becker, 1981). Occupational segregation is therefore an outcome of household specialization in 'domestic' or 'market' (paid) work. With two people and two sets of tasks to be achieved, it is best for each individual to spend all or most of his or her time on one set of tasks, and for them to exchange their respective surplus output, rather than for each to divide the time between both tasks. Here there is an echo of the 'women's two roles' discussion in sociology in the 1950s and 1960s. In this debate, women's problems in relation to employment were defined as being centred on the difficulties of combining 'domestic' and 'work' (employment) roles (Myrdal and Klein, 1956). Human capital explanations of the gender division of labour have been empirically criticized on two counts; both normative or cultural, as well as economistic. First, examples have been cited of women in occupations which are technically skilled, but of low *status*, as a consequence of the supposed inferiority of women (Craig, Garnsey and Rubery, 1985). (Such evidence has led to a growing emphasis on the sex-typing of jobs in the workplace, rather than only within the domestic sphere, and the social construction of 'skill' more generally (Phillips and Taylor, 1980; Game and Pringle, 1984).) Second, the economic 'efficiency' of *excessive* specialization by household members has itself been challenged (Owen, 1987). Women's supposed efficiency (and thus specialization) in relation to domestic work is derived from their biological capacity to bear and breastfeed children. However, Owen argues that as recent evidence suggests that the time needed to achieve these biological ends is in practice decreasing rapidly domestic specialization by women may not be particularly efficient.

Some Marxist accounts have suggested that male and female roles in the household, and in the formal economy, may be seen as functional for the capitalist mode of production overall (Seccombe, 1974). Women's domestic labour in the home, it is argued, makes an indirect contribution to the realization of surplus value in providing (at a lower than market price) the replacement/replenishment costs of the (male) labour force. It is perhaps paradoxical, but the Marxist-inspired domestic labour debate had much in common with the 'new home economics'. The latter explained the prevailing domestic division of labour with reference to individual preferences and household rationalities. The former argued that these preferences and rationalities are in fact constraints resulting from the demands of the capitalist economy. Both, however, take the division of labour between men and women in the private and public spheres largely for granted. The domestic labour debate has been much criticized (Barrett, 1980). The specificity of *capitalist* exploitation may be queried given that women have (historically and cross-culturally) been subject to social and economic exploitation in other times and contexts; and in any case, capitalism's needs may not always be best served by confining women to the domestic sphere.

Arguments which emphasize the significance of the nature of the female labour supply are complemented by demand side arguments which stress the significance of labour market segmentation and other institutional factors. One of the earliest attempts to use the insights of dual labour market theory in order to give an account of men's and

women's location in the structure of employment is found in the work
of Barron and Norris (1976). 'Primary' sector jobs are characterized
by stability, better pay and promotion prospects in the internal labour
market; in contrast 'secondary' sector jobs are unstable, poorly paid,
with few promotion prospects. They argue that the high visibility,
unstable work patterns, low economism and lack of training of
women makes them 'secondary' workers; men in contrast, are to be
found in the 'primary' sector. Such simple 'dualist' formulations have
been criticized (Dex, 1985) and labour market theory considerably
elaborated. Radical theorists have argued that segmentation is part of
a 'divide and rule' employer policy, and more recently, the
Cambridge Labour Studies Group (Roberts, Finnegan and Gallie,
1985) have linked segmentation processes to the broader environment, including crucially, the domestic economy of the household.

The Cambridge group argues that the workforce and unions are
significant elements in determining the occupational structure; this
approach is a useful and necessary modification of earlier 'capitalist
conspiracy' theories where the employer was supposedly all-
powerful (see Braverman, 1974). Worker power is given by a firm's
primary position in the product market but is also conditioned by
social, political and other institutional factors. Similarly, labour
power is socially constructed, primarily by the domestic economy
and thus the low wages of women and the young must be seen as a
consequence of their position within the household. The work of the
Cambridge group has emphasized the need to elaborate a multi-factor
explanation in order to understand the structuring of employment.
This general approach, which stresses the heterogeneity of inputs into
occupational structuring, has much in common with the arguments
developed in Chapter 1. However, like other labour market
explanations of gender segregation, there are some difficulties in
discriminating between women and disadvantaged workers as a
whole, and gender-specific roles within the household are not
explained. The emphasis upon the social structuring of economic
activity which is a distinctive feature of the work of the Cambridge
group is a major strength; but nevertheless their research has tended
to focus primarily upon the economic realm as such, rather than the
exploration of how the normative and cultural prescriptions which
shape this realm are developed.

The problem of explaining gender specificity, however, would not
be encountered by feminist arguments saying, in effect, that both the
structuring of the labour force, and the processes which maintain this
structure, are a consequence of patriarchal processes. The division of
labour within the household is seen as an outcome of men's power

over women, whilst in the workplace, men more or less consciously operate so as to exclude women from more remunerative and prestigious occupations, and render those tasks and occupations that women *do* perform as low status 'women's work'.

Hartmann (1979), as we have seen, has argued that the occupational structure is the outcome of the workings of two systems of capitalism and patriarchy, and Walby (1986) (see also Strober, 1984) has taken dual systems analysis further in an ambitious attempt to develop a theory of patriarchy which would also provide an account of occupational segregation. The systematic exclusion of women from more advantageous positions within paid work (thus making it difficult for individual women to maintain independent households), is the major device through which women are 'persuaded' to remain within the patriarchal mode of production. Thus occupational segregation, in this view, becomes functionally necessary in order to sustain the patriarchal mode of production.

As has been argued in Chapter 1, Walby's claim to have established the existence of a 'system' of patriarchy is doubtful; rather she has massively documented instances of patriarchal behaviour. However, she is entirely correct to emphasize the importance of exclusionary behaviour of men against women in the structuring of the division of labour in employment. A common feature of most accounts of occupational segregation, whether 'conservative' neo-classicist or 'radical' labour market theories, is that they view women as being at a disadvantage in the labour market 'because of' their domestic responsibilities. This statement might initially appear as common-sensically self-evident; nevertheless, the point should be made that expressed this way, it is female 'deficiencies' which are the cause of their poor labour market performance, although the victim may not necessarily be held personally responsible for her inadequacies. Walby's achievement has been to emphasize the extent to which the occupational structure has been 'gendered' as a result of male exclusionary practices in the *public* sphere, rather than just by the fact that women still have to 'await their liberation from the family' (Giddens, 1973).

This summary, therefore, has reviewed a number of theoretical explanations of occupational segregation. First, there are explanations which emphasize the continuing significance of 'masculine' and 'feminine' statuses and roles, which are carried over into the occupational structure. These explanations of sex roles can be primarily normative, or seen as resulting from constraints imposed by the workings of the (capitalist) economy. Second are those which emphasize the workings of the labour market – either from the perspective of individual men and women as rational producers and consumers, or from that developed by theories of labour market segmentation. Third, the location of women in employment is explained as a consequence of male domination in both the public and private sphere. All of these approaches have been vulnerable to some kind of criticism. However, it will be argued that, nevertheless, none of these explanations should be abandoned in their entirety. No single theory can encompass the complex reality of occupational segregation. In particular, at the level of the occupation or industry, instances of segregation will be more appropriately explained by some approaches than others. Together, the factors described above contribute to the totality of occupational segregation. Their relative impact on particular sectors of employment may be further grasped through the exploration of the *processes* of occupational segregation.

Processes of occupational segregation

As a first step in the examination of these processes, we may begin with Hakim's distinction between 'horizontal' and 'vertical' segregation. Horizontal occupational segregation exists when men and women are more commonly working in different types of occupation. Vertical occupational segregation exists when men are most commonly working in higher grade occupations and women are most commonly working in lower grade occupations' (1979, p. 19). Horizontal segregation is maintained by the *recruitment* of men and women to different jobs, vertical segregation by either differential recruitment or the confining of women to lower grades within internal labour markets.

Horizontal segregation is maintained by the recruitment of men and women into sex-typed, 'masculine' and 'feminine' occupations. The occupational order ranges from higher-level occupations such as nurses, teachers, and professional engineers, to lower-level occupations, such as refuse disposal workers, and school dinner ladies. Although it is true that 'male' jobs are usually ranked higher than 'female' jobs, nevertheless, a female profession such as nursing will be ranked higher than, say, the all-male occupation of refuse disposal.

Milkman has argued that sex typing is subject to cultural inertia: 'Once a job becomes "male" or "female", the demand for labour to fill it tends to expand or contract as a sex-specific demand, barring major disruptions of labour supply or a basic restructuring of the labour process' (1983, p. 160). The persistence of sex typing suggests that established patterns of horizontal segregation at the lower levels of the occupational structure will be least likely to undergo radical change. To take an example from the shoe industry, an advertisement for a 'clicker' (cutter) in Norwich or Northampton (two centres of the shoe trade) would not produce any female applicants, and men would not seek to work in the closing room (machining shoe uppers). This cultural inertia is well illustrated by an item in a Norwich paper (*Eastern Daily Press*, 28 May 1988). A photograph of an elderly man surrounded by middle-aged women is sub-titled 'Girls [*sic*] better machinists says factory manager'. The text continues:

> The boot of equality is on the other foot according to veteran shoe factory manager . . . Mr Fuller – who retired yesterday after 50 years of making shoes – should know. He spent those five decades working with women machinists. 'You can say all you like about equal opportunity and equality of the sexes. But the girls are far better at machining, and attempts to introduce men into shoe factory closing rooms will never succeed except in very rare cases' he said.

Ethnographic studies of individual workplaces have demonstrated the pervasiveness of gender identities in such face-to-face groups (Purcell, 1986). These kinds of practices, no doubt, contribute to the higher incidence of segregation at the workplace level. As has already been noted, within broad occupational categories (say machinists) it will often be found that male machinists' jobs are considered skilled, whereas female machinists work at unskilled jobs. Thus the sex-typing of occupations is a contributory factor to the general lowering of the occupational status of women's work.

Besides the recruitment of men and women into sex-typed occupations and the sex-typing of jobs within particular workplaces, horizontal segregation may also be a consequence of the crowding of women, as 'disadvantaged workers', into low-level occupations. Women are in the majority in jobs such as casual agricultural work, or office cleaning, because they are cheap labour, rather than because they are *women*. 'Sex-typing' and 'crowding' are two different processes through which occupational segregation is manifest. All too often, little distinction is made between the two, particularly in aggregate-level discussions. Therefore, although many women are deemed unskilled via the sex-typing of women's occupations, it is also the case that many women are constrained by their lack of qualifications and market opportunities; that is, the crowding of women into low level occupations also reflects the nature of the female labour supply.

Historical and contemporary evidence nevertheless demonstrates that male exclusion practices have been very significant in denying women access to particular jobs. Social closure is defined by Parkin as 'the process by which social collectivities seek to maximize rewards by restricting access to rewards and opportunities to a limited circle of eligibles' (1974, p. 3). The principle of exclusion has often been gender alone; that is, women were barred from particular occupations simply because they were women. However, male exclusion practices have also operated indirectly, by denying women access to job training or other pre-entry requirements. Thus the registers of many professional bodies were closed to women in the UK until the Sex Disqualification (Removal) Act of 1919. Such formal practices, however, are susceptible to the liberal-feminist strategy of the 'qualifications lever'. If occupational labour markets are maintained via credentialist exclusion, then equal opportunity legislation which gives women access to the relevant credentials may facilitate a change in the sex composition of the occupation, and this would require neither disruptions of the labour supply nor restructuring of the labour process. Direct exclusion on the basis of gender alone has clearly been of considerable significance in respect of horizontal segregation.

Vertical segregation divides into two categories. Firstly, men and women may be differentially recruited into vertically ordered categories within the *same* occupation. A good example here would be schoolteaching, where women predominate in the (lower status) teaching of young children in infant and primary schools, whereas men predominate amongst secondary schoolteachers and teachers in higher and further education. Such vertical segregation by recruitment is similar to horizontal segregation. It is a consequence of hierarchical structuring within the occupation in question and may be described as vertical segregation via the external labour market. Vertical segregation is also maintained via the internal (organizational) labour market. Men and women may initially be recruited at a similar occupational level, but whereas men proceed upward through a career structure, women do not. Well-documented examples of such vertical segregation are to be found in large white-collar bureaucracies such as banks, insurance companies and so on (Blackburn, 1967; Heritage, 1983; Crompton and Jones, 1984). Women have not progressed through such career hierarchies because of their lack of formal qualifications, broken employment patterns, etc. There is also ample evidence that women have been excluded by male managers from gaining access to the internal job hierarchy. Vertical segregation via the operation of the internal labour market may be described as vertical segregation by internal exclusion. Teaching may also be called upon to provide evidence of this process. At every level *within* the teaching profession, the proportion of men in headships or senior positions is disproportionate to their presence in that level as a whole.[2]

In summary: horizontal segregation includes both sex-typed occupations for which only women (or men) would apply as a matter of convention, as well as jobs into which women are 'crowded' as cheap labour. (Of course, sex-typing may well be a consequence of explicit exclusionary practices in the past.) Vertical segregation includes both the direct recruitment of women into permanent lower-level occupations within hierarchically structured occupational categories, as well as credentialist and patriarchal exclusion within internal labour markets.

It has been suggested that horizontally segregated, sex-typed occupations are least susceptible to change; 'Once an occupation has been "sex-typed", normative and other forces operate which maintain segregation' (Murgatroyd, 1985). Paradoxically, sex-typing may protect female workers from substitution by even cheaper labour. This is not the case in respect of the crowding of women into lower-level jobs, where they may be replaced by other categories of disadvantaged labour such as young people or immigrants.[3] For example, in the hotel and catering trade, young people of both sexes are increasingly being used as flexible, casual, part-time labour.

Where horizontal segregation, and vertical segregation by recruitment, is maintained via credentialist exclusion, then the liberal feminist strategy of equal access has the capacity to change the gender structure of the occupation in question.

In the case of vertical segregation, women who are directly recruited into the lower levels within occupational categories are likely to stay there if these 'lower levels' constitute qualitatively different, sex-typed *jobs*. Primary school teachers cannot easily become secondary school teachers, physiotherapists cannot be quickly transformed into orthopaedic surgeons. However, the presence of higher-status men within the same broad occupational category might have two consequences for women in lower-status occupations. First, the proximity of higher-status occupations will contribute to the status enhancement of those at the lower level. Second, the comparison with men doing similar types of work may lead to collective pressure to raise the return to 'women's' occupations, once the assumption of women's 'natural' inferiority has been challenged. For example, (following the Equal Pay (Amendment) regulations of 1983) the all-female profession of speech therapy is currently (1988) pursuing, through the courts, an Equal Value claim. Vertical segregation within internal labour markets is susceptible to the 'qualifications lever'. Progress through internal labour markets is controlled by a number of factors including length of service, personal qualities, work experience and job-related qualifications. Hierarchies have to be rationally justified, and in contemporary societies formal qualifications express a principle of rationality which is characteristic of 'modern' in contrast to 'traditional' societies and their organizations. However, the very rationality of such exclusion processes makes it difficult to deny access to those who have acquired the necessary qualifications, whether they are male or female.

In the most general terms, this discussion of the processes of occupational segregation describes the interplay of economic and socio-cultural factors in structuring both the occupational division of labour and the location of men and women within it. It will be a difficult, if not impossible, task to separate out, or evaluate the relative significance of, economic and socio-cultural factors. Cultural beliefs about gender and work will obviously have an important impact on women's and men's employment. The domestic division of labour, including childcare, reflects the belief that the mother is the best carer for young children, and women's employment patterns tend to be discontinuous as a result. The belief that men are superior to, or should dominate women underpins much vertical segregation; women's 'better' qualities of kindness and caring are associated with jobs in which women predominate. Cultural assumptions are materially manifest in two closely related phenomena: sex-typing and statistical discrimination. The former, as we have seen, is found in horizontal and vertical segregation by recruitment – men apply and train for 'men's jobs', women for 'women's'. Statistical discrimination describes the practice of employers who assume that women will, because of their stereotypically 'feminine' qualities, be unreliable or otherwise inadequate as employees; women will have higher rates of absenteeism, be more likely to leave, and so on. According to this explanation, 'employers practice . . . discrimination against women solely on *economic* grounds and presumably would ignore gender if they came to recognize that their cheap screening device was too costly in terms of misapplied human resources' (Reskin and Hartmann, 1986, p. 42, our emphasis).

The interdependence of the economic and the social is a theme which recurs constantly in the social sciences. For example, in organization theory there is a longstanding contrast between on the one hand the rational, individual maximiser model associated with 'scientific management' and the work of F.W. Taylor; and on the other, the emphasis on group belonging and regulation developed within the 'human relations' tradition and associated with the work of Mayo and his colleagues. (Perrow, 1972.) (Rather crudely, this contrast is often described as that between Weber's account of bureaucracy and Durkheim's account of social solidarity.) It is not surprising that an emphasis on the complementarity of these two perspectives should characterize the approach of those who have worked on the topic of women and paid work (Beechey, 1986; Rubery, 1988), as the impact of normative assumptions on women's employment patterns are immediately apparent on any empirical examination. (Normative assumptions also structure men's employment patterns, but for as long as male employment was regarded *as* the norm, this fact was not consciously explored by sociologists.) It has been argued that women are more predisposed than men to be fatalistic as far as their employment experiences and opportunities are concerned – that is, to perceive no possibility of radical alteration in their individual circumstances (Purcell, 1986). Such a predisposition reflects the impact of normative constraints on women. As Purcell and others have argued, as individuals, women are less 'empowered' than men, both as a consequence of their legal, political and moral status in the past, and in respect of the different informal responsibilities for other people which are placed on them inside and outside the domestic unit.

In his discussion of the concept of fatalism Lockwood makes a distinction between 'conditional fatalism', stemming from a person's recognition that he or she is in the grip of circumstances beyond the control of any single individual, and 'moral despotism', where fatalism results from the individual's socialization into an ideology that provides a comprehensive account, and/or a system of beliefs, which explain the circumstances in question. As conditional fatalism and moral despotism have the same outcomes, it will be difficult, if not impossible, to distinguish between them empirically. Nevertheless, the distinction is an important one, and may be used to draw a contrast, for example, between the part played by conditional factors (male exclusionary practices, government policies, a lack of educational opportunities, etc.) in structuring women's labour force participation, and that which results from genuinely-held beliefs about the position of women in society and the expectations and responsibilities attached to these beliefs. In such instances, 'constraints' will not actually be *experienced* as such.

In the previous chapter, it was argued that the division of labour (and thus the occupational structure) should be conceived, because of the 'duality' of the social structure, as both the medium and the outcome of social acts. This idea makes it possible for the investigator to grasp the fluid and changing nature of occupational order, rather than treating it as static. The *de facto* fluidity of the occupational structure will be a continuing reference point in the discussion that follows. However, it would clearly be impossible to achieve a simultaneous examination of all of the economic and socio-cultural 'inputs' into this structure. In the next section of this chapter, therefore, the insights of labour market segmentation analysis will be used to develop a model of the occupational structure which emphasizes its dynamic nature. It will be suggested how occupations emerge out of the interactions of individuals and groups seeking reasonable (if not always maximum) returns for their efforts. Thus there will be an emphasis on 'economic' behaviour, albeit constrained and influenced by 'social' factors.

In Chapter 3, both the conditional factors and moral beliefs affecting the position of women in Britain since the end of the Second World War will be examined. Here there will be more of an emphasis on the socio-cultural context – although, again, it is in fact not possible to separate the social from the economic; rather, it is a question of emphasis.

Developing a model of the occupational structure

Figure 2.1 brings together within a single framework both the nature of the labour market and the characteristics of the individuals within it. It is bounded by two axes: CD describes the labour market (or opportunity structure); AB focuses upon particular characteristics of individuals located within the structure: skills, credentials and qualifications.[4]

Very broadly, the structuring of the market for labour may be viewed as the product of the interaction between individuals offering labour and skills: employers, and consumers. Entrepreneurial options, that is, self-employment, are specifically included in this approach. The skills and qualities offered by individuals range from those incorporating extensive qualifications in high demand, to the unskilled possessing only minimal qualifications. The axis AB in Figure 2.1 represents this dimension of occupational structuring. The possession of valued skills and/or qualities clearly places the individual in a favourable market situation. In neo-classical terms it represents the 'human capital' of the individuals who are 'economically active'. Occupational *groups* may seek to enhance their market

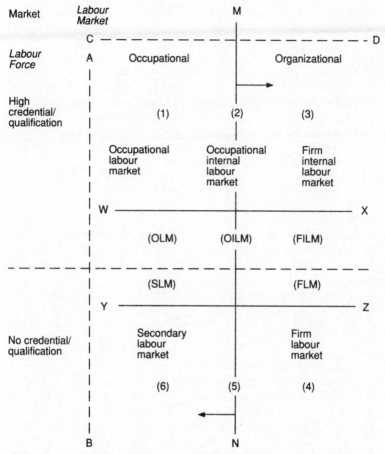

Figure 2.1 *A preliminary model of the occupational structure*

situation by 'scarcifying' the quality/qualification in question, as well as restricting access to employment. It is a feature of such processes of crystallization and closure that the boundaries of the occupation in question are (relatively) firmly drawn – for example nurse, doctor, plumber, electrician, etc. AB represents a continuum of skills etc., and the broken line which divides it indicates its approximate mid-point.

CD, the other axis of Figure 2.1, distinguishes between occupational and organizational labour markets. These terms discriminate between, on the one hand, that section of the market characterized by extensive (voluntary and involuntary) mobility and on the other, that where employment opportunities are restricted to and controlled by firms or organizations. This axis, in contrast to AB, seeks to incorporate the insights of the labour market segmentation approach. Within the model are located two further continua. WX and YZ, which are subdivided to describe the segmentation of the labour market as a whole.[5] The continuum WX includes occupational labour markets (OLMs), occupational internal labour markets (OILMs), and firm internal labour markets (FILMs). OLMs include individuals whose skills and qualifications provide a market shelter which enables them to move between jobs without incurring any employer penalty – indeed, such moves may be part of the individual's career progression. Jobs in OLMs will be clustered towards the upper levels of the occupational hierarchy, including, for example, professionals or skilled craftsmen.

OILMs can include occupations similar to those found in OLMs.[6] In OILMs, however, they are linked to the internal labour market of the organization – for example, the accountant or the corporation lawyer. There is a considerable literature documenting the experience of professionals in organizations that suggests that their expectations and attitudes are rather different from those of non-specialist senior employees (Rueschemeyer, 1986). The highly skilled and qualified are also found in FILMs, which are characterized by limited entry ports combined with movement up job ladders facilitated by formal and informal on-the-job training and experience. The former includes the development of industry and/or corporation specific qualifications which enhance the process of 'encirclement' and thus inclusion of highly qualified staff. 'The employers' most effective counter-strategy against the claims of skilled workers is to confine them to tight internal labour markets under their own control' (Kreckel, 1980, p. 541). Thus employees are held within specific organizations, or categories of organization (for example, local authorities). Some of the best documented examples of FILMs in Britain are to be found in the major clearing banks (Crompton and Jones, 1984). FILMs are also characteristic of corporatist, 'Japanese style' management, and, as Ouchi (1981) has argued, tend to promote the development of the highly-trained generalist rather than the mobile specialist characteristic of OLMs and OILMs.

The continuum YZ represents individuals at a relative dis-advantage in that they lack *formal* skills and qualifications, either general or job-related. However, some jobs within firms requiring firm-specific knowledge may offer considerable job security, even if there is little in the way of opportunities outside the organization and only limited opportunities within it. Such firm labour markets (FLMs), therefore, are distinguished from FILMs both by the extent of career progression (promotion) which is possible, as well as the likely fates of individuals excluded from them. Workers in FLMs, however, have a considerable advantage over those exposed in the 'submarket for everyman's qualifications' (Kreckel, 1980) – the secondary labour market (SLM). 'All jobs in the secondary labour market lack the elements, or sources, of structure that define the other markets: job ladders, development of skill or knowledge, significant investment in training by either the employer or the employee, limited entry or notable entry requirements, and options for firm-specific tenure' (Althauser and Kalleberg, 1981, p. 136).

Figure 2.1 is further divided by MN, which suggests the 'structuring interface' between employers and employees. The direction of the arrows at the top and bottom of the line indicates the variations in directional pull at different skill and qualification levels. Where the workers in question have scarce and desirable skills, then segmentation theory suggests that employers will tend to pursue policies of encirclement and inclusion in FILMs; where skills are absent and/or generally available, workers will seek to establish secure FLMs, and a constant threat at the employers' disposal will be exposure in the SLM. An extensive literature in industrial sociology and industrial relations has described how economic recession has pushed more workers into SLMs, and how organized labour has been able to secure advantages in FLMs when product markets are stable and order books are full (Rubery, 1978). However, recent developments in Britain suggest that the assumptions underlying the direction of these arrows should perhaps be modified. There has been intensive political encouragement, together with state material aid, directed towards the development of individual 'occupational' strategies involving forms of self-employment. Similarly, pressures in favour of subcontracting will have worked against strategies of encirclement, resulting in a rightward movement of the MN axis overall.

In summary, therefore, Figure 2.1 describes the simultaneous structuring of occupations by the conflict between employers and their representatives on the one hand, and employees and trade unions on the other, as well as competition between different groups of employees, at different levels of the structure. In respect of the latter, the argument has often been made that such competition, as expressed in strategies of closure, fragments and splinters a putative working class. A similar argument may be developed in respect of a putative service class, which would be located along the WX axis.

This model of occupational structuring is culturally specific; in the broadest terms, it describes a contemporary capitalist industrial society. Given the realities of occupational segregation, women and men will be differentially located within it. The assumptions inherent in statistical discrimination (that feminine qualities render women inadequate employees) have been used to justify the location of women in secondary labour markets. SLMs also offer employment flexibility, and working hours (including part-time work) that can be fitted in around domestic responsibilities. Women are over-represented in this sector of the labour market. For example, women are 67 per cent of employees in hotel and catering and 76 per cent of employees in other catering, cleaning, hairdressing and other personal service jobs.

Sex-typing will tend to be associated with occupations which have relatively clear boundaries. (If the boundaries of an occupation are fuzzy, then it is also likely to be unclear as to whether is is a 'male' or 'female' job.) There is a range of 'caring' occupations such as speech therapy, nursing, physiotherapy, etc. often described as 'semi-professions' (Etzioni, 1969) and classified in the census as 'lower professional', that are sex-typed, female occupations. Typing and secretarial work is also sex-typed. Whilst it is certainly the case that many women doing such work are under-valued and under-paid, a qualified typist and/or secretary will usually have little difficulty in finding a job, and should certainly not be viewed as a member of the 'secondary' labour force. Sex-typed occupations which require pre-entry training and qualifications will tend to be clustered in occupational labour markets (OLMs) which are characterized by considerable, and usually voluntary, mobility. Flexibility and mobility is a characteristic of women's employment overall which, therefore, will tend to be concentrated along the occupational dimension of Figure 2.1, from the flexible instability of the SLM to the flexible stability of jobs in OLMs.

However, as we have seen, sex-typing is by no means confined to jobs for which higher-level training is required. The sex-typing of unskilled or semi-skilled jobs at the workplace will be organized around specific tasks or parts of the labour process. As with occupations requiring specific training, boundaries have to be drawn if a job is to be identified as 'male' or 'female'. Given that this is the case, it could be suggested that the sex-typing of jobs at the lower end of the occupational hierarchy will be associated with organizational labour markets, that is, FLMs. Women in manufacturing have traditionally been concentrated into women's occupations, even in those industries, such as textiles, clothing and footwear, which have a high proportion of female employees (Coyle, 1982). Examples would be the historical distinction between spinning and weaving in the Lancashire cotton industry, or between 'clicking' and 'closing' in the shoe industry described earlier. Such traditional areas of women's employment have also been associated with specially developed flexible working patterns such as the 'twilight shift'.

Concluding summary

The recurring theme of this book is straightforward – that at any moment in time, occupational segregation is being reproduced by cyclical practices which are the outcome of past conventions regarding the 'proper' relations between the sexes, the particular characteristics of national economies, and so on, as well as transformed by divergent practices such as the 'qualifications lever'. Occupational segregation is itself a source of stability, and conventional gender identities will be reinforced by work in sex-typed occupations. The orthodox division of labour between women and men in the public and private spheres will also be reaffirmed by jobs which offer the opportunity to combine domestic with paid work – that is, flexible conditions of working, part-time hours, and so on.

In this chapter, insights deriving from a range of theories purporting to explain occupational segregation have been combined in order to examine the location of women in the occupational structure as a whole. This is a product of the past sex-typing of occupations and conventional assumptions relating to the domestic roles of women, formal and informal exclusionary practices, and fluctuations in both the demand for labour and the nature of female labour available.

Sex-typing will tend to be associated with occupations which have relatively clear boundaries. It will, therefore, be associated with strategies of exclusion and closure. Thus the sex-typing of occupations – as opposed to the crowding of women in secondary labour markets – might be expected to occur along the AC diagonal: in OLMs, OILMs and FLMs.

Many jobs which are sex-typed, as already noted, will offer hours which are convenient as well. However, this is also a characteristic of many jobs in the SLM – work in the catering trade, casual agricultural work, part-time retail employment and so on. Thus women's employment will tend to be concentrated along the occupational dimension (AB) of Figure 2.1: from the flexible instability of the SLM to the flexible stability of jobs in OLMs.

It has been suggested that discrete occupational boundaries are integral to the process/maintenance of sex-typing. Overt exclusionary practices have to be oriented around an identifiable occupation, and in a similar fashion, exclusion based upon traditionalist assumptions has had to be constructed in respect of a specific task. Where exclusionary practices are legitimized by formal, rationalistic criteria (for example, qualifying examinations) then access to these (formerly) 'male' occupations may be achieved via the 'qualifications lever' which operates along the WX continuum.

Where exclusion has rested upon traditionalist assumptions and practices at the level of the locality or firm, then these practices are susceptible to pressures towards flexibility etc. which are increasingly felt by a workforce already weakened by economic recession. Many of these 'women only' jobs are also associated with declining industries such as textiles and footwear. Thus sex-typing may be eroded, but the size of the SLM is increasing (Hakim, 1987; Dale and Bamford, 1988). At the *aggregate* level, little change in occupational segregation may be noted.

These assumptions, together with the more general assumptions contained in Figure 2.1, have been investigated via a series of case studies. (The numbering of these case studies corresponds to their location within Figure 2.1).

Pharmacy (1) is a non sex-typed occupation, for which women are qualifying in ever greater numbers, and which offers a wide range of employment opportunities in flexible occupational labour markets. Historic patterns of internal segregation have developed within this occupation. Accountancy (2) is an occupation which women have been entering at a rapid rate since the mid-1970s. It offers opportunities for both 'occupational' and 'organizational' careers, but organizational careers put most strain on the conventional domestic role as far as women are concerned. Building society management trainees (3) are exemplars of organizational careers for which formal qualifications are increasingly required; women are gaining these qualifications but still face problems associated with male exclusionary practices. Cashier-clerks within building societies (4) are almost entirely women, recruited at a time of massive expansion of the building society branch network in the 1960s and 1970s. The school meals service (5) is an all-female occupation in decline as a consequence largely of political factors. Finally, the hotel and catering industry (6) is an expanding sector of the secondary labour market, largely indifferent to the gender of the unqualified labour it recruits.

Given the significance of normative and cultural factors in the structuring of women's employment, an historical perspective is necessary in order to understand its patterns of development and change. Patterns of sex-typing, for example, are likely to reflect the particular configuration of ideas relating to gender proprieties at the time that particular occupations emerged out of the division of labour. Before we begin our exploration of the case studies, therefore, Chapter 3 will briefly summarize the nature of, and changes in, 'women's estate' in Britain since the Second World War.

Notes

1 Dingwall, 1983. The term 'subjective economy' is one he takes from Friedson, and it broadly corresponds to the domestic or private sphere 'where . . . labour is not part of any system of economic exchange although symbolic, and occasionally material, rewards may accrue' (ibid., p. 622).

2 See the report of the NUT/EOC: 'Promotion and the woman teacher', March 1980, together with an empirical updating: 'Women in teaching: a decade of progress?', NUT Research Unit, April 1987.

3 It has been argued that the cheapness of female labour derives from the fact that most women are 'component wage' earners, rather than from their gender as such (Siltanen, 1986). This observation may often be valid, but it should not be allowed to obscure the fact that once cultural sex-typing *has* occurred, it assumes a reality which may over-determine purely economic calculations. Economists have distinguished three hypotheses which seek to explain the underlying trends in women's labour force participation: these are (i) women as a 'buffer' or 'flexible reserve', (ii) job segmentation (or sex-typing) and (iii) as a substitute for more expensive categories of labour. However, as is argued in Rubery (ed.) (1988), these perspectives are complementary rather than contradictory.

4 There is some ambiguity here as skills may be socially constructed and, indeed, a considerable literature on women's work has demonstrated how 'women's' skills have been socially defined as inferior. Nevertheless, it is as misleading to treat skills as mainly socially constructed as it would be to assume that they are mainly determined by 'rational' factors, and qualification levels do provide a reasonable measure of this aspect.

5 The labels used to describe these segments have been adapted from Althauser and Kalleberg (1981). Similar arguments have been developed by other authors, including Kreckel (1980) and Loveridge (1987). For an excellent review and empirical application of labour market segmentation theory see Dale (1987). The extensive use of broken lines, arrows, etc. in describing Figure 2.1 is to reinforce the point that although the model is two-dimensionally divided up into segments and areas, *these should not be treated as watertight compartments.*

6   Although Althauser and Kalleberg's concepts are used here, the distinction being made between OLMs and OILMs is different. The distinction that Althauser and Kalleberg draw between OLMs and OILMs is that the latter incorporate job ladders, whereas the former do not although some degree of market shelter is afforded. By implication, OILMs are 'superior' to OLMs; jobs in OLMs require less training than jobs in OILMs. In this discussion, however, OLMs and OILMs include similar occupations, which may be carried out within occupational or organizational labour markets.

3 Women in Britain: the post-war context

Introduction

The last chapter, which focused upon occupational segregation, examined in some depth arguments which have been developed to explain the location of women in the occupational structure. This exploration included the development of a model of the production and reproduction of the occupational structure, and the way in which ideas and assumptions relating to masculinity and feminity are incorporated in it. In the empirical case studies of industries and occupations that follow in this book, the structuring of occupations will be further examined. However, the experiences of women in particular occupations cannot be adequately grasped unless set in a context of the broader structure of gender relations, or the 'gender order' (Connell, 1987).

The concept of the gender order, unlike the more specific notion of patriarchy, begins from the premise that there will be a considerable variation in gender relations, both over time and between different societies. Not only may the structures of labour, power, and cathexis (or the construction of emotionally charged relationships with other people) be different, but so are their combinations. It may be argued that Connell's framework is rather loosely defined, and over-reliant on a straightforward empirical description of the links between the structures in question, rather than the specification of the theoretical relationships between them. Nevertheless, his arguments do provide some elements of framework around which to organize a discussion of the changing situation of women in Britain since the Second World War.

Connell emphasizes that the structure of gender relations may be internally contradictory, that is, that the patterns of relationship in the different structures may come into conflict with each other (1987, p. 96). Generalized notions of strain, tensions, contradictions, etc. are widely employed in the social sciences. In the case of the development of the women's movement, a relevant and well-documented example of the outcome of such a contradiction is to be found in the history of nineteenth-century feminism in the United States (Eisenstein, 1981; Bouchier, 1983). Women had taken a leading role in the movements working towards the abolition of slavery. The parallels between the women's own circumstances and those for whom they were campaigning became only too apparent, and their treatment within the abolitionist movement created many tensions. For example, female abolitionists were not permitted to address public meetings on a trip to England and were concealed behind a curtain. The ideology of the American constitution was contradicted by the legal status of slavery, and the work of the abolitionists was contradicted by the treatment of women activists within the movement. As a consequence, abolitionists were prominent in the development of nineteenth-century feminism.

The scope of the investigation in this chapter is relatively circumscribed. To provide a complete description of the gender order in Britain since the end of the Second World War would be a considerable undertaking. This brief discussion, therefore, will seek to highlight those aspects particularly relevant to the participation of women in paid employment.

In respect of the structure of power, state policy will be given considerable emphasis, particularly its role in the construction of two, rather different, female identities: 'mother' and 'citizen'. Mother-child relationships are of enormous significance in the structure of cathexis. However, in practice the duties of the 'good mother' have shown much variation. With the development of the Welfare State in Britain during this century, state policies have had a considerable impact on the structuring of this role. However, immediately after the Second World War, women in Britain were receiving contra-dictory 'messages' about their position. On the one hand, there were moves towards the achievement of full citizenship (including educational provision) which guaranteed and enhanced their right to participate in the public sphere of paid employment; on the other, women were also being told that their 'real' work lay in the private, domestic sphere of home and children. This is a particular instance of a persisting tension between the ideology of bourgeois liberalism, which proclaims freedom, and equality for all citizens in societies where structural constraints on achieving material equality still persist (Merton, 1965).

The many facets of the state

Chodorow has argued: 'Because women are themselves mothered by women, they grow up with the relational capacities and needs . . . which commit them to mothering. Men, because they are mothered by women, do not' (Chodorow, 1978, p. 209). Thus, she argues, mothering reproduces women's responsibilities and their continuing location in the domestic sphere. Whilst there is much to say in support of this analysis, it is nevertheless the case that the extent to which women are *confined* to the domestic sphere is not only a consequence of this simple reproduction within the family. Furthermore, a reduction or modification in the extent of mothering by individual women will be likely to change its nature. Although some kind of mothering is universal, ideas of *motherhood* are not, and changes in the latter will affect the former.

In Britain, state policies have long held the mother personally responsible for the care of her children. Thus campaigns to reduce infant mortality, for example, were directed at the education of the mother, rather than the provision of alternatives to maternal care or material state support. In the inter-war period, infant mortality was seen as a failure of motherhood. Maternal and child welfare services were concentrated on educating the mother in personal hygiene, and the working mother was held to be 'feckless' (Lewis, 1980). This close association of women with welfare was carried over into the development of the Welfare State after the Second World War. Welfare legislation was a key element in the development of what Marshall (1951) has described as 'citizenship'. He identified citizenship as having three components: civil, political and social. Civil citizenship was achieved with *habeas corpus* and political citizenship with the franchise. Social citizenship may best be summed up as representing a minimum standard of welfare and the move towards equality of opportunity for all citizens; major moves were made in this direction both during the Second World War and by the reforming Labour government which was elected in 1945. These included the consolidation and expansion of state benefits after the Beveridge Report (1942), and other reforms such as the Butler Education Act (1944), which made free secondary education universal. In short, the development of the Welfare State represented, for Marshall, the development of social citizenship.

The universal rights of all citizens could not actually be denied to women. Indeed, it can be argued that in some instances women benefited disproportionately from the introduction of universalistic criteria. For example, places in secondary education for girls had to be rapidly expanded in order to meet the requirements of the Act. However, in the case of social welfare, state policy had the effect of consolidating the material circumstances which confined women to the home.

Wilson has argued in respect of Beveridge that 'the principles underlying the Report were not those of socialism, but were the principle of insurance; the principle of the subsistence income; and the principle of the sanctity of the family' (1977, p. 148). The report anticipated that 'during marriage most women will not be gainfully employed'; married women were thus regarded as their husbands' dependants, and exempted from unemployment and sickness benefit contributions. Unsupported mothers (unless widows) were not included in the social insurance scheme, and were forced to rely on supplementary benefit. However, family allowances were endorsed by Beveridge, who was, like many others, concerned at the fall in the birth rate which had occurred during the inter-war period. Therefore, Beveridge argued,

> The attitude of the housewife to gainful employment outside the home is not and should not be the same as that of the single woman. She has other duties . . . In the next thirty years housewives as mothers have vital work to do in ensuring the adequate con-tinuance of the British Race and of British Ideals in the world. (cited in Wilson, 1977, pp. 151-2).

In the thirty years and more that have elapsed since Beveridge, one of the major social changes has been the increase in the employment of married women. However, it may be argued that social policies initiated in the 1940s are still one of the major means by which gender inequalities within the family are sustained (Land, 1983).

At the same time as the Beveridge Report, however, moves were being made in the area of employment towards a legislative equality of treatment for men and women in the public realm. The Royal Commission on Equal Pay (1946) and the Whitley Council report on Marriage Bars (1946), continued the laborious process of dismantling statutory discrimination – which had actually been intensified by the introduction of marriage bars (in response to recession) during the inter-war period. Walby (1986) has argued that 'the dropping of the marriage bar during the war was the single most important effect of the war on gender relations' (pp. 247-8). But the barriers were not formally removed, in many institutions, until the 1950s. The debates of the period may be read in two ways: both as reflections and reinforcements of the male-dominated status quo, but also as evidence of a gradual movement towards the realization of orthodox liberal feminist aims. After the traumas of the Second World War, and with the beginnings of the 'cold war' era, it may be suggested that the prevailing ideological climate in Britain was, in any case, highly receptive to ideas in favour of individual freedoms and equality of access. Arguments suggesting that biological grounds were a firm basis for inequalities of treatment would be unlikely to be well received. The linkage of the moral claims of individualism with the national interest is evident in an influential Memorandum of Dissent to the Royal Commission on Equal Pay (1946). Arguing strongly for the validity of equal pay, the Memorandum concluded: 'the claims of justice between individuals and of the development of national productivity point in the same direction' (p. 196).

Moves towards formal equality in the public realm, however, were accompanied by contradictory pressures in the domestic (or private) sphere, as has been illustrated by the treatment of married women in respect of social insurance. Many women employed in the war effort had been returned to domesticity upon demobilization. In Britain, as we have seen, the government was committed to a policy of pro-natalism, after the substantial decline in the birth rate during the inter-war period. An indirect strategy was developed which attempted to enhance the attractions of maternity and domestic life, rather than, for example, the direct strategy of making contraception unobtainable (the latter, in any case, had unfortunate fascist overtones). Not only pro-natalism, however, but also developments in the ideology of motherhood served to reinforce this elevation of domesticity. Infant mortality had once been perceived as the major issue, and the attention of the experts had been directed mainly at improvements in health and hygiene. With a reduction in infant mortality, however, attention began to be moved towards psychological, rather than physiological, problems. John Bowlby, a Kleinian-influenced social psychologist argued that the nature of the mother-child bond was central to the mental health of the future adult (1953). His work was widely interpreted to mean that *any* separation of mother and child was potentially damaging. In a 1958 pamphlet, for example, entitled 'Can I leave my baby?' the advice he gave suggested that, apart from the possibility of a brief shopping trip, the answer was 'no' (cited in Riley, 1983, p. 10). 'Scientific' psychological theories were reinforced by popular handbooks of childrearing such as Dr Spock:

> In most cases, the mother is the best one to give him this feeling of 'belonging', safety and security . . . If a mother realizes clearly how vital this kind of care is to a small child, it may make it easier for her to decide that the extra money she might earn, or the

satisfaction she might receive from an outside job, is not so important after all.[1]

The practical reality of child-rearing has probably always owed more to parental instincts and preferences than textbook knowledge (Newsom and Newsom, 1963) but, perhaps paradoxically, 'scientific' theories of the child and mother are more likely to have had an impact on official policy than common-sense practice. Nevertheless, whatever the precise reasons and however inadequate it may have been (Summerfield, 1984) the network of state nursery provision for young children established during the war was dismantled after it.

The decades after the Second World War, therefore, were ones in which the messages being received by women regarding work and employment were contradictory. On the one hand, slow moves were in progress towards their treatment (in principle) as equal 'citizens' in the market place. On the other, mothers (and most women are actual or potential mothers) were repeatedly being told that their real 'work' lay at home in caring for their children. Riley has succinctly expressed the situation as follows: 'women were, rhetorically, both over-personified as mothers and desexed as workers' (1983, p. 18). Meshing with these contradictory cultural prescriptions were the requirements of the postwar economy, which was booming.[2] In Britain, the solution to these contradictions was that married women *did* return to the labour force, but increasingly as part-time workers and usually after having partially completed their 'real' work, the rearing of children. It should be stressed, however, that it is not being suggested that the popularizing of Bowlbyian theories of child-rearing was a deliberate ploy to keep women tied to the domestic sphere. Nevertheless, it is being argued that, in Britain, the state played an important part in the development of an ideology which made individual *mothers* responsible for their children. When the focus of child-rearing shifted from its more physiological to its psychological aspects, therefore, individual mothers were yet again the major targets. The notion of maternal responsibility exerts a 'moral despotism' (Lockwood, 1982) over women qualitatively different from the institutional restraints to which women were (and to an extent still are) subject. This is not to cast women as dupes, nor to question the positive reality of the mother-child bond. In Britain, the context was such as to be likely to reinforce the conditions of 'conditional fatalism' (ibid.) as well.

The argument that the tension between the tedium of isolated domesticity and increasing opportunities for, and rights in, employment was an important factor underlying the development of 'second wave' feminism in the 1960s has been well-rehearsed (Friedan, 1975; Eisenstein, 1981; Bouchier, 1983). In the UK, the social citizenship of women was confirmed by legislation, including the Equal Pay Act of 1970, which was implemented in 1975. In 1983, the Equal Pay (Amendment) Regulations (which came into force in 1984) extended the principle of 'equal pay for equal work' to include 'equal pay for work of equal value' (the efficacy of this latter principle, however, is still being tested in the courts). The Sex Discrimination Act of 1975 made direct and indirect discrimination on the grounds of sex unlawful. (Indirect discrimination refers to a condition which, although applied equally to men and women, is in fact significantly more difficult for a woman to fulfil.) The Employment Protection Act of 1975 gave protection from unfair dismissal on the grounds of pregnancy, and a right to reinstatement without loss of status after maternity leave (these provisions became operational in 1976 and 1977). Knowledge of and access to contraception had been growing since the Second World War (Lewis, 1984) and in 1974 it was finally made available, free, under the National Health Service. Abortion had been legalized in 1967.

As many have argued, the impressive-looking enumeration of legislation concerning the rights of women in respect of both employment and the control of their bodies leaves no ground for complacency. Maternity leave provision has actually been eroded (Amendment to the Employment Protection Act: Statutory Maternity Pay (General) Regulations 1986). The Equal Opportunities Commission, set up at the time of the Equal Pay and Sex Discrimination Acts to promote opportunity and investigate cases of possible discrimination, has been under-resourced and poorly supported by government. Rights (and access) to legal abortion have been almost continuously under attack from well-organized pressure groups. A succession of private member's bills and legal cases have aimed to narrow the conditions for abortion, reduce the time limit during which a legal abortion may be carried out, and establish the rights of the putative father. Nevertheless, most of the provisions of the 1970s still remain in place and as far as legislation is concerned, the decade must be regarded as the equal of that which granted the suffrage to women (1918–28). These legislative changes were accompanied by significant developments in the level and pattern of education and training undertaken by women, to which we now turn.

Education and qualifications

Education was one of the first areas which attracted the attentions of academic feminists in the 1960s and 1970s. This was doubtless due to the fact that educational practice tended massively to reinforce gender stereotypes. Influential academic work on feminism during this period relied heavily on socialization and the concept of role in giving an account of gender (Oakley, 1972). Educational provisions fitted in with these explanations very well. Histories of charitable and state education for girls demonstrated that whereas boys were educated for work, girls were educated for domesticity. In the 1940s, 1950s and early 1960s, practical subjects for boys were woodwork and metalwork; needlework and cookery were reserved for girls. Infant reading schemes were constructed around the nuclear family, where mother stayed at home and looked after Janet and John (or Peter and Jane, or Simon and Elizabeth) whilst father went out to work. This stereotyping of educational provision, it was argued, was reflected in the examination and post-school performances of boys and girls within the educational system (Byrne, 1978; Deem, 1978). Fewer girls than boys went into higher education, and further education (where proportionately more girls gained access) was dominated by gendered training such as for nursing and secretarial work. Boys gained technical qualifications, and predominated on day-release courses essential to the pursuit of a long-term career. In 1963, on the basis of trends then current, the Robbins Report predicted that by 1980, 10.7 per cent of male school leavers, but only 5 per cent of female would have achieved three A levels and thus higher level university entrance qualifications.

However, despite a long history of gender stereotyping, recent trends suggest that education may be assuming an important role in breaking down occupational segregation for a growing number of women. In the first place, girls' school leaving attainments have improved considerably relatively to boys. As summarized elsewhere (Crompton and Sanderson, 1987, p. 136), fewer girls than boys leave school with no qualifications at all, and in 1981–2, 28 per cent of girls, but 25 per cent of boys left school with 1–4 O levels, and 11 per cent of girls, but 9 per cent of boys, left school with five or more O levels. In the same year, 10.7 per cent of young men, and 9.2 per cent of young women, left schools or further education colleges with three or more A level passes. The male figure is exactly in line with Robbins's predictions, that for young women has been far exceeded. Past trends suggest that around 10.5

per cent represents a plateau in A level attainment, and the data for males indicate little deviation from this figure since it was achieved in 1975–6. The proportion of female leavers with three A levels, however, has increased from 7.3 per cent to 9.2 per cent over the same period (1975–1982). Of course, important differences by subject still persist (women predominate in arts subjects, men in sciences) and these are very significant given the differential impact of cuts by subject in higher education.

The improvement in girls' school leaving qualifications has been a smoothly rising curve although the gradient of the curve has increased somewhat in recent years. There have been substantial fluctuations, however, in the pattern of further and higher education and qualifications for women. These are largely a consequence of the massive increase, followed by an equally massive cut-back, of teacher training places in the 1960s and 1970s.

The expansion of state education after the Second World War, followed by the raising of the school leaving age, had created an increased demand for teachers of all kinds. School teaching is highly segregated by gender; women predominate in the teaching of infant and junior school children, men in secondary and further education. Until the 1980s teacher training was of two kinds: (i) non-graduate initial teacher training in specialized institutions (training colleges), which provided the majority of non-secondary school teachers, and (ii) postgraduate certification, often in university departments of education. Teacher training establishments have had the status of institutions of higher education since the first were established in the nineteenth century. They were also a poor relation within the system. Training colleges were originally denominational, linked to the provision of basic education for the poor (state elementary school education), rather than that provided by the grammar or public schools. In the nineteenth century, the training colleges provided the only form of higher education available to women when they were barred from entering the universities. During the twentieth century both local authorities and civic universities began to make provision for the education of teachers, and local authority provision came to dominate teacher training after the 1944 Education Act. Most colleges followed the pattern initiated by the first Anglican foundations – isolated institutions on green field sites, with grandiose buildings harbouring what were often very poor academic standards. Training colleges were, however, cheap and Robbins (1963) calculated that whereas a university student cost £660 a year, a teacher training student cost £255.

For nearly three decades after the Second World War, teacher training was *the* route into higher education for young women, as illustrated in Table 3.1. In 1965 there were thirty-eight thousand male, but only fifteen thousand female, first-year, full-time undergraduates admitted to British universities. However there were twenty-six thousand first-year female students at teacher training colleges, compared to only ten thousand men. During this period, the training colleges were described as 'a traditional form of higher education for working-class women' (Robinson, 1968, p. 17). In the 1970s, however, this avenue was abruptly blocked.

Whereas in the mid-1960s nearly twice as many women went into initial teacher training as went to universities, by the early 1980s, the number of women going into initial teacher training had more than halved and was only just over a third of the numbers going to university. The significance which initial teacher training once had for higher education for women may be further illustrated by another summary statistic: in 1970, 73 per cent of all female enrolments on advanced courses in non-university further and higher education institutions were in teacher training; by 1982, this proportion had dropped to 14 per cent (Crompton and Sanderson, 1987).

These summary cuts in initial teacher training were a consequence of a number of factors, including government cuts in educational provision in response to the deepening recession, a decline in the

Table 3.1 *First year full-time students in universities and initial teacher training, by sex (thousands)*

		university undergraduates	initial teacher training
1965–6	men	38	10
	women	15	26
1970–1	men	44	14
	women	21	34
1975–6	men	49	13
	women	27	29
1979–80	men	52	6
	women	34	12
1980–1	men	52	6
	women	34	11
1981–2	men	50	6
	women	33	12

Source: 1983, HMSO. Adapted from *Education Statistics for the UK*, Table 23.

birthrate, the slowing down of teachers leaving the profession in the years following the Houghton pay awards, and sheer bad management (Hencke, 1978). Given the importance of teacher training to women's higher education, considerable disquiet was expressed as to the differential impact the cuts would have on women (Bone, 1980). Indeed, women's opportunities in the non-university sector did suffer a temporary setback – and it will be remembered that these cuts were applied at a time when the supply of well-qualified female school leavers was rising. However, contrary to some expectations, women's share of further and higher education faltered only slightly. As is demonstrated in Table 3.1, they have continued to increase as a proportion of university undergraduates and, in the non-university sector, women have improved their representation on BEC/TEC courses, professional training courses, and other advanced and degree courses. The number of women has also increased on day and block release courses, particularly in the finance industries and in public administration (Crompton and Sanderson, 1987).

As far as education is concerned, therefore, it would seem to be an area where females are beginning to achieve some kind of parity with males – at least in respect of formal school leaving qualifications. There has been a narrowing of the male/female differential in post A level education and qualifications. This is a perhaps unexpected by-product of the massive drop in the availability of initial teacher training opportunities. Developments in the teacher training area have been stressed not only because of its significance for women's higher education from the 1950s to the early 1970s, but also because it may be argued that teacher training played a significant role in perpetrating gender segregation at the higher levels of the occupational structure. There are, of course, many positive aspects to teaching as far as women are concerned. There has been equal pay for women for many years and, although women are under-represented in promoted posts, it was for a long time one of the few occupations where women could achieve positions of responsibility. Nevertheless, as Deem has argued, 'If teaching has provided some women with an opening into a professional career, it has done so without fundamentally changing the position of those women in the sexual division of labour in British society' (1978, p. 109). Teaching, particularly the teaching of young children, not only reinforces cultural norms relating to 'women's work', but also means that the woman, as wife and mother, can fit her paid work around the requirements of home and family. Although the opportunities which teaching offers have clearly been advantageous to many women, nevertheless the expansion of this occupation has enabled higher education and employment opportunities to be taken up by women without any real modification to the kinds of gender roles, and the domestic division of labour, which had been established after the Second World War. To put it another way, the female domination of this expanding occupation will have played its part in maintaining the status quo between the sexes despite the improvements in education and opportunities for women in and from the 1940s onwards.

The sudden and drastic cut in teacher-training places, it would appear, has 'bumped' a substantial number of well-educated women into professional education and training other than teaching (Crompton and Sanderson, 1986). As women begin to qualify and enter into other occupations, the complementarity between paid work and domestic responsibilities such as is found in teaching can no longer be assumed. The working day in a bank or insurance company is not structured around a timetable appropriate to the demands of a husband and family. Indeed, it may be suggested that the difficulties faced by such women – who, by virtue of their education and training, may occupy relatively influential positions in the occupational structure – may be a source of pressure for change in the division of labour in both the narrower and broader senses.

Employment

The growth of, and contemporary developments in, the structure of women's paid employment have been extensively documented in recent years (Hakim, 1979; Martin and Roberts, 1984). Throughout the inter-war years, economic activity rates for women remained remarkably stable at around 38 per cent, and in the years immediately following the war, rose only slightly despite wartime mobilization, to 43 per cent in 1951 (data taken from Hakim, 1979[3]). However, by 1971, activity rates amongst women of working age had risen to 55 per cent and by 1981 reached 61 per cent. This increase in female employment has been largely an increase in *married* women's employment. Throughout the inter-war period the proportion of married women working did not rise above 10 per cent. It will be recalled that in any case marriage bars were widespread, and married women were positively discouraged from employment during the recession (Walby, 1986). However, by 1951 the proportion had risen to 22 per cent, to 42 per cent by 1961 and 52 per cent by 1980.

Women's participation in the labour force varies markedly by age, closely reflecting the domestic responsibilities of married women –

or rather, women with children. Hakim describes the emergence of the 'two-phase' employment profile amongst women. In the inter-war decades, economic activity rates amongst young women were high (over 70 per cent) but declined sharply in the 'marital years', that is, from the early 20s, levelling out to a plateau of about 20 per cent which would have included mainly unmarried and/or childless women. By 1961, however, there emerged the two-phase or bimodal work profile. Activity rates were high amongst younger women, and declined throughout their 20s. From the age group of about 35, however, activity rates increased sharply until, by the 40–50 year age group, they equalled the participation rates of the youngest women. This second peak was largely composed of women returning to the labour force once their children were of school age, and was reflected in the sharp rise in the participation rates of married women. More recent evidence (Dex, 1984) suggests that younger cohorts of women are moving beyond the two-phase pattern described above. Increasing numbers of women, it would seem, are returning to work between births and the total period spent out of the labour force during child-rearing is compressed.

As the pattern of women's formal economic activity is so closely bound up with child-rearing and domestic responsibilities, it is not surprising that much of women's employment is part time, an arrangement which facilitates both 'public' and 'private' sphere work – whether this is viewed unproblematically as fulfilling 'women's two roles' (Myrdal and Klein, 1956) or as 'double exploitation' (Eisenstein, 1981). Beechey (1986) has summarized the pattern of part-time working as follows:

> The 1984 Labour Force Survey showed that 88% of all part-time employees are women . . . Nearly 45% of women working (and 55% of married women) work part-time, compared with (about) 4% of working men. It is women returning to work who comprise the majority of part-time workers. Most part-timers are married, and mothers in particular tend to work part-time. (Beechey, 1986, p. 93).

Part-time work follows the pattern of occupational segregation described in the last chapter. Part-time work in manufacturing industry is declining overall (although very important in particular industries with a long tradition of 'women's work', for example, clothing, food processing) but is increasing in the service sector, the fastest growing category of women's employment. It is particularly prevalent in 'personal service' occupations: cleaning (including office and hospital cleaners, etc.) and cooking (for example, waitressing, and in restaurants, canteens, the school meals service), as well as retail and some clerical and related occupations. Beechey and Perkins (1987) argue that many of these jobs have been constructed as part-time, married women's jobs. When flexible working is required of 'women's work', then part-time jobs are created. However, flexibility in 'men's' jobs is achieved through overtime working, or the hiring of (male) full-time temporary workers. This is true even of sectors where women predominate, such as the health service.

Women's employment in Britain, therefore, has developed in a way that has facilitated, for many of them, the combination of their two roles over the cycle of their work and domestic lives. It could be argued that, besides often being a particularly exploitative form of women's employment, part-time work also serves to perpetrate and reinforce the existing gender division of labour in both the public and private spheres. Thus part-time work may be seen as a way in which the requirements of capitalism and patriarchy may both be met, resolving the tensions described by Walby (1986).

This (apparent) functional fit between part-time work and the reconciliation of women's two roles might seem to be such an obvious solution as not to warrant further explanation. Cross-national variations in the extent of part-time working amongst women, however, suggest that it is too simplistic. Although women are more likely to work part-time in all countries, Britain has one of the highest rates internationally (OECD, 1985). Comparisons may be drawn between Britain and France, which have very similar proportions of women in the labour force. However, 1983 labour force survey data showed that whilst 42 per cent of employed women in Britain work part-time, this is true of only 20 per cent of French women (Dale and Glover, 1987). A number of explanations have been offered to account for this variation. Amongst the most important appear to be the provision of child care facilities (both pre-school and school age) by the French State, as well as fiscal and social insurance policies which do not make part-time work particularly attractive to French employers. In Britain, on the other hand, part-timers who work less than sixteen hours a week are not covered by the Employment Protection Act, and part-timers are often not eligible for bonus schemes, pension benefits, or holiday pay. These kinds of comparisons suggest that the French state policies have had a considerable effect on the level of part-time employment amongst women. In Britain, in contrast, a lack of state support for working mothers, together with policies which have emphasized the responsibility of individual mothers for the welfare of their children, has led to lower levels of full-time working amongst mothers.

The implication of this Franco-British, and other international comparisons, will be discussed further in the last chapter of this book. This kind of evidence serves, however, to further emphasize the variable nature of gender relations. These variations are to be found not only at the aggregate level of the nation state, but also between women of different ethnic origins within the same country. A survey carried out in the early 1980s revealed that 75 per cent of West Indian women between the ages of 25 and 34 were economically active, as compared to 54 per cent of white women, 88 per cent between the ages of 35 and 44 compared to 70 per cent of whites, and 83 per cent between 45 and 54 compared to 65 per cent of whites (figures cited in Beechey, 1986, p. 83). Participation rates for Asian women were closer to those of whites but slightly lower, but the participation rate for Muslims was extremely low at all ages. West Indian women are more likely to work full-time. They are more frequently the sole or major supporters of their households than white women. (It may also be noted that white single mothers in paid employment are also more likely to work full-time.) The extent of this variation might be used to argue that it is particular national and/or economic circumstances, rather than gender *per se*, which structures the pattern of women's employment. For example, Siltanen, on the basis of empirical evidence derived from her study of the British Post Office, which employs a considerable minority of black women, has argued that it is primarily financial need and relations to household maintenance that structures the distribution of people to occupations, rather than gender. Thus married white women (and unmarried adult men living with their parents) require only 'component wage' jobs at lower rates of pay. In contrast, married white men and black women assuming the responsibilities of breadwinner require full wage jobs. She argues, therefore, that gender is *not* a 'generally valid category in relation to the structuring of employment and a theory of equality' (1986, p.118).

These cross-national and inter-ethnic variations in female employment have been used to support the argument that patriarchy should not be seen theoretically as a universal system. It is gender relations that are universal, rather than a specific form of patriarchy. As has been argued in Chapter 2, a distinction should be drawn between segregation in employment which arises as a consequence of women's characteristics as 'labour' taken in a neutral sense (for example, their crowding, along with other categories of disadvantaged labour, into lower-level occupations), and the normative or cultural sex-typing associated with occupations held to be 'feminine'. Siltanen's argument provides an insightful account of how variations in family responsibilities between different groups of women – and men – structure their labour force participation. Her work might be regarded as a micro-level case study which emphasizes the same kind of arguments as those of the Cambridge Labour Studies Group (Craig, Garnsey and Rubery, 1984), who have laid a similar emphasis on the 'domestic' structuring of the labour force. These arguments are, however incomplete, as they tend not to incorporate the cultural stereotyping of occupations. This factor may have been more important in the past, but the occupational structure still bears the massive imprint of past socio-cultural practices.

Summary and conclusions

Besides giving an account of recent developments in Britain, this chapter has also used the example of women's employment to carry further forward the argument that the market – and thus the occupational structure – is as much a social as an economic construct. Thus at any moment in time the pattern of women's employment will reflect both existing as well as past assumptions relating to gender.

Gender assumptions are also reflected in contemporary social science literature. For example, in the 1950s, a respected textbook in the sociology of work (Caplow, 1954) noted two major normative sanctions structuring women's employment: '(1) that it is disgraceful for a man to be directly subordinated to a woman, except in family or sexual relationships; (2) that intimate groups, except those based on family or sexual ties, should be composed of either sex but never of both' (p. 238). The emphasis given to these normative sanctions has changed, but the occupational structure still bears their imprint. In the same vein, although 'the woman's two roles' literature was, by the standards of the times, progressive in respect of women's employment, Myrdal and Kleins' discussion of 1956 took it for granted that women would assume the major responsibility for the care of children.

In their description of the attitudes of employers, Beechey and Perkins (1987) have provided ample evidence that *employers* do not regard the labour force as gender-neutral, and discriminate between different categories of potential female employee depending upon age and stage in the family life cycle. However, female employees are not a static, even if internally differentiated, category. As we have seen, there have since the Second World War been substantial changes in the nature of the supply of female labour, as well as changes in the cultural prescriptions surrounding it.

These changes, it has been suggested, have in part stemmed from the fact that the messages being received by women as wives and mothers on the one hand, and as public citizens on the other, were in conflict. Brenner and Ramas (1984) have suggested that the 'exigencies' of biological reproduction should be given due weight in explanations of the structuring of occupations; that the nineteenth-century burdens of pregnancy and lactation, for example, placed extensive limitations upon the public sphere work of which women were capable. However, their critics have argued that biological consequences are not just physical, and that the *social* consequences of biology are themselves negotiated. Postwar developments in contraception and abortion legislation have modified the purely physical aspects of biology, but of equal, if not more, importance, has been the social construction of motherhood and child-rearing. In the decades after the Second World War, women were under considerable pressure from a whole range of 'authorities' to devote long hours to the *personal* care of their young children. In contrast, the growth of 'social citizenship' ensuring the rights of all individuals progressively 'desexed' (at least in theory) women in the market place and public sphere more generally; marriage bars were removed, girls given more equality of access to secondary education, etc. These contradictions were exacerbated by the rising demand for labour in the 1950s and 1960s.

During the 1970s (a decade which, paradoxically, was to witness a sharp down-turn in the demand for labour with the advent of the recession) legislation was achieved on equal pay, fertility control, and the outlawing of gender discrimination. This legislation may be viewed as in part a continuation of the growth of 'citizenship', but was also a consequence of the pressures of 'neo' or second wave feminism which emerged, in part, from the contradictions described above. (That such legislation has remained on the statute book, especially that relating to fertility control, is almost certainly due to continuing feminist pressure.)

For the majority of women in Britain, however, cultural and economic contradictions have been resolved on the practical level by a temporary retirement from paid employment during their child-rearing phase, combined with part-time working for a period on their return to the labour force. However, although both the patterning of employment, and more direct experience of work, might have reinforced this solution, it might also enhance further the contradictions experienced by many women. Indeed, for some women, education for equality has had far-reaching effects. This has been particularly the case when a major avenue of occupationally segregated (and gender reinforcing) employment for better-educated women – school teaching – was abruptly closed off in the 1970s.

The possible consequences of the increase in the number and proportions of well-qualified women in non gender-specific (or sex-typed) occupations will be explored via case studies of pharmacy, accountancy, and the building society industry. This erosion of segregation via rational and legalistic strategies (the 'qualifications lever') at the higher levels of the occupational structure, however, has been accompanied by the persistence, if not growth, of the 'secondary' labour force. Therefore, although the decades since the Second World War must be seen as positive as far as women's rights are concerned, there are also indications of an increasing dualism within the labour force which may be particularly pronounced in respect of female employment. The development of the flexible labour force has received considerable attention in the debates surrounding the supposed end of 'organized capitalism' (Lash and Urry, 1987); these will be further examined in respect of an industry which has long been the ultimate in flexible employment – hotels and catering (Chapter 7).

Notes

1 Cited in Friedan (1975).
2 It is paradoxical that whilst the Ministry of Labour was appealing for more women workers, the Ministry of Health was extolling the virtues of domesticity (Riley, 1983, 133 f., 172 f.).
3 'Economically active' is a Department of Employment definition which includes individuals in work or seeking employment. The argument has often been made that such a definition will tend to underestimate the number of women both in employment and/or seeking work. Women who work at home (for example, child-minding, home-working) or seasonally (for instance, in agriculture) may not be registered as in employment. Similarly, women who become unemployed may not go on to the unemployment register for a number of reasons (ineligibility for unemployment benefit, decision to undertake further family commitments, etc.)

4 Qualifications and occupations: the example of pharmacy

Introduction

In Chapter 2, it was argued that if women have, historically, been kept out of occupations by virtue of their lack of qualifications (either because of overt gender exclusion, or through simply not getting them), then when women *do* acquire the qualifications in question, the logic of credentialist exclusion suggests that access to the occupations is likely to follow. If it does not, then the legitimacy of the qualification will be undermined. A long established liberal feminist strategy, therefore, has been the use of the 'qualifications lever'. Women, by proving themselves to be the intellectual equals of men, have revealed discrimination on the basis of sex alone as irrational.

Following the Sex Disqualification (Removal) Act (1919), the major professional bodies have gradually admitted women. Women have remained a small minority in most professions, however, with the exception of 'female' professions such as nursing. There can be little doubt that, even in the case of girls who were educated to a relatively high level at secondary school, there have been considerable pressures directing them into these 'suitable' occupations for women. During the course of the research, extended, unstructured interviews were conducted with thirty-six professionally qualified women.[1] A recurring theme amongst the older women was the pressure on them, despite their position as academic 'high-flyers', to take up 'suitable' careers in nursing or teaching. For example, a woman pharmacist (born 1940) commented:

> I can't remember a single teacher that actually tried to make you ambitious . . . I used to always think that unless you wanted to be a nurse or a school teacher, they really couldn't imagine that you would possibly want to do anything else. (FL)

There has also been continuing direct discrimination in employment (for example, the marriage bar in the Civil Service which prevailed until 1946), combined with the fact that it was not sufficient for a woman to qualify on the same level as a man, she also had to resemble a man, as closely as possible, in other aspects of the professional's working life. This implied a long-term, continuous, 'linear' career. The minority of well-qualified, high-ranking professional women, therefore, have tended to be unmarried or, if married, to have no children. (However, this pattern appears to be changing.)

In some professions, part-time work has provided an alternative to the 'linear' career. 'Women's' professions such as nursing and teaching have a long tradition of part-time opportunities (agency nursing, supply teaching). Part-time work for the professionally qualified is usually available if the occupation in question rests upon the delivery of a particular skill, and may be part of a flexible, *qualified* career in an occupational labour market (OLM). That this pattern may be relatively common amongst well-qualified women is suggested by Dex's analysis of the Women and Employment Survey evidence, which showed that, of professional women who worked part time, a considerable proportion worked very few hours (1988, p. 126–7). Pharmacy, the profession discussed in this chapter, is not a sex-typed, 'woman's' occupation. However, it offers extensive opportunities for part-time working of all kinds.

Qualifications

Neither qualifications nor professions are homogeneous entities. Qualifications may be grouped into two broad categories: first, academic and second, job related – vocational or professional. General academic qualifications (O levels and GCSE, A levels, degrees), are most often acquired whilst in full-time education. Universal secondary education means that, in principle, all citizens in the UK have access to academic qualifications up to A level. (Further education in the UK is not universal.) It has been suggested that the wide availability of general academic qualifications may result in their relative devaluation. For example, Collins (1979) has argued:

> The survival of the traditional educational credential . . . seems to be increasingly tied to the efforts of women to break out of their subordinate occupational position, while male employment may well be shifting into a separate set of trades-and-business controlled credentialing institutions. (Collins, 1979, p. 194).

The 'diploma disease' that is, the devaluing of a qualification when excessive numbers obtain it (Oxenham, 1984), where individual rationality can lead to collective irrationality, is always a possibility in an unregulated educational market. However, there is ample evidence that women in Britain are beginning to acquire occupationally specific 'trades and business' qualifications and, in any case general educational qualifications are usually a prerequisite for access to training for job–related, vocational and professional qualifications.

Job–related qualifications extend over a range from City and Guilds qualifications in a wide spectrum of practical subjects, for example: catering or carpentry; RSA examinations in typing and office practice; through ONC, OND, HND, HNC (now BEC/TEC/BTEC) to professional examinations in law, accountancy and medicine.[2] 'In house' qualifications should also be included, although they may not be transferable between different jobs. The distinction between general academic and job–related qualifications is not absolute. Some A level and degree subjects, for example, are oriented towards particular occupations (for example, accountancy, law).

Job–related qualifications may be required as a 'licence to practice'. Professions such as medicine and dentistry cannot be undertaken by the unqualified. These are occupations practising the most complete form of credential exclusion. Access is restricted to those who possess the appropriate qualification, the standards of which are closely monitored by the profession.

'Occupational' qualifications bestow a notional equivalence of competence amongst practitioners which is of great significance to the ideology of professionalism. In theory, all qualified professionals have reached a certain level of expertise; skills are acquired as a consequence of professional training and transfer of knowledge rather than from day-to-day experience accessible to all. This individual possession of specialized occupational skills, as argued in Chapter 2, gives a considerable degree of protection in the occupational market. Such skills may facilitate frequent job changing and part-time work as well as self-employment as an independent practitioner. This feature is another element of historical importance in the ideology of professionalism: the image of the independent professional, providing a service to a client (the 'fiduciary' relationship). However, today most professionals, even those with 'occupational' qualifications, work in organizations: in firms of chartered accountants, in National Health Service hospitals, and in industry and services more generally. The qualified professional, therefore, has the option of moving from the 'practitioner' level to develop a linear career within either the profession or organization (becoming a partner in a professional firm), or developing a career in industry (for example, the pharmacist who moves into drug company management).

However, part-time professionals do not usually move out of the basic 'practitioner' level while they are part-timers, although their professional status will be maintained whilst in part-time employment.

Although the discussion has so far been focused upon professional qualifications, it should be stressed that even where not required as a licence to practice, occupational qualifications nevertheless give the individual a degree of market shelter. A secretary or plumber who possesses the relevant formal qualifications will usually find it easier to get a job than one who does not. In some cases, occupational qualifications may be acquired as a means of progressing through organizational hierarchies. In Britain accountancy provides a good example of a professional training which is widely regarded as a general qualification for management, and three of the major accountancy qualifications are most usually acquired whilst the student is in full-time employment (see Chapter 5).

Some professional qualifications are tied more directly to an organizational career strategy, and the general term 'organizational' qualifications will be used to describe these. They include those of the Institute of Bankers, Chartered Insurance Institute, Chartered Building Societies Association and so on. Although these qualifications are administered and monitored by external, independent bodies, it would be rather misleading to view them as examples of *occupational* exclusion. In these instances it is the employers who, through their encouragement (and in some cases, insistence) that their employees gain the qualifications, are controlling access and movement through the organizations' internal labour market (Crompton and Sanderson, 1986; Crompton, 1987). Such credentials are clearly an important element sustaining the process of vertical segregation by exclusion discussed in Chapter 2, and empirical research has shown that women have been actively dissuaded from acquiring them (Crompton and Jones, 1984). Organizational qualifications are associated with firm internal labour markets (FILMs). Both occupational internal labour markets (OILMs) and FILMs share similar characteristics, including job ladders and movement up a hierarchy associated with incremental knowledge and skill. However, whereas FILMs are controlled by employers, OILMs are strongly influenced by the people who hold jobs in the occupation (Althauser and Kalleberg, 1981, p. 130). This influence may be direct, as in respect of the standard and level of the occupation itself, but also indirect in that a competent occupationally qualified professional will usually have few difficulties in taking his or her portable qualifications elsewhere.

Occupational or 'licensing' qualifications, therefore, are associated with occupational labour markets (OLMs), including independent practitioners, and OILMs; organizational qualifications are associated with FILMs. These distinctions, however, denote a continuum from the occupational to the organizational dimension, rather than watertight analytical compartments, and most professional occupations would be able to provide individual examples drawn from all three categories across the WX continuum. OILMs, in particular, may be pulled in the direction of the occupation or profession (the professional with the organizational career – either within the profession or organizing other professionals); or on the other hand, towards the organization or firm (the organizational careerist with full or part professional qualifications, for example, the accountant as manager).

Women and qualifications

Women in Britain have, by the latter half of the twentieth century, gained a formal equality of access to professional qualifications in Britain. As discussed in the previous chapter, female school leavers have, by the 1980s, achieved virtual educational parity with males, although important differences by subject still remain. Of even more interest, it might be suggested, is the recent (and considerable) increase in the proportions of women gaining professional and job-related qualifications. For example, women were 30 per cent of first-year enrolments in medicine in 1970, but 45 per cent by 1983; 7 per cent of new members of the Institute of Chartered Accountants in 1975 but 23 per cent by 1984; 2 per cent of successful candidates in the final examinations of the Institute of Bankers in 1970, but 21 per cent by 1983; and 19 per cent of successful Law Society finalists in 1975, but 47 per cent by 1984 (Crompton and Sanderson, 1986).

These are all examples of women gaining access to what had been previously considered 'male' occupations. However, women have always predominated in some occupations requiring relatively high levels of pre-entry qualification and long periods of training, such as nursing and social work. 'Female' professions such as these have often been described as 'semi-professions', a designation which reflects the initial sex-typing of the occupation in question. A profession which has been sex-typed as 'female' will tend to be rated lower, and receive a lower level of reward, than one which is 'male', or gender-neutral. (These two designations are virtually the same (Simpson and Simpson, 1969; Hearn, 1982).) An interesting example of the effect of past sex-typing is given by the comparison between pharmacy, speech therapy and optics. Pharmacy and optics have not been sex-typed as 'female' professions (although increasing numbers of women are qualifying for both). Speech therapy, on the other hand, developed initially as, and has remained, a virtually all-female occupation. All three are degree-level professions, requiring further postgraduate training before certification. Little distinction can be drawn, therefore, between the levels of skill (in a technical sense) required for these professions. The levels of material reward, however, are rather different. Basic grade speech therapists in the NHS commence at just under £6000, basic grade pharmacists at over £7000. The maximum for a senior grade speech therapist is under £10,000; a senior pharmacist earns well over £12,000 (1986 figures). The contrast with optics is even greater: a newly-qualified optician in the private sector can earn £20,000. It has elsewhere been argued that, if a profession has a low level of material reward as a consequence of initial sex-typing as 'female', then the only strategy available to practitioners is to work collectively to raise the reward level (Crompton, 1987). Attempts are currently being made by the MSF (Manufacturing Science and Finance Union) to pursue this strategy on behalf of speech therapists under 'equal value' legislation, using pharmacists as a direct comparison.[3]

Sex-typing cannot be used to explain differentiation *within* an occupational group. If a man trains as a nurse or a speech therapist, he will receive the same rate for the job as a woman. Women within male-dominated professions, however, tend to be concentrated in the lower categories of employment, that is, at the practitioner level. For example, women predominate as school teachers, men as head teachers, inspectors, local authority education officers and lecturers in colleges and university departments of higher education. Within the medical profession, a similar distribution by category also occurs. In 1981, women were 28 per cent of junior hospital doctors, and 26 per cent of doctors working in general practice and community health, but only 16 per cent of senior hospital doctors, and 13 per cent of those employed in universities and institutes (source: DHSS, Civilian Doctor Statistics, Great Britain, 1981[4]). Professional work also includes private practice in OLMs where the level of material reward may be very substantial. However, women have tended to be employees rather than employers in private practice. Thus, as Carter and Carter (1981) have argued for the United States (where the increase in women gaining professional qualifications has been even more rapid than in Britain), the relative gains made by well-qualified women may be considerably less than those of men at the same level of qualification.

Teaching, medicine, and the health service professions more generally all furnish occupational careers. The particular skills they represent are required across a wide spectrum of geographical locations. It has been noted that many professionally qualified women will develop occupational careers which include extended periods at the 'practitioner' level, particularly during part-time employment. A recent study of doctors, for example, has shown that whilst the proportion of female doctors in employment was practically the same as that of male doctors, 57 per cent of the women had worked part-time at some point in their career, compared with 10 per cent of the men (Allen, 1988). Part-time professionals will not suffer a drop in their occupational status, but part-time work is often not considered particularly relevant to a 'linear' career, which is more usually developed within an organizational context.

Within organizations, professional and job-related qualifications are increasingly required in order to gain access to senior positions. However, these positions are themselves an important power resource. 'Property in positions' may be regarded as a resource independent of property in skills and credentials, not least because access to positions does not depend on formal credentials alone. As Collins (1979) has argued,

The overriding fact is that an organisational career is made in a political environment, and success goes to those individuals who recognise that fact and act on it most assiduously. The one who makes it to the top is the organisational politician, concerned above all with informal ties, manoeuvering toward the crucial gate-keepers, avoiding the organisational contingencies that trap the less wary. (1979, p. 31).

Women, it may be argued, are at some disadvantage as far as this kind of activity is concerned. Men predominate at the higher levels of most organizations, and organizational hierarchies are not sympathetic to women (see, for example, Kanter, 1977; Hearn and Parkin, 1987). Thus, even if women gain the kinds of organizational professional qualifications required to pursue an organizational career, organizational exclusion may hinder their progress. In general, however, the greater the extent that the position and remuneration associated with an occupation depend on formal qualifications and/or the delivery of a precisely-defined skill, rather than 'property in position', the less determinant the gender of the individual concerned will be to both the standing and reward of the occupation in question.

Pharmacy: history and development[5]

The Pharmaceutical Society of Great Britain was founded in 1841 and the professional qualification (MPS) is given by membership of this society. Under the terms of the National Health Service, only a qualified pharmacist can dispense Health Service prescriptions. The society was founded by the chemists and druggists who, although not offering a formal qualification, had been licensed to trade in drugs and poisons since 1815. Their rights to sell medicines had been challenged by the Society of Apothecaries, a qualifying body which had been founded in 1617 and required a seven year apprenticeship. The apothecaries were also in contention with physicians and surgeons for the control of the emergent medical profession, a battle they eventually lost. (It is ironic that today the Society of Apothecaries persists as a licensing body for dispensers, who are qualified but low-level assistants to Pharmacists.)

At the time of its foundation the profession's journal argued: 'Had they [the chemists and druggists] submitted to be under the government of either College [Physicians or Surgeons] and particularly under that of the Society of Apothecaries, they would have degraded themselves and lost sight of their interests' (*The Chemist*, vol. 2, 1842, p. 149). The Pharmaceutical Society set up its own training school for student pharmacists in 1842 and a royal charter was granted in 1843. The Pharmacy Act of 1852 provided for the maintenance of a Register of Pharmacists by the society; registration was granted upon the production of a certificate satisfactory to the society's council. The Act also restricted the titles 'Pharmaceutical Chemist' and 'Chemist and Druggist' to registered members of the society. The 1868 Pharmacy Act required students to pass an examination set by the council of the society, and the Pharmaceutical Society was confirmed as the only registering body. Registration was made compulsory, and all those who intended to trade in medicines and dispense prescriptions had to be registered.

Moving into the twentieth century, the National Insurance Act of 1911 ensured that pharmacists (rather than doctors) 'should become the principal dispensers of medicines prescribed for beneficiaries under the Act'. In 1919 the basis of a new examination system was established, which remained in place, with modifications, until 1967. Initially the training was in two parts (Part I general (including science and a foreign language), Part II materia medica and prescribing) and twenty-five institutions were approved to teach it. A Bachelor of Pharmacy degree was introduced at the society's school in 1924, which in 1948 was integrated into London University. This year also saw the setting up of the National Health Service, and the move from a standard two-year to a three-year full-time course. In 1958 one year's in-service training was made mandatory. Pharmacy became a degree-entry profession in 1967.

In many respects the development of pharmacy reads like a textbook example of the process of professionalisation: the founding of the learned society, the granting of the royal charter, the establishing of exclusive rights for an area of practice, steady enhancement of the length and levels of qualification required, and so on. However, it would probably be true to say that, nevertheless, pharmacy has historically fallen short of the top rank of professional esteem. The close association with 'trade' fell short of the gentlemanly ideal which predominated at the time the professions were crystallizing as identifiable occupations.[6] The 'collegiate professions' (Johnson, 1972) of law, medicine and the church had a history of association with high-status clients and ancient universities which chemists and druggists did not. Aristocratic families were quite willing, indeed eager, to place their younger sons within the armed forces and higher civil service, but it is unlikely that many younger members of the aristocracy trained as pharmacists. Although, therefore, pharmacy has successfully maintained and improved its academic standards of training and qualification, and although the level of material reward for individual pharmacists can be considerable, pharmacy would still probably not be ranked at the top of the 'first division' professions.

The Pharmaceutical Society's survey of members in 1985 gave a membership total of just over thirty thousand. This contrasts with a census total of just over twenty thousand (1981). The main reason for this discrepancy is that any qualified pharmacist, in or out of employment, may remain on the register, or re-register on payment of a fee. Retired pharmacists pay a reduced fee, yet remain on the register, and in 1985 nearly five thousand registered pharmacists were recorded as 'not in paid employment'. There will also be pharmacists working in other occupations who will nevertheless remain as registered, and some pharmacists working in industry may not record their occupation as such in the census.

As has been noted, pharmacy is a degree-only discipline taught in universities and polytechnics. Science A levels are required for entry to the degree course. Interviews with qualified pharmacists suggested that the training involved in a pharmacy degree is extremely hard work. The hours of class attendance and practical work are long, with frequent examinations which have to be re-taken in case of failure. Pharmacists are trained, rather than educated. Graduate pharmacists undertake a pre-registration year after which they are fully qualified. The registration year may be worked in either hospital or community pharmacy (which has also been described as 'retail' and 'general practice'). A pharmacist who began a degree course immediately after A levels, therefore, would be fully qualified by the age of 22. Once qualified, the salary levels obtainable in community pharmacy are not inconsiderable for young people in their 20s – figures of up to £18,000 p.a. were suggested during the course of the research.

The number of community pharmacies (or retail outlets) has declined in recent decades, although the multiples (such as Boots) have flourished. Besides industry and other pharmacy-related occupations three main employment alternatives are open to the newly-qualified pharmacist: (i) within the Hospital Service, (ii) as an owner or an employee in independent community pharmacy, or (iii) as a manager or 'practitioner' within a multiple such as Boots. All three of these alternatives offer long-term 'linear' careers. These careers could assume a wide variety of forms, from the entrepreneurial option in the occupational labour market, to an organizational option with a major company like Boots or within the Hospital Service, teaching, or research in academia or industry. The regulations relating to the sale of drugs and dispensing of prescriptions require a qualified pharmacist to be in attendance at all times, so there are also many opportunities within community and hospital pharmacy for short-term, full-time and part-time work as a relief pharmacist or locum; in short, practitioner work is freely available.

The total number of qualified pharmacists in employment has remained remarkably stable over the years, when taken against a background of changes such as the expansion of medical services, demographic change, etc. However, this stability masks considerable changes in both working patterns and gender distribution within pharmacy.

Women in pharmacy

Women were first admitted to membership of the Pharmaceutical Society in 1879, when Isabella Skinner Clarke and Rose Coombes Minshall were successful (on their third application) in gaining admission to the society. The debate surrounding their admission laid heavy emphasis on 'rational' criteria and what may be viewed as considerations of natural justice. Apparently the society's charter did not include the male personal pronoun, and so it was not possible to exclude women on the basis of this technicality, as was subsequently the case in accountancy (Silverstone, 1980, p. 20). It was argued that the women were *entitled* to membership since they had fulfilled the entry requirements, that is, passing the examination set by the society. The President of the Council remained opposed, but the council consoled itself with the thought that most members would not object to qualified ladies joining and, in any case, very few were likely ever to apply.

For many years their hopes were fulfilled and women remained a small minority of pharmacists up to and including the Second World War. In 1941 their numbers were estimated at about 10 per cent of a membership of twenty-five thousand. By the early 1950s, however, female membership had increased to 15 per cent and, by the early 1960s, to about 20 per cent. These estimates are derived from the Register, and will therefore tend to be an overestimate of female pharmacists actually practising. The apparent discrepancy in pharmacy numbers between the census and the profession's own records has already been noted. Another problem with census data is that, until the 1971 census, the occupation of 'pharmacist' was not recorded separately from 'dispenser'.[7] The Pharmaceutical Society has carried out surveys of the membership at intervals since 1964. These provide an excellent source of data but, prior to that date, only gross estimates derived from numbers on the register are available. Even though these figures should be treated with caution, however, it is apparent that women were substantially increasing their representation within the profession during the immediate postwar period. This trend has continued unabated and indeed accelerated in the decades that followed. While female membership of the pharmacy profession increased by approximately 5 per cent per decade in the 1940s and 1950s, since the 1970s and 1980s the rate of increase has reached 10 per cent (Table 4.1).

It should be stressed that information drawn from the register will underestimate the number of women *trained* as pharmacists, given that many have lapsed from membership during the breaks for child-rearing, etc. This point is demonstrated by Universities Central Council on Admissions (UCCA) and Department of Education and Science (DES) data on the recruitment of student pharmacists. Women have actually been a (small) majority of undergraduate admissions to pharmacy in the universities since the early 1970s, and in the polytechnics since the early 1980s. In 1983, for example, women were 373 (62 per cent) of the 597 UCCA applicants accepted and 760 (51 per cent) of 1,486 enrolments in polytechnics. As an interesting sidelight on the impact of rational, examination-linked 'credential-ism', we were told that the quality of female applicants to pharmacy

Table 4.1 Men and women in pharmacy: selected years, by occupation

	1963 %		1972 %		1977 %		1981 %		1985 %	
	Men	Women	Men	Women	Men	Women	Men	Women	Men	Women
(1) community pharmacy	84	16	82	18	77	23	71	29	67	33
(2) hospital pharmacy	45	55	37	63	44	56	40	60	38	62
(3) industry	95	5	95	5	89	11	85	15	78	22
(4) other	82	18	77	23	83	17	77	23	76	24
(5) total (a) no.	20,284	4,378	18,400	5,380	16,498	5,971	16,315	7,809	16,194	9,455
(b) per cent	82	18	77	23	73	27	68	32	63	37
(6) no paid employment	70	30	53	47	67	33	64	36	65	35
(7) overall total (a) no.	21,401	4,861	20,010	6,800	19,604	7,504	19,130	9,373	19,164	11,089
(b) per cent	81	19	75	25	72	28	67	33	63	37

Notes:

Data derived from the *Pharmaceutical Journal*, vols. 193, p. 124; 209, p. 228; 219, p. 462; 228, p. 131; March 1986, p. 265. Data for 1963 and 1972 were collected via a sample survey of members; for 1977 onwards, as part of a retention from an application form completed by all members. The apparent fluctuations in row 6 (no paid employment) are a consequence both of changes in classification and rules relating to the subscriptions of non-working but registered pharmacists. Row 5 and above, therefore, represent the most accurate estimates of gender distribution.

However, it is also apparent that some pharmacists recording no occupation *do* work part-time (see, for example, *Pharmaceutical Journal*, 1972, p. 230, Table 6), although the numbers are small and do not affect major trends. The figures in this table, therefore, should be regarded as fairly accurate estimates, rather than as giving precise numbers.

was superior to that of males, and the gender differences between pharmacists in university and polytechnic training was cited in support of this argument. The registration figures show, therefore, a continuous increase in the proportion of women qualifying as pharmacists since the Second World War. This gradual increase is in sharp contrast to the trends discernible in other professions, particularly the finance professions, such as accountancy and banking. It has been argued in Chapter 3 that the sudden cutback in teacher training which occurred in the 1970s was a significant factor 'bumping' relatively well-educated women into other professions at this time, and the trends for women in the finance professions would certainly support this hypothesis. Rising levels of education amongst women will have been an important factor improving the rate of professional take-up in any case, and the increase in the proportion of female pharmacists has also accelerated since the 1970s. This earlier growth of the numbers of women in pharmacy suggests, perhaps, that the profession may have been particularly attractive to women.

Indeed, this was found to be the case. As an occupation, pharmacy has not been sex-typed. It requires a high level of scientific competence, and the training is rigorous. However, as far as women are concerned, it must have always appeared to have had one notable advantage – the wide availability and flexibility of employment. As we shall see, the history of women in pharmacy has been characterized by this flexible, part-time employment, and women's employment patterns are quite different from men's. That this has long been a feature of the profession is illustrated by the comments of a qualified pharmacist now in her late 40s:

> one of the very first woman pharmacists I met . . . I must have been about 14–15 . . . and my mother had some cousins and they had a friend or relative staying with them . . . and this lady was a pharmacist. She said to me – I'd just decided so I was 16 probably – it's an ideal career for a woman, she said, you can always pick up odd day's work, week's work, year's work, whatever you like or not, and she said, you get paid £20 a week for doing it! (NB)

Thirty years later, the situation has apparently changed very little, as is suggested by a young hospital pharmacist in her early 20s:

> We were told in one of the lectures [i.e. whilst an undergraduate] that it was quite interesting actually for lecturers to see the proportion year by year because as years went on there were more and more women and our year probably had 60 per cent female and 40 per cent male. The year before us it was about 50–50. (Int: Why did they think it was like that?) JP: Yes, because it was a very

attractive career for a woman to go for because it's very flexible, you can leave it, have a family and go back into it because there are always plenty of jobs there to go back into. (JP)

Flexible employment opportunities, therefore, have been a major factor underlying the gender structure of employment in pharmacy, but this is not the whole story. Using the same raw data as in Table 4.1, in 1985, 73 per cent of practising pharmacists were working in community or retail pharmacy, 16 per cent in the hospital service, and 5 and 6 percent respectively in industry and other pharmacy occupations.[8] More women work within the hospital service and Table 4.1 shows considerable segmentation by gender within types of employment. Men have always predominated in community pharmacy; women, on the other hand, have predominated in hospital pharmacy within the NHS. These sex differences in employment in pharmacy reflect gender stereotypes. It is felt that success in community pharmacy requires qualities of toughness and entrepreneurship, as well as capital, if the individual wishes to set up as an 'independent'. Management careers in Boots require appropriate managerial qualities. In contrast, the hospital service is seen as more caring and, perhaps paradoxically, more 'professional'.[9] Thus in 1963, for example, women were 55 per cent of hospital pharmacists, despite being only 18 per cent of those on the register and in employment. Conversely, women were 16 per cent of community pharmacists, below their representation in the total population.[10] However, there are indications that this aspect of gender segmentation is becoming less apparent than in the past. For example, comparing the 1963 and 1985 figures, the proportion of women practising pharmacy has increased overall by 19 per cent, but the proportion of women in hospital pharmacy has increased by only 7 per cent, and the proportion of women in community pharmacy by 17 per cent.

Although women have predominated numerically in hospital pharmacy, even when only a minority of the profession, they were and are concentrated in the lowest grade of hospital employment. Women have worked within the hospital service as practitioners, leaving the linear career routes, or occupation internal labour markets, open for the men. In 1984, for example, whereas a majority of male hospital pharmacists aged 36–40 were on Principal grades, a majority of *female* pharmacists within the same age group were on basic grades.[11] Possibly because hospital pharmacy *has* been regarded as a 'woman's job', salary levels on basic grades are low. (In 1986, basic grade rates were between £7,000 and £8,000). A pharmacist who is promoted within the hospital service, however, can anticipate a reasonable salary. In 1986, the average salary for a staff grade pharmacist was £12,000, and for a Principal considerably more.[12]

A similar pattern is revealed in community pharmacy. Table 4.2 demonstrates that although 44 per cent of the pharmacists employed by Boots are women, they are concentrated on the lowest rung of the professional hierarchy. This is 'pharmacists employed solely in professional duties', 'practitioners' with no managerial responsibilities.

Table 4.2 *Boots Company plc: pharmacists employed by job category and sex (retail division), 1987 (numbers)*

Function	Men	Women	Total
district/development manager and above	172	14	186
store/support managers	1,205	353	1,558
management trainees	96	151	247
pharmacists employed solely in professional duties	342	880	1,222
Total	1,815	1,398	3,213

Although male and female pharmacists have exactly equivalent qualifications, therefore, women pharmacists tend to be found in the lower levels of employment within the profession. Mention has been made earlier of the fact that an important feature which made pharmacy an attractive job for a woman was the flexibility of employment in pharmacy, and the widespread availability of part-time work. The regulations governing chemists and druggists require the presence of a pharmacist in order that drugs may be dispensed, and there is a permanent demand from both community pharmacy and the hospital service for locums to cover for rest days, holiday periods, and even the lunch hour. In most industries and occupations, part-time work is poorly paid. In the case of part-time employment amongst pharmacists, however, pay levels will not be particularly depressed. The going rate for a locum pharmacist (£60 a day in 1988) is a considerably more than adequate level of income, although not matched by those of higher-level linear careerists and/or successful entrepreneurs. No gender differential exists in part-time remuneration rates.

Amongst the women pharmacists interviewed who had had children, all had worked part-time when their children were young. The ready availability of part-time employment meant that work could often be fitted around the availability of child care, rather than the other way round, as is more usually the case:

While they [her two children] were still fairly small, my husband
used to have Monday afternoon off and I used to work on a
Monday afternoon in a community pharmacy, and I used to work
on a Wednesday morning as well, and I used to leave them both
with a child-minder just for the half day a week . . . and I also used
to work at the hospital occasionally during the summer months
when they were short of staff and they would go to the hospital
playscheme. (SMc)

However, although pharmacy represents a 'good' part-time job,
particularly for a woman, one feature it does share with other part-
time work is the fact that it is not relevant to a linear career. Indeed,
until recently part-time pharmacists in the Hospital Service were not
even eligible for promotion, and Boots has a policy that management
level and above must work full-time. Part-time work, therefore, has
been an extremely important factor reinforcing the 'practitioner'
status of women in pharmacy. (In addition to full-time working,
geographical mobility is required in order to pursue a career with a
company such as Boots.)

The trends illustrated by Table 4.3, however, suggest that the
pattern of part-time employment is changing. More men appear to
be taking up part-time work, whilst more women are working full
time. Age-specific data, which are available for 1981 and 1985, reveal
an extremely interesting pattern. Part-time employment amongst
men is concentrated in the older age groups: 22 per cent of male
pharmacists aged 60–4; 58 per cent aged 65–9; and 78 per cent of those
over 70. (These 1985 figures all show a slight increase over 1981.)

Table 4.3   *Employment in pharmacy by gender and extent of occupation
(percentages)*

		Men	Women	Total
1969	full-time	90	52	81
	part-time	10	48	19
1972	full-time	90	51	81
	part-time	10	49	19
1977	full-time	87	57	79
	part-time	13	43	21
1981	full-time	85	59	76
	part-time	15	41	24
1985	full-time	84	60	75
	part-time	16	40	25

Source: see notes Table 4.1, also *Pharmaceutical Journal*, November 1969,
p. 613.

Amongst female pharmacists, however, the majority are working part time from the 35–9 age cohort onwards. However, as Table 4.3 demonstrates, the proportion of female pharmacists working full time has increased, and a comparison of recent data suggests that the underlying trend might be changing. Table 4.4 shows that the increase in part-time working with age amongst the younger age cohorts of women is less than in previous years. In 1981, for example, 53 per cent of female pharmacists were working part time between the age of 30 and 34, whereas by 1985 the proportion of part-time workers in this age group had fallen to 43 per cent. This trend has been associated with an increase in the number of women moving out of 'practitioner' roles within the profession. The proportion of women in store and support management in Boots, for example, has increased from 12 per cent to 21 per cent between 1977 and 1987.

Table 4.4 *Part-time working among younger female pharmacists (percentages)*

Age	Most recent year of qualification	1981			1985			Most recent year of qualification
		FT	PT	Total nos	FT	PT	Total nos	
under 25	(1980)	96%	4%	1,099	98%	2%	1,080	(1984)
25–9	(1975)	83%	17%	1,785	85%	15%	2,219	(1979)
30–4	(1970)	47%	53%	1,002	57%	43%	1,538	(1974)

Source: see notes, Table 4.1

In summary, therefore, the pattern of women's employment in pharmacy demonstrates that, although this is an occupation where the formal qualification levels of men and women are absolutely equal, women are nevertheless heavily concentrated at the 'practitioner' level within the profession. This concentration is in large part a consequence of the fact that the flexible employment opportunities available in pharmacy have enabled women, through a combination of intermittent and part-time work, to combine their domestic roles with continuing employment in pharmacy. There is clear evidence of change over the last decade. Even more women have qualified as pharmacists, and proportionately more are rising through managerial hierarchies and staying in full-time work. Employment patterns in pharmacy, therefore, seem to be responding to developments in the wider social context – that is, the growing independence and 'career-mindedness' amongst women (Dex, 1988, chapter 2).

It has been argued that, even in the absence of sex-typing, the experience of employment may serve to complement, rather than come into conflict with, the conventional division of labour between men and women (Chapter 2). Thus flexible occupations, like pharmacy, facilitate the combination of domesticity and near-continuous employment for qualified women. However, this arrangement also serves to reproduce the gender order as a whole, in that women are subordinate to men within the profession. It may, of course, be disputed whether women pharmacists have 'chosen' their particular combinations of work and domesticity, or whether it has been forced upon them as a consequence of male exclusion practices. Evidence relating to male exclusionary practices across a wide range of occupations suggests that this argument should certainly not be rejected out of hand. However, qualified pharmacists are in a better position to make such a choice than most women; they can achieve levels of pay which would enable them to maintain an independent household, or pay for child care if they wished to do so.

Many, perhaps the majority of, women seek employment which enables them to combine paid work and child care, not out of a sense of constraint, but out of a genuine belief that mothers are the best carers for their children. The 'moral despotism' associated with motherhood will often have e.actly the same practical outcome as the material constraints on women brought about by male exclusionary practices, lack of state support for mothers with children, or whatever else. Empirical evidence for this suggestion can be found in the Women and Employment survey, which found that traditional attitudes were more likely to be present amongst part-time than full-time women workers (Martin and Roberts, 1984, p. 172). Dex has recently (1988) re-analysed the data with a view to exploring whether women work part time because they have more traditional attitudes, or whether their attitudes are a consequence of the fact that they work part time and their traditional roles are therefore reinforced. As might have been expected, an exhaustive analysis failed to resolve conclusively this chicken-and-egg question, although there was a small but significant relationship between less traditional attitudes and increased hours of work. The whole tenor of Dex's argument serves to emphasize the reciprocal relationship between women's work and their attitudes to work and employment: 'as women gained more work experience, they seemed to exhibit traditional attitudes about women's roles less frequently and positive attitudes towards women working more frequently' (1988, pp. 151–2). At the aggregate level, this trend might reasonably be anticipated. However it has been argued that particular occupations will be of varying significance within this overall trend. Occupations which positively facilitate stereotypically feminine roles, or conventional combinations of work and domestic responsibilities, might be expected to have less of an impact as far as changes in attitudes and behaviour are concerned. Internal contradictions found within the overall structure of gender relations in employment, on the other hand, are liable to produce changes at the micro level.

In the particular case of pharmacy, the question may be raised as to whether women entering the profession have deliberately selected the occupation because of its compatibility with a 'traditional' combination of work and employment. As we have seen, this assumption is certainly widespread, and the (male) principal pharmacist of a teaching hospital said (in 1987): 'When I talk to schools, or a group or whatever on careers, the flexibility for married women is something I usually mention . . . It is a profession you can pick up again into a whole array of levels – from one day a week up to full time.'

Some women, however, had not deliberately entered the profession because of its flexibility, although they had of course become aware of the fact: 'I looked at it as being a woman in the professions because it was a little bit more unusual but in pharmacy I didn't [seek flexibility]. But now looking at it, it is a very good profession for a woman to go back to' (SG).

Once established in the occupation, whatever an individual woman's prior orientations as far as her most favoured combination of employment and domesticity might have been, the ready availability of 'suitable' female employment clearly facilitates the conventional option. As we have seen, the majority of women pharmacists have in practice followed an employment pattern characteristic of the new orthodoxy established amongst women in Britain by the second half of the twentieth century: a period of full-time employment, followed by breaks in employment and flexible working with the advent of children.

The evidence reviewed in this chapter demonstrates that this dominant pattern of employment amongst female pharmacists was established from the beginning, at the historical moment at which women became a substantial minority within the profession (the 1950s and 1960s). At this time, even more emphasis than at present was laid upon the individual *mother's* responsibility for her children. All of the women pharmacists with children who were interviewed had taken on the major responsibility for child care, whilst maintaining, to varying degrees, an active professional life:

Once (you've) made a decision that yours isn't going to be a major career, and you're going to look after a family, as long as you can tie the two, which you can do very well . . . I can do the two very well, and I didn't want to be not around when the children were young. I want to be in mainly when they come home. (NB)

Similarly, a woman pharmacist more than twenty years younger expects to give up work when she has a family:

I wouldn't speak for other people, but personally for any children I have I think it's in their interest that I give up work and look after them . . . I might feel a little frustrated at home but I believe that I'll take on a different role. (JP)

However, she knows that when she does give up work . . .

The good thing about pharmacy, you can do locums, and you can pick and choose really. There are so many jobs going and I possibly might do a morning or an afternoon every so often but not on a regular basis . . . Retail pharmacists will often phone the hospital [where she works] and say, have you any staff that want to do locums . . .? There are more jobs than there are pharmacists. (JP)

In general, therefore, when pharmacy is described as 'a good job for a woman', it is explicit that, like teaching, it is an occupation where she can 'do a job' whilst 'remaining a woman' – bringing up her children and attending to her domestic responsibilities. Creeping feminization has not yet produced any major disruption in gender relations within the profession; the transformation has been achieved in the absence of major technological change, or the radical restructuring of the labour and product markets – all factors which have been argued to be closely associated with occupational feminization (Murgatroyd, 1985).

The pharmacy profession, it might be suggested, has responded to exogenous rather than endogenous changes. The increase in the number of women going into pharmacy was and is in part a consequence of the rising qualification levels amongst girls. Amongst the women pharmacists interviewed, pharmacy was seen as an occupation which was 'scientific' but 'caring'. The point was often made that pharmacists were 'failed medics'. Formal gender exclusion was common in medical schools throughout the 1950s, 1960s, and possibly 1970s; this does not seem to have been the case in pharmacy since the Misses Clarke and Minshall made their breakthrough in the nineteenth century.

Women who went into pharmacy in the 1950s and 1960s found little difficulty in combining their work and family lives. In the 1980s, however, the pharmacy profession is adjusting to changes in the wider society. The later a woman trained as a pharmacist, the more likely she is to be working full-time during the child-rearing years (Table 4.4), suggesting that an increasing number of female pharmacists may embark on linear careers. As a Boots staff manager has argued (1987): 'In the UK, women's interest in pursuing long-term progressive careers alongside their family responsibilities is a fairly recent phenomenon and it will take time to work through.'

Further evidence to support this hypothesis is given by a comparison of the occupational distribution of male and female pharmacists in the UK and Canada, where Boots has a wholly-owned subsidiary. In Canada, 37 per cent of women pharmacists are in store management positions and above, in contrast to only 26 per cent in the UK. The difference between men and women in the level of part-time working is also less pronounced – although, because of longer trading hours, more pharmacists in Canada work part-time. It is argued, by Boots management, that these differences reflect the longer period that equal opportunity initiatives have been established in North America. The increase in the level of full-time working in the UK, and of women moving into the lower of the management positions within pharmacy, suggests that more women will be moving into higher management in the future. This is certainly widely anticipated within the profession (*Pharmaceutical Journal*, March 1987).

Even as women show signs of moving into management, however, gender stereotyping is recreated and reproduced. For example, the Staff Director of Boots, addressing a professional gathering in 1987, referred to the 'communication and interpersonal skills that are so necessary in community pharmacy and which will become increasingly important in the future'. He further suggested that women are 'on the whole better equipped in this respect. They seem to have greater social confidence and appear more skilled in personal communication'. Thus, yet again, pharmacy appears to be an occupation where a gender transformation may be achieved without a significant restructuring of gender stereotypes.

Although a major survey of attitudes was not part of the research, it is nevertheless noteworthy that there seemed to be little evidence of resentment amongst women pharmacists at gender discrimination in employment: 'Women tend to leave and have families and come back part-time or don't come back at all, so they don't get the same opportunities, by choice, to get to the top' (JP). Low status is clearly being perceived as a consequence of a freely-chosen, flexible option and is therefore not actively resented. Indeed, one of the strongest complaints concerning colleagues was made of a female district pharmaceutical officer, described as 'very go-ahead, a whizz-kid type of spinster who didn't really have much time for the married ladies with children; she was, and still is, very much a queen bee' (GS). Flexible employment opportunities, however, are linked to those situations where a continuing, corporeal, pharmaceutical presence is required, that is, hospital and community pharmacy. The minority of pharmacists who work in the pharmaceutical industry (5 per cent) will have organizational careers, and there is no reason to anticipate that women in these situations have been less prone to organizational exclusion than women working in other organizations. A woman (without children) who has built a successful career in industry describes her situation in 1967:

> I was a bit tired of the factory because . . . they weren't going to promote a woman to anything that was worth having. . . it wasn't developing a career, it was just frustration really. I didn't particularly want to run the factory or anything, I just couldn't see why lads who'd been there eighteen months should be reckoned to be able to do it when there was two of us, two women, and . . . at one time we ran five departments between us and, when they finally got people to take the other heads of departments, they all without exception got promoted ahead of us, and we thought that was a bit poor so we both left at the same time . . . I still think it's very hard in industry on the production side to do much as a woman . . . packaging is OK, but large-scale production – it's all men. (VJ)

Organizational exclusion may obviously have a very significant impact on women's opportunities – although, as we have seen in the example above, the possession of an 'occupational' qualification may mean that its most negative effects may be avoided by the individual, who can simply leave. Pressures to change the situation are likely to be greater when this option is not available, as we shall see in our discussion of higher-level employment in organizations in the finance sector.

Notes

1   The Joseph Rowntree Memorial Trust sponsored research ('Women professionals and part-time work') which enabled us to carry out thirty-

six extended interviews with professionally qualified women. This research has been reported in 'professional women's careers' in S. MacRae (ed.), *Keeping Women In*, Policy Studies Institute, 1989. A listing of the interviews used in this book has been included as Appendix A.

2 Royal Society of Arts, Ordinary National Certificate, Ordinary National Diploma, Higher National Diploma, Higher National Certificate, Business Education Council, Technical Education Council, Business and Technical Education Council.

3 The claim was and is being pursued by ASTMS (Association of Scientific, Technical and Managerial Staff) (now MSF), who recruit both pharmacists and speech therapists within the NHS. See ASTMS: 'Speech therapists: the case for equal pay' and 'Speak up for speech therapists' (both undated).

4 This kind of evidence has been used to argue that the breaking down of occupational segregation and gender stereotyping may not be invariably beneficial for women. If an occupation is all female, then at least the hierarchy that administers it will be female as well.

5 Pharmacy is one of a cluster of occupations where women have much increased their representation in recent years. These include: medicine, dentistry, optics, veterinary science. Preliminary work carried out on these professions revealed trends very similar to those in pharmacy. The empirical data in this chapter have been drawn from a number of sources. The Pharmaceutical Society of Great Britain was kind enough to allow the use of its library and archives. Interviews were also carried out with representatives of the society, the major retail organization employing pharmacists (Boots the Chemists), local pharmacists working as entrepreneurs, employees, and in the hospital service, the area officer responsible for hospital pharmacy. We are grateful to all of these informants for their information and advice.

6 See, for example, Jane Austen's ironic discussion of the Gardiners in *Pride and Prejudice* (Penguin, 1972, p. 177). It must be noted that pharmacy is an occupation with a strong Asian, often Ugandan Asian, representation. This combination of gender, ethnicity and association with 'trade' would make a fascinating study but cannot be pursued here.

7 The occupation of dispenser is today virtually an all-female occupation. O levels or Grade 1 CSEs are required as entrance qualifications for training, which requires two years' work under the supervision of a pharmacist and examinations at TEC level. Dispensing qualifications are held completely separate from professional pharmacy training, and cross-over between the two is not possible. Although reliable data are not available, dispensing was once apparently a male, as well as a female, occupation, and dispensers possessed more responsibility and authority. The exclusion and subordination of dispensers may be viewed as a part of the process of the professionalization of pharmacy.

8 The relatively small proportion of pharmacists employed in the NHS, however, is not an entirely reliable indication of its overall significance

to careers in pharmacy. All pharmacists have to work a pre-registration year (as practising pharmacists) before becoming fully qualified, and the hospital service, together with the larger concerns in community pharmacy (such as Boots and the Co-op) is the major source of such pre-registration contracts. Thus the number of pharmacists passing through the NHS at some time or other is well in excess of the total numbers employed at any one point. In any case, pharmacy is an extremely flexible occupation, and moves between employers and employment sectors are very common.

9   See the *Pharmaceutical Journal*, vol. 236, no. 638b, 28 June 1986. The news that Boots was about to abandon its requirement that all Boots managers should be pharmacists was described as 'probably not very important'. The larger Boots stores were described as 'far removed from pharmacy' and 'the equivalent of supermarkets'. In contrast, the decision by the North Lincolnshire Health Authority to advertise for a non-pharmacist to take over the management of the hospital pharmacy service is described as 'misconceived', to be 'strenuously' opposed on the grounds that only a professional pharmacist was capable of managing 'pure' pharmacy.

10   This argument was originally developed in an earlier publication (Crompton and Sanderson, 1986). Since the data were gathered for that paper, full details of the 1985 survey of pharmacists have become available. Although they do not suggest a radical restructuring of the previous argument, they do indicate that the rate of change in gender segregation within the profession is more rapid than anticipated. These (1985) data have been used in this chapter.

11   Information from 'Staffing the NHS Hospital Pharmaceutical Service': discussion document for regional pharmacy officers' meeting, November, 1984.

12   In April 1974 the Guild of Hospital Pharmacists merged with ASTMS (Association of Scientific, Technical and Managerial Staffs), and subsequently negotiated a much improved pay package and career structure. Better pay and prospects within the hospital service, it would seem, resulted in a short-term increase of men within the service, but the proportion of male pharmacists has fallen back as both have declined in subsequent years (see Table 4.1, row 2).

5 Qualifications, occupations, and organizations: the example of accountancy

Introduction

In the last chapter, pharmacy was found to be a profession which has been 'feminizing' gradually since the end of the Second World War. The entry of women into this previously male-dominated occupation, however, has occurred without giving rise to any major transformations in gender relationships. The widespread availability of (full-time and part-time) employment at the 'practitioner' level within this 'occupational' profession has resulted in the incorporation of women into the lower levels of professional employment, although in the younger age cohorts more women appear to be pursuing linear careers. Accountancy, however, is very much a new profession for women. Up until the mid 1960s under 1 per cent of the membership of the Institute of Chartered Accountants in England and Wales (ICAEW) were women. The entry of women into membership began to 'take off' in the 1970s, and today (1987) 39 per cent of younger members (aged between 23 and 26) are women. Female members of the ICAEW, however, are concentrated in this youngest age group and represent only 10 per cent of ICAEW membership overall.

There are other important differences between pharmacy and accountancy. Pharmacy is an occupation characterized by rigorous credential exclusion. There is a single, long-established and universally acceptable qualification; the number of pharmacists trained in Britain is a function of the number of places available in universities and polytechnics. As we have seen, the numbers of qualified pharmacists have remained remarkably stable since the Second World War. In contrast, the number of men and women qualifying as accountants has been increasing rapidly. There is no single occupational qualification. Although the various accountancy bodies co-operate with each other in some important respects, there are also elements of competition both for students and in their claims to represent 'the profession'.

In the case of pharmacy, much of the work that is available at the 'practitioner' level stems from the legal requirement for the pharmacist's presence at the point of dispensing. The accountancy profession embodies a similar requirement (the services of a chartered accountant are legally required for auditing purposes) but only a relatively small amount of accountancy employment will be so generated. A wide range of careers are available in pharmacy but, nevertheless, much pharmacy work is associated with service delivery, and with 'occupational' careers. Accountancy, in contrast, is more likely to be associated with organizational careers, and indeed, it is the single most common qualification amongst management in this country. Accountancy has been described as being 'the recording of data, usually numerical, which relate to economic events. It also involves the communication of these data to those who would use them' (Freear, 1984, p. 1). This 'recording of data about economic events' is carried out by large numbers of people (assisted by electronics), not all of whom will be trained or qualified accountants. Many of the unqualified will be working as bookkeepers, wages clerks, and so on, and many will be women. Whereas no one would describe himself or herself as a pharmacist unless qualified, many 'accountants' may not have formal qualifications.

A number of related issues will be explored in this chapter. Will the women now qualifying in ever-increasing numbers for this profession eventually end up in lower-level, practitioner roles within OLMs, as has been the case with pharmacy? Two issues are of significance here: first, the timing of the increase in women's entry into this profession. It has occurred at a historical moment (the late 1970s onwards) when issues of gender equality have had a high profile. Second, there is a relative lack of 'practitioner' options, particularly within the organizational context, for the qualified accountant. The latter brings into sharp focus the question of organizational exclusion within firm internal labour markets (FILMs); that is, the exclusion of women by men from access to higher-level and better-paid positions within the organization.

Accountancy: history and development[1]

In the discussion that follows, there is a primary emphasis on accountancy as an occupation, one which has systematically excluded women in the past, and to which they are now gaining access.

However, as well as describing an occupation, 'accountancy' can be used in a more general sense to refer to an integral aspect of the capitalist mode of production – as when, for example, Braverman describes the development of 'entire industries . . . whose activity is concerned with nothing but the transfer of values and the accounting entailed by this' (1974, p. 302). The extent of the emphasis laid on this function, and the expansion and development of the occupation as such, are clearly interlinked. Nevertheless, a distinction should be maintained between an examination of 'accounting' in the abstract and an investigation of the profession of 'accountancy' in particular. There has developed a recent critique of accounting which, like Braverman, links its operations to those of the social relations of the capitalist mode of production (for example, Tinker, 1980). On this reading, the occupation would be identified as carrying out a particular role on behalf of capitalism. However, others have suggested that the independent audit has always been an element in the control of 'agency costs' – that is, the possibilities of opportunism open to an agent who does not personally own the capital involved (Watts and Zimmerman, 1983). Such agency costs, it is argued, are a universal consequence of the delegation of authority and are to be found in pre-capitalist, as well as capitalist, organizations. On this reading, the occupation is viewed from a value-neutral perspective as a technical specialism. However, the occupation may be seen as acting in its own interests to further the power and influence of its 'own' speciality – as in, for example, the argument that British industry has been dominated (to its disadvantage) by financial, rather than production managers.

The role of accounting in capitalist production, and the development of accountancy as an occupation or profession, have been brought together in a recent analysis which argues that the success of accountancy as an occupation or profession is directly linked with the proximity of accountants to the 'function of capital'. (Johnson, 1980; Armstrong, 1985, 1987). Accountants in Britain, Armstrong argues, have consolidated and developed a strategic role in British industry. From their initial role in company liquidations, their position was further enhanced by the Companies Act of 1862, (known as the 'accountants friend', it gave accountants a crucial role in the liquidation process)[2] and in the increasing significance of the audit in British capital investment. From the strong base which had been established by their role in the audit, the development of cost accounting was much encouraged, Armstrong argues, by state strategies of production management during the two world wars. As a consequence of these and other developments, British industry emerged as dominated by the financial manager rather than the engineer.

However, whatever the theoretical significance of the occupation to the structure and functioning of capitalist society, an empirical fact that cannot be disputed is the considerable increase in the number of individuals qualifying as accountants in recent years. A number of professional qualifications are available, corresponding (very broadly) to different areas of expertise within the accountancy profession as a whole. Table 5.1 gives details of origins, membership, student membership and growth over the last decade.

The oldest qualifying associations are: the Chartered Accountants, that is, the ICAEW; the Scottish Institute, (there is also a smaller Irish Institute); and the Chartered Institute of Public Finance and Accountancy. These older bodies reflect the emphasis on the auditing role within the early accounting profession. Membership of the ICAEW is the major qualification sponsored by the professional accountancy firms. Members are admitted to the ICAEW via a training contract, once known as an articled clerkship. The numbers entering the ICAEW, therefore, are regulated by the availability of training contracts, and the number of students is well below that of full members. The number of training contracts, however, has been

Table 5.1   *Year of formation, membership and registered students of the major accounting bodies, 1976, 1986 (numbers in thousands)*

	Year formed	1976 Members	1976 Students	1986 Members	1986 Students
The Institute of Chartered Accountants in England and Wales (ICAEW)	1880	62	15	85	16
The Chartered Association of Certified Accountants (ACCA)	1903	16	61	20	75
The Chartered Institute of Management Accountants (CIMA, ex-ICMA)	1919	15	35	27	44
The Institute of Chartered Accountants in Scotland	1853*	9	2	12	1.5
The Chartered Institute of Public Finance and Accountancy (CIPFA)	1885	8	4	10	2.5

* Strictly speaking, the combined institute was granted its royal charter in 1951, an amalgamation of three Scottish bodies, the earliest of which was the Edinburgh Institute founded on the date indicated. Table adapted and updated from Renshall (1977); 1986 data provided by the qualifying bodies.

rising steadily (see Table 5.3). The Chartered Institute of Public Finance and Accountancy (CIPFA) does not require a training contract, but only admits persons employed in public service (for example, national and local government). Thus the numbers qualifying are tied to the availability of such employment and, like the ICAEW, the number of students is below that of full members. (Cutbacks in the public sector can be seen reflected in the 1986 figures (Table 5.1).)

The Chartered Institute of Management Accountants (CIMA), once the Institute of Cost and Management Accountants, and the Chartered Association of Certified Accountants (ACCA) do not require a training contract for entry into membership; these qualifications are usually undertaken by persons already in employment. The CIMA qualification tends to be associated with manufacturing industry, ACCA with the service sector (for example, insurance). They correspond more closely to 'organizational' qualifications, that is, qualifications undertaken in the pursuit of an organizational career rather than work as a sole practitioner or in an occupational career. Part qualifications are also relevant to an organizational career strategy – and indeed, the mere fact of being registered for taking them may be sufficient to convey the seriousness of the individual's career strategy to his or her employer. Thus, in the case of CIMA and ACCA, the number of student members is far in excess of those with the full qualification. Overseas members and students also make a substantial contribution to the membership of these bodies, much of whose income derives from this source.

In respect of registered members, however, Table 5.1 shows that the older Chartered Institutes predominate. Approximately half of all male chartered accountants over the age of 35 are working in commerce or industry. The Chartered Institutes appear to dominate not only in respect of their size, but also their status. The 'technical' value of the different qualifications, (that is, the difficulty of passing the examinations), however, is generally agreed to be equivalent. Below the six major accountancy bodies is a 'second division' of certifying bodies, many of whom rely heavily on overseas students as a source of income. The major certifying body, the Association of Accountancy Technicians, is sponsored by ICAEW, CIMA, CIPFA and ACCA. It offers a lower-level qualification, not requiring a training contract, to O level entrants.

The figures for membership and student membership given in Table 5.1 do not account for overlapping membership of the different institutes, neither do they exclude overseas members or students. In 1976 Renshall estimated that of the 113,000 registered 'units' in the five main British bodies, there were approximately 79,000 members active and resident in Great Britain (Renshall, 1977, p. 27). Estimating the number of professionally qualified working accountants, therefore, is a difficult business.

A qualified accountant would be regarded unambiguously as a 'professional' with respect to occupational status, and in recent years, the qualifying bodies have been involved in an overall strategy of professionalization. Both the Cost and Management accountants, and the Certified accountants, have acquired their Royal Charters in recent years, and the ICAEW is on its way to becoming an all-graduate profession. The larger accountancy firms now recruit only graduates to training contracts, and indeed, accountancy is currently the largest single source of graduate recruitment. In respect of professionaliza-tion, the emphasis on credentialism and closure often associated with this strategy suggests that the occupational group concerned will also 'scarcify' the skill in question by regulating access, limiting numbers, and so on (Wright, 1985, p. 76). In the case of accountancy, however, there does not appear to have been any sustained attempt to limit the quantity of qualified accountants produced – which would in any case be difficult to achieve as there is no single professional body.[3] The broad census category (unit group 002) shows an increase of 24 per cent (to 211,100) between 1971 and 1981. If there has been a strategy on the part of the profession, therefore, it appears to have been one of expansion, rather than regulation. Accountancy skills have not been 'scarcified', rather the demand for them has continuously expanded – perhaps as a consequence of an occupational strategy, as Armstrong (1985) has argued.

The structure of professional qualifications in accountancy could be described, in any admittedly loose fashion, in a way which corresponds to the distinction which has been made between occupational and organisational qualifications. The ICAEW qualification (and that of the Scottish and Irish bodies) trains accountants for public practice, as professionals giving a direct service to clients. It thus constitutes an occupational qualification, and all who obtain it will spend some years working in public practice. In contrast, management and certified accountants (CIMA and ACCA) train whilst in industrial and/or commercial employment; their qualifica-tions are obtained within and on behalf of their employers, rather than for sale to the general public. CIMA and ACCA, therefore, may be described as organizational qualifications. (CIPFA, as we have seen, is a rather special case given its exclusive link to the public sector.)

However, the actual pattern of employment amongst qualified accountants is such as to blur the distinctions drawn above. As we shall see, ICAEW statistics show that from their mid-30s onwards, a majority of members are employed in commerce and industry. A similar crossover is observable amongst members of the other accountancy bodies; an ACCA qualified accountant, for example, could work independently for clients as a tax consultant.

Accountancy, therefore, offers a range of employment possibilities which in some respects parallel the work opportunities in pharmacy. Public practice could include part-time work managing the tax and/ or business accounts of a limited number of clients either as a sole practitioner or an employee. It could also include full-time employment at the 'practitioner' level, or in a senior position as a partner in an accountancy firm. Work is also available within industry, commerce, finance or the public sector, either as an accountant or in general management. Part-time opportunities, however, will not be freely available in such employment, which will tend to be associated with linear careers.

Women and accountancy

What cannot be at issue is that accountancy is a male-dominated profession, but women have recently increased their membership of all of the major professional bodies. Previous research has shown that women were 6 per cent of ACCA new members in 1975, but 21 per cent by 1984; 6 per cent of successful CIPFA finalists in 1975, but 36 per cent in 1984, and only 3 per cent of successful CIMA finalists in 1975, but 16 per cent in 1983 (Crompton and Sanderson, 1986). Much of the empirical discussion in this section, however, will relate to the ICAEW. Not only have more women qualified within this, the largest, professional body, but the ICAEW also has the best set of membership statistics and affords the only possibility of longitudinal comparisons.[4]

Women were only admitted to membership of the Institute (ICAEW) in 1920, after the Sex Disqualification (Removal) Act of 1919. Silverstone (1982) has documented the sustained efforts of the (male) chartered accountants to exclude women. Not all of the accountancy bodies were as resolute as the ICAEW. ACCA, for example, was created in order to make a professional qualification available to those unable to pay the premium necessary for an articled clerkship, and in keeping with this policy of open access, first admitted women in 1909. Few women, however, undertook the qualification even after their admission had been made possible. The first woman ICAEW member was Miss Mary Harris Smith, a practising accountant who had first applied for membership in 1888. She had previously been refused membership on the grounds that the use of 'he' and 'his' in the profession's charter could not be interpreted to include women. (It will be remembered that the fact that the Pharmacists' Charter did not so exclude women was one of the grounds on which women gained entry to the Pharmaceutical Society in 1879.) For many decades after her admission, however, accountancy remained a male-dominated profession. In 1945 only 105 women were members of the Institute; this had increased to 342 by 1960.

Table 5.2 shows that the number of registered members of ICAEW has more than doubled over the last two decades. It also gives details of the phenomenal increase in the number of women members. If the overall number of members has more than doubled since 1965, then the number of women members has increased no less than fourteen times in the same period.

This increase has been particularly marked since the 1970s. Seven hundred and two new women members were taken on to the register between 1970 and 1975; 1,558 between 1975 and 1980, and 3,508 between 1980 and 1986. In 1986 women were 25 per cent of new members admitted to the Institute. Table 5.3 suggests that the proportion of women members will continue to increase at this very rapid rate. It gives details, provided by an international firm of chartered accountants, of the gender distribution of students recruited to training contracts. From the mid-1970s, all students have been graduates, although some non-graduates were still being admitted in the early 1970s. The larger firms train approximately 60 per cent of all ICAEW accountants.

It would appear, therefore, that the feminization of accountancy is proceeding very rapidly. However, because accountancy has for so many years been a male-dominated profession, the overall proportion of women on the ICAEW register (home members only) is still only 10 per cent. If present rates of recruitment continue, the major changes still lie in the future.

These future trends are difficult to predict on the basis of existing figures. Their recent entry into the profession means that female

Table 5.2 *ICAEW – Membership, selected years*

Year	1945	1955*	1965	1975	1980	1986
Total membership	13,332	18,772	40,759	61,718	71,677	84,543
Women members	105	182	464	1,413	2,971	6,479

* Part of the increase from this date is due to the merger of ICAEW with the Society of Incorporated Accountants from 1958 onwards, which added 10,076 members, 36 former members, and 3,321 students.

Table 5.3 *Students recruited to training contracts by gender, selected years*

			Men	Women	Total
Autumn	1972	no:	91	14	105
only		%	87	13	100
Autumn	1975	no:	134	32	166
only		%	81	19	100
	1980	no:	198	60	258
		%	77	23	100
	1985	no:	215	96	311
		%	69	31	100
	1986	no:	200	120	320
		%	62	38	100

Source: Touche Ross & Co.

accountants are overwhelmingly young, thus their age profile differs markedly from that of male accountants. Eighty-two percent of female accountants are under 36, in contrast to 35 per cent of the men. (It should be noted that the expansion of the profession means that, even amongst men, the age distribution is skewed toward the lower age ranges.) The career profile of qualified accountants shows considerable variability by age. Amongst the most recently-admitted members (between 1 and 4 years of membership), 55 per cent are employed in a practice, 4 per cent are partners in practice (or sole practitioners) and 27 per cent are in commerce or industry. After 10 and up to 14 years of membership, however, only 9 per cent are still employees in practice, 33 per cent are now partners or in sole practice and 51 per cent are in commerce or industry. This distribution continues up to retiring age. We would expect, therefore, to find female accountants over-represented as employees in a practice (the 'practitioner' option within accountancy) by virtue of their age distribution.

The implications of this difference in the age distributions of male and female accountants were not fully taken into account in an earlier empirical investigation of the work and career patterns of female accountants. Silverstone (1980) was conscious of the fact that the relative youth of her sample would tend to over-emphasize the significance of the 'practitioner' option, but no controls for age were built into her subsequent data analysis. In 1977 a postal survey was carried out of half of the women ICAEW members, with a response rate of 71 per cent (616). Silverstone's results showed that, in 1977, 61 per cent of women members were working full time, 26 per cent part time, and 13 per cent were full-time housewives. The women's employment was concentrated in public practice (64 per cent in total,

79 per cent of those working part time), and only 15 per cent were working in industry, commerce and finance (1980, p. 39). In public practice, women predominated as employees, and only 15 per cent were partners or in sole practice. In contrast, data from the Solomons Report (1974) showed that 30 per cent of ICAEW members overall (and they would have overwhelmingly been men in 1972 when this information was gathered) were partners or in sole practice in public practice, and 47 per cent (as compared to 15 per cent of women in 1977) were employed in commerce, finance or industry.

This 1977 investigation, therefore, suggested that female accountants were adopting the 'practitioner option', as employees, or self-employed accountants, in public practice. Silverstone's discussion notes these emerging trends. Public practice was seen as advantageous for women because of the part-time opportunities it offered, thus enabling domestic roles to be combined with employment. Indeed, the whole tenor of her discussion was oriented towards the assumption that a 'good' profession for a woman was one which, like pharmacy, enabled her to continue in some kind of employment whilst assuming the major responsibility for the care of her children, if any. It was noted that women tended to specialize in tax, rather than auditing, which would further facilitate their domestic role. As she commented:

> Taxation has the advantage of enabling its practitioners to lead a fairly regulated life whereas auditing involves working at the client's premises, which may be far from home, involve an absence of several weeks and often considerable stretches of overtime. (Silverstone, 1980, p. 40).

However, Silverstone also makes it clear that her respondents had experienced substantial discrimination from men, which would have made organizational careers difficult. Such discrimination had been direct; one woman, upon qualification, 'was offered even less [salary] than others [male] who took Part II at the same time and *failed*' (1980, p. 42); and men did not like being subordinate to women: 'Even my own husband rejected a woman as a company accountant because she would have been in charge of men' (p. 44). Many felt that they had to prove themselves better than men in order to achieve even a minimal equality of treatment. Thus this earlier research suggests that a combination of domestic role expectations and male exclusionary practices would seem to have been laying the foundations of gender segmentation within this occupation even as women were entering it. These assumptions, however, are derived from an analysis which did not take into account what would have been the extreme youth of the female membership at the time. Neither was the age-related pattern of the male career incorporated into the argument which, despite its other strengths, was grounded in the assumption that women would take prime responsibility for home and family and, therefore, that their careers would be different from those of men.

Since 1977 the number of female members of the ICAEW has more than trebled, and home membership figures now stand at six thousand or more. Current membership statistics (1986) reveal both continuity and change. A greater proportion of women members (22 per cent) are employed in commerce and industry than in 1977 (15 per cent), but this figure is still well below that for men (45 per cent). Women are still far more likely to be employees in a practice (40 per cent) than men (17 per cent). These comparisons, however, are still rendered problematic by the very young age distribution of women ICAEW members. Although the data in Table 5.4 is not ideally accurate,[5] age-specific breakdowns suggest that the variations in the patterns of men's and women's employment are by no means as substantial as gross comparisons would suggest. Table 5.4 suggests that older (over 55) accountants are marginally more likely to work in public practice, and less likely to work in commerce or industry, than younger. However, accountants aged over 55 are very much a minority of all accountants. The table illustrates very clearly the strong association, for both sexes, between age and the likelihood of employment in commerce or industry.

However, the crucial age break, as far as employment in industry is concerned, appears to be around the mid-30s, and the vast majority of female accountants are younger than this. Table 5.4a gives finer age breakdowns for the younger age groups. It can be seen that, although sex differences in employment are still apparent, the similarity between the sexes is greatest in the younger age groups, where the majority of female accountants are located. By their late 20s, it would seem, a quarter of female accountants are already working in commerce or industry, in contrast to 32 per cent of their male peers. This kind of evidence does suggest that the 'practitioner' option in accountancy, although taken by more women than men, is not as prevalent as might have been expected on the basis of Silverstone's work.

It is clear that there have been considerable changes over the last decade. In the late 1970s, the increase in women qualifying for the accountancy profession had just become apparent; equal opportunities legislation had only just come on to the statute book. As we have seen, Silverstone's discussion assumed that a 'good' professional job for a woman was one where she could successfully combine her 'two

Table 5.4   *ICAEW members, 1986: employment, location and age, home members only (percentages by row)*

Age:	partner in practice/ sole practice		employed in a practice		commerce or industry		other		total nos.	
	M	F	M	F	M	F	M	F	M	F
Under 36	15	8	36	44	37	20	13	28	20,555	4,482
36–45	36	31	8	22	50	28	5	19	20,443	793
46–55	38	41	4	18	52	30	6	11	11,558	157
55+	45	44	7	13	40	19	8	24	6,899	62

Table 5.4a   *1987 figures*

Age:	M	F	M	F	M	F	M	F	M	F
23–26	(0.4)	(0.3)	39	41	8	6	52	53	1,612	623
27–31	7	5	45	50	32	25	12	20	9,888	2,651
32–36	26	18	23	32	47	28	4	22	10,487	1,617
37+	39	34	6	21	49	27	5	18	37,994	1,011

Source: ICAEW membership statistics. These are collected via a retention form attached to the subscription and the response rate is 94%. Details relating to partnerships/employment in public practice and commerce or industry are likely to be accurate. The 'other' category includes (a) those not responding to the questionnaire (6%), (b) those not in permanent employment and (c) those recently admitted to membership who have not yet been sent a questionnaire, as well as those in other employment such as teaching. The distribution of ICAEW members between the latter three categories is not known, and will clearly have a substantial impact on the percentages in the younger age ranges.

roles' because of the availability of part-time work. Part-time work in accountancy, however, is generally available only in public practice, either as an employee or as a sole practitioner. Current trends in the employment of ICAEW members, however, suggest that up to a third of female ICAEW members will be employed in commerce, industry, or finance; that is, they will have *organizational*, rather than occupational careers. (This proportion will be even higher for the other accountancy institutes, CIPFA, CIMA and ACCA, which are organizationally based.) Organizational careers, however, do not facilitate the 'two roles' option to the same extent as that of a practitioner does (Crompton and Sanderson, 1986). It is in respect of these organizational careers, therefore, that we might expect to find more conflict over orthodox gender assumptions and thus an increased likelihood of divergent gender practices.

Organizational exclusion

In Chapter 2, a distinction was drawn between horizontal and vertical occupational segregation by recruitment (that is, the direct recruitment of men and women to different jobs) and vertical segregation by internal exclusion. In the latter case, women are not given access to careers in bureaucratic hierarchies. There is a considerable body of empirical evidence that women have historically been excluded from access to these firm internal labour markets (FILMs) (Kanter, 1976; Crompton and Jones, 1984; Collinson and Knights, 1986). The most stable patterns of sex segregation are those perpetuated by recruitment, that is, where men and women train and/or apply for sex-typed 'male' and 'female' jobs. Where women are being kept out of jobs which are supposedly gender neutral, such as careers in bureaucratic hierarchies, then the situation is potentially unstable.

The supposed gender neutrality of bureaucratic structures, it has been argued, is a key element in the development of the rational disciplining, and regulation of the individual, which has made 'modern' society possible (O'Neill, 1987). It has also been proposed that a central feature of modern organizations is the regulation of sexuality itself (Burrell, 1984). Indeed, he has suggested that accountancy (viewed as a function rather than as an occupation) has played a central role in this process: 'To the extent that accounting stands for an acceptance of the virtues of legality and rationality, sexual relationships at work may be perceived to be "illegal" and "irrational" by the judges of organizational normality today' (Burrell, 1987, p. 96). Central to the ideology which sustains bureaucratic hierarchies, therefore, is the assumption that sexual matters are irrelevant.

These insights may help us to understand why bureaucratic hierarchies are regarded as asexual, but they do not, of course, supply a complete account of their nature and existence. Another important feature of bureaucracies describes their role in the legitimation of authority. Rational-legal or bureaucratic authority (Weber, 1948) is justified by rules relating to open competition and the possession of skills and techniques appropriate to the bureaucratic position in question. Exclusion on the basis of individual characteristics, such as gender, will work against such a process of legitimation.

Therefore, although exclusion from access to firm internal labour markets may be in part achieved directly, as well as through mild and not so mild forms of sexual harrassment which 'keeps women in their place', it is more usually achieved through formal processes which are supposedly gender neutral but which have in the past indirectly discriminated against women. These include rules relating to formal qualifications, length of service, work experience and so on. It is these rules which, as we shall see in the next chapter, women may turn to their advantage.

Direct sexual discrimination at the level of the organization is both more pervasive and more difficult to regulate than these formal rules and processes. Professional women who adopt, for whatever reason, the 'practitioner' option as far as their working lives are concerned are reducing the likelihood that they will experience direct discrimination in the course of their working lives. Professional women pursuing organizational careers, however, are more likely to be exposed to discriminatory practices.

Silverstone's research provided many historical examples of direct discrimination against qualified women accountants. Such discrimination was felt to be less of a problem than in the past, but her respondents had experienced lower rates of pay than men for the same work, elderly male cashiers who had simply refused to communicate with a woman, and social invitations which were difficult to refuse but fraught with sexual problems. Older women accountants interviewed during the course of this research[6] reported similar problems. These included the qualified accountant who was asked, in 1958, to leave her employment with a leading firm of accountants when her first pregnancy became obvious, and the university graduate who, in the 1960s, began work as a graduate trainee with the Bank of England at 90 per cent of the men's rate and who on leaving the Bank could remember 'one of the senior people in the department when I said goodbye, they said, "perhaps it's just as well that you young ladies are going, it's too much of a distraction" ' (AT). Such women could, of course, take up forms of employment where they would not be liable to such direct exclusionary practices (for example, self-employment, perhaps part time, as a sole practitioner), or they could choose to remain in employment at the 'practitioner' level. However, amongst the younger women interviewed, their attitudes, and associated career strategies, suggested that many may not simply adopt such 'coping' solutions.

This does not mean that young women who have qualified as accountants do not experience male discriminatory practices. They do, but it would seem that they are not prepared to accept them. For example, a young woman explained her decision to leave her employment with an international accountancy firm as follows:

I can't see that they would ever promote a woman to senior manager. Even to be a senior manager is not that good in

accountancy. The only people who . . . earn really good money
are the partners . . . there's no point in staying in practice unless
you can get to be a partner. It's a sort of dead end really and I felt
it was absolutely impossible at (name of firm); they'd never have
a female partner. (LS).

She had, therefore, taken her (expensive) qualifications elsewhere, to
an organisation with, she hoped, more enlightened personnel
policies. Similarly, in the case of a young woman who would not
describe herself as a feminist ('I don't like the word feminist, to be
honest'), her experience of discrimination may well have been an
element furthering her own career:

I had the feeling that my boss in particular wasn't that struck on
women – he made a typical comment once. I took a collection to
him, one of the girls was leaving to have a baby, and I actually took
the card in; he said, 'I can't wait for the day when they bring yours
in.' I said, 'Thank you very much, do you want to get rid of me?'
He said, 'Oh no, no, but I just think that's where women are most
fulfilled, at home having a family' . . . So I thought I want to
qualify to prove him wrong and I don't think it was so much
because I was female but also at the time I was fairly unique in being
an A level trainee [the others were graduates] . . . I wanted to get
the exams to prove to my boss that I could do it, and I wanted to
prove to myself that I could do it. (MB).

Young women who are qualifying at a time when gender equality has
a high profile, it may be suggested, have a greater capacity to resist
male discriminatory practices than women who qualified in earlier
years when gender exclusion was legally and socially acceptable.
Another story gives a considerable insight into these processes. The
respondent had qualified (postgraduate, ICAEW) with an international firm of accountants and had then moved from public practice
to join a large financial institution:

I had a lot of problems with this boss. He was a professional
chartered accountant, had trained in the profession, come in about
seven years ago . . . eight or nine years now . . . but very insecure
and he did a lot to try and undermine what I was trying to do in
the department which I found impossible to deal with so, I think
it was probably this time last year, I went to talk to Personnel and
said, look, I need to talk to someone to get my side of it down on
my Personnel file because I don't want to suddenly find that I've
got black marks when I haven't had a chance to put my side of the
story and I think, by then, I'd managed to establish a reputation –

there weren't that many female accountants, and particularly not many female accountants who were very ambitious. The next thing I knew, I was being head-hunted by one of the general managers of one of the areas, discreetly taken out to lunch by somebody and then I was offered a job. (JC).

Amongst the young women accountants interviewed, therefore, the feeling seemed to be general that the long and often arduous training they had undertaken was in order to achieve a job for life. Not all hoped, or even wanted, to get to the top of their profession, but none appeared to be actually planning to take the 'practitioner option' as far as their working lives were concerned, although a number of them will probably do so.

One of the reasons why part-time work, and/or the 'practitioner' option, was not viewed with enthusiasm was that it was seen to be of low status, and/or lacking in prospects. 'If I could, I would go part-time. Obviously here that's not acceptable. Anybody who does part-time work here is in lower grade jobs, and I would be just as bored doing that as I probably would be bored at home' (MB). Similarly, another woman described a situation in her previous employment: 'There was a woman there who, she'd got a baby, she just worked three days a week, and really she would never get promoted . . . that's probably what's happened in my experience of people. When they have children, that's it, they don't really get any higher' (LS).

These assessments of the situation are, even at the end of the 1980s, broadly correct. In the financial services sector part-time work in organizations is associated with relatively low-level work, often carried out by the unqualified. A career break scheme developed by a major clearing bank, for example, ran into difficulties amongst the highly qualified because of the lack of part-time work at the appointed officer level.[7] This can be contrasted with the situation in pharmacy, where part-time work is prevalent amongst the qualified and no loss of professional status is involved.

The relative lack of part-time work available for the well qualified meant that most of the young women accountants interviewed, in contrast to the pharmacists, were contemplating a 'linear' career, either with or without children: 'I don't intend to have any family for quite a long time. I want to qualify and get established. I might not even have children, I don't know yet' (NJ). 'I'd like to get married but children might be sacrificed for my career, if my job was a lot more interesting . . . if it meant I'd have to give up . . . there probably wouldn't be any' (SE).

Amongst the pharmacists interviewed, all who had had, or

considered having, children anticipated a 'bimodal' career – that is, a short break followed by a return to (part-time) employment. Of the twenty-three women interviewed in the finance sector (banking and accountancy), however, only five had experienced or contemplated such a pattern. Their views are well expressed by a woman accountant's explanation of her decision to have only one child:

> I was 34 when I had to make the decision. Well, I've worked this far and got as far as I am, if I now leave for four or five years or whatever, it's going to be very difficult to get back in . . . I can look back over the past five years and see how things have changed here and everything is speeding up all the while and in five years time I thought, well, if it's a choice between having a 40-year-old woman who hasn't worked for four or five years as opposed to an up-and-coming, newly qualified accountant, there isn't going to be much choice in it really. (MB).

Concluding summary

In the last two chapters, two professions which offer a range of work and career opportunities extending across the WX axis of the model of the occupational structure developed in Chapter 2 have been examined. These are, occupational labour markets (OLMs), occupational internal labour markets (OILMs), and firm internal labour markets (FILMs). All of these labour markets require high levels of qualification. Women working in OLMs have a historic tendency to be concentrated at the 'practitioner' level in the professions in question; as part-time and locum pharmacists, and as part-time accountants in public practice. Such part-time work will lack career prospects, but it will be relatively well-paid, and such employment has been considered particularly suitable for women. The increase in the number of women gaining pharmacy and accountancy qualifications is one manifestation of the major changes which have affected the position of women since the Second World War, changes reflected in the growth of social 'citizenship' for women. These have included the outlawing of systematic inequalities in employment such as the marriage bar, as well as equal pay and opportunities legislation. Improvements in the statutory position of women have been accompanied by rising levels of formal educational qualifications, and their entry into professions which had been previously dominated by men. It is not being argued that male exclusionary practices have become a thing of the past, but they are more difficult to sustain than they once were.

It has been suggested that two major features might serve to reinforce gender stereotypes despite the employment of women in the public sphere – a phenomenon which was at one time considered to be a major source of divergent gender practices and thus the liberation of women (Engels, 1940). These are first, the employment of women in sex-typed, gender-segregated occupations such as nursing and secretarial work; and second, the provision of employment opportunities which enable women to combine 'two roles' – that is, paid employment as well as their domestic duties. In Britain, the most usual way in which this is achieved is through part-time work. Neither pharmacy nor accountancy have been sex-typed as occupations. However, pharmacy has been an occupation for which an increasing number of women have qualified over the last twenty or thirty years, whereas the increase in women qualifying as accountants is confined to the last decade.

In pharmacy, a pattern has been established whereby women pharmacists are concentrated in practitioner roles, and gender segmentation was very apparent. The extensive availability of part-time work is well known in the profession and indeed, many women may have trained as pharmacists because of the flexible work opportunities available. It has been argued that the flexible combination of work and family life offered within pharmacy has tended to reproduce and reinforce the gendered division of labour both within and without the profession, despite the fact that it is not a sex-typed occupation.

Accountancy is a *young* woman's profession given that women have only recently begun to qualify to any substantial extent. Although available, part-time opportunities in accountancy are restricted to public practice. Research carried out in the 1970s suggested strongly that a part-time female 'practitioner' option for women was developing, in public practice, within accountancy. However, more recent evidence suggests that the 'practitioner option' will be by no means universal, especially amongst women engaged in 'organizational' careers where part-time opportunities are in any case limited. Young women who have trained and qualified at a time when 'neo' or 'second-wave' feminism has made a substantial impact, and when equal opportunities legislation has become law, appear to be both more able to resist male discriminatory practices and more committed to a long-term career.

In summary, therefore, the evidence suggests that the combination of highly qualified women, a context where equal opportunities have a high profile, and male exclusionary and/or discriminatory practices within the organization is likely to stimulate resistance on the part of the individual. The nature of the organizational context is probably of crucial importance here. In previous research (Crompton and Jones, 1984) it was found that resentment at lack of career prospects was greatest amongst women doing the same, or very similar jobs to men, and this pattern was found amongst young female accountants. Amongst women in physically segregated clerical employment, this resentment was not particularly manifest. A similar argument may be developed in respect of the two professions discussed here. Women pharmacists are relatively isolated in their work, and in any case, gender segmentation within the profession is so well-established as to seem almost 'natural'. For women in accountancy, however, the organizational context provides ample opportunities for comparisons of the career development of individual men and women, but will not, unlike pharmacy, supply examples of other qualified professionals, men and women, in 'practitioner' roles (for example, as in the NHS or community pharmacy).

In the next chapter, these arguments will be developed further through an examination of the building society industry. As we shall see, although this industry offers extensive and flexible work opportunities for the unqualified female 'practitioner', qualified women wishing to develop a career must do so through the firm internal labour market. The operation of these FILMs has had important consequences as far as the gender division of labour within the industry is concerned.

Notes

1   The empirical data in this chapter have been drawn from a number of sources. Interviews have been carried out with representatives of all of the major qualifying bodies and the Association of Accountancy Technicians. We are grateful for their help and advice. An international firm of chartered accountants was most helpful in providing background data and further contacts within the profession, as were a local firm and the Head of Accountancy at a college of higher and further education.
2   It should be noted that the Act did not incorporate a *requirement* for independent auditing, but clearly did much to encourage this. For a summary of the relevant legislation, see Watts and Zimmerman, (1983), p. 628.
3   Students of accountancy have suggested that the rate of production of accountants has been adjusted by manipulating the pass rate, and this is certainly widely believed to be the case within the profession.
4   We would like to acknowledge the help of Frank Makin of the ICAEW for making obtainable special analyses of ICAEW membership statistics.

5 The first category of employment 'partner in practice/sole practice' incorporates what will in reality be a considerable range of employment statuses. A 'partner in practice' could be associated with an international accountancy firm; a 'sole practitioner' could be a part-time worker operating from home. The year difference between the two parts of the table is a consequence of the updating of the 1986 figures in between requests for information.

6 This work was sponsored by the Joseph Rowntree Memorial Trust. See note 1, Chapter 4, also Appendix.

7 See R. Crompton and K. Sanderson: 'Professional women's careers', reported in S. MacRae (ed.), forthcoming.

6 Organizations and their labour markets: the building society industry

Introduction

In the previous chapters, two rather different occupations have been examined. Both were 'professional' occupations requiring extensive training beyond A level standard; neither had been sex-typed as 'female'. A quantitive index of occupational segregation would measure pharmacy as a less segregated occupation than accountancy, given the substantial proportion of female pharmacists. However, as we have seen, the prevalence of 'feminine' career patterns in pharmacy belies the apparently less segregated nature of the occupation. In contrast, although accountancy is a male-dominated occupation, the emergent career paths amongst young female accountants suggest that such 'intra-occupational' segregation might not be as prevalent as women increase their representation within this occupation.

This comparison lends emphasis to the argument, developed in Chapters 1 and 2, that a multi-factor, historical approach should be developed in order to understand the changing pattern of gender relations, and thus the gender order. In the next two chapters, the argument is taken from the occupational to the industrial level. A close examination of particular occupations is likely to lead to more of a focus upon supply-side and therefore individual (and/or occupational) strategies, whereas the investigation of an industry is likely to lead to more of an emphasis upon demand-side, or employer, strategies. However, as we have already seen in the analysis of occupations, it is not possible, in practice, to draw a sharp distinction between these two aspects. Indeed, in the model developed in Chapter 2, these dimensions were explicitly combined.

In this chapter, a 'white collar' industry, where over 70 per cent of the employees are women, will be examined. The industry is characterized by a mass clerical labour force. Clerical work is the single most populous occupation for women in the UK. It will be argued that short-range, feminized, 'career clerical' hierarchies have been developed within the industry over the last fifteen years or so, that is, firm (specific) labour markets (FLMs). The significance of clerical employment to the overall structure of women's paid work can hardly be minimized; in addition, the building society industry provides an interesting example of a phenomenon which has already been discussed in relation to accountancy, that is, the use of the 'qualifications lever' by women to progress through firm internal labour markets (FILMs) at the managerial level.

It will be argued that the structure of women's employment in building societies, particularly at the lower levels of organizational hierarchies, reflects a complex restructuring of the industry involving technological change, changes in legislation, and indeed in the contextual milieu relating to savings and the ownership of capital. It will not, of course, be possible to examine in depth all of these aspects, but some essential background will be given in the next section.

Building societies: history and development

As their name implies, building societies were created initially as savings clubs for the purpose of house purchase. The earlier societies terminated once their members' needs had been met. In 1845 legislation enabled the establishment of 'permanent' societies, but the last 'terminating society' was not wound up until 1980. All building societies remained as mutual institutions until 1987. (The Building Societies Act, which came on to the statute book in 1987 has facilitated the setting up of limited companies.) Although the major role of building societies is still to do with house purchase, they have become increasingly important as savings banks. Between 1966 and 1976 the societies increased their share of the personal savings market from 8.3 per cent to 17.8 per cent (Gough, 1982, p. 20), and their share of personal sector net wealth stood at 8.4 per cent in 1983 (Boléat, 1986). They have been particularly successful in attracting the 'under-banked' working classes. Unlike the major clearing banks, building societies often retain strong regional links. Until the early 1980s, they operated a cartel on mortgage interest rates, which was agreed by the council of the Building Societies Association. Competition between societies, therefore, has been for investors, rather than borrowers. Although major financial institutions (£102 billion of assets distributed between 190 societies at the end of 1984), their contribution to employment within the financial sector is relatively modest despite very rapid expansion during the 1970s. In 1981, for example, the number of people employed by building societies was approximately 56,000 as compared to 293,000 in insurance and 367,000 in banking.

Building societies borrow from investors (savers) and advance money for house purchase. (Investors and borrowers are often the same individuals.) Historically, there has been no shortage of borrowers. Investors are recruited in part through a network of agents (estate agents, solicitors, and so on) who are paid a retainer and/or a small commission on investment brought to the societies. Agents liaise with building society managers, who are individuals expected to possess a suitable level of financial expertise and professional standing. Managers are not paid commission. Investors, particularly small investors, are also attracted in and serviced by a network of branches. The branch network expanded rapidly during the 1960s and 1970s. In 1962 there were 1,070 building society branches, 2,522 by 1972, 5,147 by 1979, and in 1984, 6,815 (Davies, 1981, p. 58; Boléat, 1986). On a day-to-day basis much branch activity resembles that of savings banks. New technology, particularly the introduction of counter terminals, has been extremely important in facilitating the extension of retail banking services. The branches are staffed largely by women, who will often have a woman supervisor. She may be known as 'Assistant Branch Manager', 'Chief Clerk' or even, in the case of 'satellite' branches, 'Branch Manager'. Branches vary considerably both in size and the extent of functions carried out at the branch. The smallest and simplest are satellite or 'feeder' branches, where a two or three woman team runs the computer terminal, linked to the decision-making centre. The decision-making centre could itself be a branch office or 'processing centre' and would be under the direction of a branch manager, area manager or district manager whose job it is to liaise with agents, authorize mortgage loans, etc. Branching has played a major part in the expansion of building society employment. As we have seen, the number of branches doubled during the 1960s, then doubled again during the 1970s. As a consequence, chief office employment increased by 35 per cent between 1970 and 1980, but branch employment increased by 272 per cent, giving an increase of 110 per cent overall (data calculated from Davies, 1981). (During a similar period, employment in insurance increased by 9 per cent and in banking by 35 per cent.) From 1980, total employment increased by a further 34 per cent to 65,404 by 1985: 18,677 men, and 46,727 women. Part-time working has also increased, particularly in the branches. In 1970 only 4 per cent of employees worked part time; in 1979 it was 11 per cent and by 1985, 19 per cent. In 1985, 73 per cent of staff in the industry worked in branches and of these, 23 per cent were part-time workers (data taken from Ashburner, 1987).

In 1900 there were over two thousand building societies; by 1985 their numbers had declined to 167. Much of the decline is accounted for by the winding-up of the older terminating societies. Mergers in recent years have also taken place in response to competitive pressures, particularly those resulting from changes in legislation devised to increase competition between financial institutions. The movement is dominated by the 'big five', all of whom have assets of over £7,000 million and five hundred branches or more. Below the big five is a second division of about ten societies with assets ranging from £3,500 to £7,000 million, all with more than a hundred branches each. The big five, and most of the 'second division', are national institutions, the smaller societies tend to be regionally concentrated.

Building societies, therefore, are growing and successful institutions within the more than healthy finance sector of British capital. For their employees, they have offered excellent opportunities for upward mobility in an expansionary climate which has hardly shown any sign of slackening. Their success has been due to a number of factors. The housing market has been expanding rapidly, and housing has also proved to be an exceptionally good investment. Perhaps because of their image as mutual institutions, they have received favourable treatment from successive governments. Investors have been well treated for tax purposes and borrowers receive tax relief on mortgage interest. From the earliest years until the beginning of the 1980s, the Building Societies Association was allowed to operate a cartel which fixed interest rates. As mutual companies, investor/shareholder pressure was largely absent, and building societies were not liable to take-over bids. These factors, taken together with the operation of the cartel, have led some to question the true status and motives of these non-profit-making mutual institutions. The expansion of the branch network, for example, has been argued to be an expression of managerial *folie de grandeur* rather than a manifestation of competitive effort (Barnes, 1984).

At the same time as building societies were expanding their branch network the major clearing banks were undergoing a period of rationalization and branch closure. It has been suggested that the building societies are, in a sense, simply repeating a 'natural history' in the growth and development of financial institutions that was largely accomplished by banks in the nineteenth century (Davies, 1981, p. 71). However, this comparison is inappropriate. The expansion of branch banking occurred before computerization. Thus each bank branch represented a 'microcosm' of banking, with a full range of staff, including bank managers empowered to negotiate loans and investments (Crompton and Jones, 1984). The structure of branch banking, therefore, was expensive to create and maintain in respect of both staff and facilities.

In contrast, the expansion of the building society branch network occurred at a time when computing technology was available. During the 1970s, efficient terminals linked to a mainframe at regional and/or head office were developed, and the further development of mini- and microcomputers means that advice on financial matters such as underwriting and mortgage quotes can be given by an efficient machine operator. These technical innovations, as we have seen, have made possible the development of satellite, feeder or retail branches and much branching activity has been of this kind. As noted earlier, satellite branches are effectively shop-fronts, often run by an all-female staff, and controlled from the processing centre or regional office. It is difficult to be precise as to the extent to which the creation of the building society branch network has depended upon satellite branches. Figures on the number of staff per branch, however, suggest that well over half the branch network is composed of satellite branches and amongst the smaller societies branching may have been entirely achieved via the creation of satellites (Boléat, 1986, p. 13). In a later section of this chapter, it will be argued that the timing of branch expansion in the building society industry was an important factor in the creation of short-range clerical hierarchies, or FLMs, which are dominated by women.

Technological developments have clearly been of major importance in the restructuring of the industry, but changes in legislation are likely to be of equal, if not more, significance. In the discussion of branch expansion, mention has already been made of competition between banks and building societies; recent legislation (The Finance Act 1986 and the Building Societies Act 1987) has been designed to break down functional specialization between different financial institutions with the aim of increasing competition within the finance sector as a whole. In respect of the services offered this is clearly beginning to happen. Major changes lie in the not too distant future. One of the two largest societies (the Abbey National) has already taken the decision to become a public company, and further mergers are expected. Clearly, these trends will narrow the differences in operations and employment practices between financial institutions. Evidence gathered from three very different societies during the course of research revealed a basic similarity in operating mechanisms and gender practices, despite considerable dissimilarities between the societies concerned, of which the most apparent was size.[1] Different organizations might have different labels for the same job, or carry out the same process in different organizational (and spatial) locations, but the underlying processes were the same in all three societies.

Building societies are white-collar bureaucracies. Women predominate in the lower clerical grades, and men in the managerial hierarchy. The similarities between their occupational structure and other white-collar organizations such as banks and insurance companies is considerable, although the manner in which this outcome was achieved has varied between the different institutions in the financial sector (Crompton and Sanderson, forthcoming). In the concluding remarks to the previous chapter it was suggested that a consciousness of, and action to resist male exclusionary practices is most likely to occur when women are discriminated against whilst in direct competition with men. In the case of the building society industry, evidence of such practices occurred at this point of direct competition: the recruitment of management trainees.

Firm internal labour markets

A variety of strategies has been used to block women's access to the upper levels of bureaucratic hierarchies. The most straightforward is direct exclusion, when vertical segregation is achieved through barring career grades to women. Since the Second World War, however, indirect exclusion has been more common. Women are not formally barred from the positions in question, rather, access to them is regulated via a series of requirements and expectations (formal qualifications, irregular overtime working, geographical mobility and so on) which women find it difficult to fulfil. Finally, women may be excluded through the relatively informal practices which have been developed to protect men's 'property in positions' (Collins, 1979; see also Chapters 4 and 5 above). Thus vertical segregation by internal exclusion may be achieved through indirect exclusion using formal or informal criteria.

Kanter's (1977) analysis of power at 'Indsco' provides a classic account of the 'cycle of powerlessness' in which women in organizations find themselves, as a consequence, entrapped. One route to power is through activities which are seen as extraordinary, and are highly visible – for example, the sales coup. Power is also acquired by forging alliances, particularly with 'sponsors' or 'mentors' who are highly-placed within the organization, as well as with peers and subordinates who themselves might be high-flyers.[2] Women fail on all counts. They tend to be in jobs which are routinized, and present few or no opportunities for extraordinary or visible behaviour. Most higher-level positions in organizations, in part as a consequence of the workings of indirect exclusionary rules, are held by men, who are reluctant to sponsor women. One of Kanter's informants made a revealing comment: 'Boy wonders rise under certain power structures. They're recognized by a powerful person because they are very much like him. He sees himself, a younger version, in that person . . . Who can look at a woman and see themselves?' (1977, p. 184). Women who *do* have power are widely viewed as mean, bossy and dictatorial, thus further lending a justification for their exclusion from power which might be supported by both men and women. However, as Kanter argues, the 'mean and bossy woman boss . . . is a perfect picture of people who are powerless. Powerlessness tends to produce those very characteristics attributed to women bosses' (ibid., p. 202). Lacking access to mentors or the plum organizational positions, women in organizations are forced back to excessive reliance on rules and procedures and/or 'negative power' – the ability to filter or distort information.

Indirect exclusionary practices such as qualification and mobility requirements are often embodied in formal rules and regulations. Indeed, the greater the pressure to achieve organizational equality for women, the greater the likelihood, in a situation where sex discrimination is illegal, that the impersonal, formal nature of these rules will be stressed. That is, internal labour markets are liable to become even more 'bureaucratized' in response to pressure from feminists.[3] If requirements for credentials such as job-related qualifications have been used systematically to exclude individuals, then entrance cannot be denied to those who have them. Because expert power is the most socially acceptable form of power, then it may be more dangerous for the organization to deny its legitimacy than to admit the previously excluded group. Thus liberal feminists have attempted to set up a 'cycle of rationality' to combat the 'cycle of powerlessness' described by Kanter. If rational procedures are challenged in their own terms, then a common organizational response is to make such procedures even more rational and systematic. Thus the feminist strategy of the 'qualifications lever' has been extended from professional bodies and into firm internal labour markets. In the next section, we will examine in some detail an important example of this process: the EOC investigation of the Leeds Permanent Building Society.

Informal male exclusion practices are well-known and established but difficult, if not impossible, to catch within the net of legislation. These include women's lack of access to informal networks, clubs, and so on, as well as the kinds of personal pressures described by the young women accountants in Chapter 5. The two women journalists who attempted to use legislation to prevent El Vino's management from refusing to serve them at the bar counter were not pursuing a trivial matter, as was suggested at the time. The business and professional world is largely male, and during the course of this empirical research, women's ability (or lack of it) to cope in the social circumstances of traditional male dining clubs, bars, etc., was mentioned frequently. It is not merely a question of the ease of social contacts but also, as the previous chapter demonstrated, of more intimate, interpersonal pressures, often with sexual overtones, which impede the organizational progress of women (Collinson and Knights, 1986). An awareness of these kinds of problems is acknowledged in the provisions of the Sex Discrimination Act which allows employees to 'give special encouragement to, and provide specific training for, the minority sex' in cases where there have been few or no members of one sex in particular work in their employment for the previous twelve months (EOC Code of Practice, April 1984). A women's training 'industry' has grown up to meet these requirements.

Management training is an area which has been relatively neglected by more academic social science research and theory.[4] It has been argued that 'management' is not distinguished by an identifiable body of theoretical knowledge and thus cannot be considered to be a profession (Esland, 1976). Thus, critics have suggested, if no such body of knowledge exists, how can it be taught at the university level? Radical critics have been even more dismissive; Braverman, for example, describes 'human relations' theory and industrial psychology as being the 'maintenance crew for the human machinery' (1974, p. 87) and no more. It is paradoxical, therefore, that although there has been a considerable debate about the extent to which Taylorism or 'scientific management' represents the 'bedrock' of modern work organization, as Braverman argued, there can be little doubt that the 'human relations' approach has remained the bedrock of much modern management training (Peters and Waterman, 1982).

Our empirical knowledge of management training for women is rather sparse (Wickham, 1986), despite the fact that in recent years it has absorbed a considerable quantity of corporate and government resources.[5] The courses for women offered by one of the foremost institutions specializing in such training lay heavy emphasis on assertiveness training, time management, and so on, with titles such as 'Learn how to sell yourself' and 'Dealing with people effectively'.[6] The four-day residential development course for women is advertised as being 'for women who are seen by their company as having management potential but are lacking the self-confidence to push themselves onwards'. It is clear, therefore, that such courses have the object of advising women as to how they may surmount the organizational disadvantages of being female, and combat the informal (male) pressures which have inhibited their career development.

Despite the relatively high profile which management training for women has achieved in the business world, however, some scepticism is still apparent as to its actual effectiveness. It is felt that employers have a tendency to finance women on training courses as a sop to equal opportunities, rather than with the serious intention of promoting them to positions of real authority. Some support for this view may be derived from the results of empirical research carried out within the institution described above.[7] It was found that, amongst the older women sponsored by employers, women who had had a career break were sent on the less expensive, one-day courses, whilst older women without a career break were more likely to be sent on the more expensive, four-day courses.[8] In short, the greater the woman's 'human capital', the more willing the employer appeared to be to invest in it further. Negatively, this finding could be used to emphasize the intractable nature of the informal (male) pressures to which women are subject. Positively, however, it might also be used to lend support to the liberal feminist strategy, of first, forcing an expression of the rules governing access to positions, then testing them, as in the discussion which follows of the case of the EOC (1985) investigation of the Leeds Permanent.

Management trainees

Building society management, especially above the level of office manager, is generally an all-male occupation. Particularly amongst branches (and societies) which specialize in the larger accounts (that is, customers), it is doubtless felt that the most appropriate person to deal with the bank managers, solicitors, and accountants, who are the most usual contacts with these customers, should be male. However, masculinity is not in itself a sufficient qualification; the individual has also to be socially acceptable and of similar status to the professionals with whom he has to interact in the course of his work. Thus a competitive, standardized, and rational selection procedure has been established. The industry also sponsors professional examinations (the Chartered Building Societies Institute, CBSI). The very rationality of these selection procedures, however, has proved to be problematic as far as male exclusion practices are concerned.

In all three societies researched for this book, the most usual career route was via direct entry as a management trainee. There are exceptions – men and women can in theory progress from the clerical ranks to management but it would be relatively unusual for the move from clerk to full manager of a non-satellite branch to be achieved. There are, in any case, only a tiny minority of male clerks. The small societies will not usually have a management training programme, and will recruit non-satellite branch management and above from the larger societies who 'home-grow' their trainees. Management trainees were required to register for the CBSI or similar qualification in the three societies researched, but no strong sanctions appeared to accompany a failure to complete the course.

In April 1977 a woman who had been interviewed for a post as a management trainee with the Leeds Permanent Building Society complained that she had been discriminated against on the grounds of her sex during the course of the interview. The case was taken up by the Equal Opportunities Commission, who undertook a thoroughgoing investigation of the process of recruitment in the Leeds in 1978. They found that, of the 412 women and 1,382 men who applied for management traineeships, 58 per cent of the men, but only 39 per cent of the women were called for interview. Thirty per cent of the men interviewed were offered a second interview, as compared to 4 per cent of the women. No women were offered jobs as management trainees as compared to 145 of the men.

The evidence gathered by the EOC provides a rich and fascinating account of the processes of male exclusion. Lest this be thought of as an isolated example, Table 6.1 gives details of the recruitment of management trainees by the Cloister Building Society, who seem to have been more aware of the potentialities of Equal Opportunities legislation than the Leeds Permanent.

In 1974, 42 management trainees were recruited by the Cloister Building Society, of whom none were women. In 1975 (the year of Equal Opportunities Legislation) 39 management trainees were recruited, of whom 10 were female.

In 1978, as we have seen, nearly 1,800 people applied for 145 management traineeships with the Leeds Permanent. Direct discrimination on the basis of sex was illegal, universalistic criteria had to be employed in order to sift applicants. In the case of the Leeds, three criteria were laid down in the job advertisements: (i) age (precise

Table 6.1   *Cloister Building Society: recruitment of management trainees by gender*

	Men		Women		Total	
	nos	%	nos	%	nos	%
1960–9*	158	93	12	7	170	100
1970–4†	199	98	5	2	204	100
1975–9	169	67	84	33	253	100
1980–5‡	30	35	57	65	87	100

Notes: * Data for 1961, 1962, 1963 not available.
    † Data for 1972 not available.
    ‡ Between 1980 and 1982 the Cloister virtually ceased recruitment of management trainees.

specifications varied between the 20–30 age limits); (ii) educational requirements (a minimum of 4 O levels including Maths and English), and (iii) a sound financial or commercial background. In respect of these characteristics there were no differences between the men and women who applied. However, women who possessed all three of the characteristics specified stood *less* chance of being offered an interview than men who had none of them. In the words of the Commission, 'since the singular lack of success of female candidates in gaining interviews and jobs could not be explained by any lack of the relevant criteria sought by the Society its Managers directly discriminated against women applicants because of their sex' (EOC, 1985, p. 26).

It is clear, therefore, that the process of male exclusion has historically shaped the gender/occupation structure within the Leeds Permanent (Table 6.2) and, it is probably reasonable to assume, within the building society movement as a whole. (It should be noted that after the EOC investigation the Leeds made a number of changes to its prescriptions for employment and instructions to managers regarding interviewing practice (EOC, 1985, pp. 69–72)). However, of as much interest as the exclusion processes themselves is the way in which they were achieved using overtly rational criteria. The official criteria for selection were all gender neutral but the arguments employed by the Leeds Managers show ample evidence of their difficulty in maintaining even a facade of rationality.

For example, 'Shirley I' (EOC, 1985, pp. 89–90) was one of the seven female applicants who was recommended for a second interview. Nearly 23 and single, she had eight O levels, three A levels, five years' work experience with a major clearing bank and was an Associate of the Institute of Bankers. At her first interview, she was described as 'very presentable' in appearance, 'well-spoken', 'relaxed', and

Table 6.2   *Number of staff employed by the Leeds Permanent Building Society in 1977*

	Male		Female		Total	
	nos	%	nos	%	nos	%
Management and managers	281	27	1	–	282	14
Assistant managers and supervisors	50	5	17	2	67	3
Area representatives	39	4	0	0	39	2
Management trainees	80	8	0	0	80	4
Chief clerks	282	27	1	–	283	14
Clerical, typing general duties	314	30	897	98	1,211	62
Total	1.046	100	916	100	1,962	100

(Adapted from Table 0.1, p. 3, EOC Report, 1985).

'confident'. At her second interview, she was described as only 'fair' in appearance, 'nervous' and 'lacking in confidence' – in short, it was necessary to re-define her personal qualities to provide a rational basis for exclusion. Some managers found this particular kind of rationality more difficult to achieve than others, as with the Branch Manager who reported that, of another candidate:

> Miss N. is perfectly prepared to meet our mobility requirement and has no reservations in meeting professional people. As I *cannot* fault her academically, I feel I *should* put her forward to the Regional Manager for interview. (EOC, 1985, p. 326, our emphasis).

By its very nature, the Leeds Permanent investigation had a unique focus upon formal procedures and written records. It did not set out to examine informal exclusionary practices, although, as we have seen, such informal assumptions were in fact latent in the manner in which the formal procedures were operated. It provides an interesting empirical illustration of the argument which has been developed above, to the effect that the more the organization relies upon rational criteria to allocate the individuals within it, the more susceptible is the employment structure to the liberal feminist strategy of the 'qualifications lever'. This strategy may be quite explicit. The (female) training officer in the Cloister, for example, regarded the society's policy statement that, by 1990, no promotions would take place without relevant qualification, as a major breakthrough for women. Much as unions, particularly craft unions, have secured the position of their membership through the bureaucratization of internal procedures, so this training officer hoped to secure the position of women in management.

The EOC investigation of the Leeds caused a considerable *frisson* within the building society industry (as well as demonstrating direct exclusion, the EOC also secured the removal of the mobility requirement for management trainees, which had operated as an indirect exclusionary rule). The case was discussed in the industry's journal, and a confidential six-page memorandum was circulated to all members of the Building Societies Association giving advice on the consequences of the investigation – advice which included the recommendation that societies carry out their own internal investigations to ensure that direct and indirect discrimination was not taking place. These pressures towards change, however, have been comparatively recent and it would be unwise to assume that results will be rapid. In the case of the Abbey National, for example, a recent report revealed that, despite some years of overtly 'affirmative' action, women in the Abbey National had penetrated only as far as the assistant branch manager level in the Abbey job hierarchy. At this level, however, the change had been considerable. In 1975 there were 520 assistant branch managers, of whom 20 (4 per cent) were women; by 1985, out of 723 ABMs, 432 (60 per cent) were women (IR-RR, 1985). This apparent penetration of the lower managerial grades, however, masks what has in fact been a major transformation of lower-grade work and the creation of the 'woman's job' of the cashier-clerk.

The feminization of clerical work

Clerical work is often cited as an example of an occupation which has been effectively feminized during this century. Late nineteenth- and early-twentieth century clerks were usually men. The relative status and material returns to different kinds of clerical work varied. At one pole were clerks such as those in major financial institutions such as insurance companies and clearing banks, where sponsorship was often necessary to get a job in the first place, jobs were secure and attached to responsible clerical, or even managerial, careers (Supple, 1970). At the other were industrial and commercial clerks, where wages were low and employment precarious (Anderson, 1976). These differences in the status and remuneration of male clerical jobs persisted into the period immediately after the Second World War, when a majority of clerks were still men. They were extensively discussed in Lockwood's influential book, *The Black Coated Worker*, first published in 1959. Lockwood's theoretical discussion focused upon both the class situation of clerks in general, and variations within the clerical category. It stimulated an extensive debate in class and stratification theory which continues today.[9] By the time of the 1981 census, however, over 70 per cent of all clerks were women. The feminization of clerical employment has been variously interpreted by different authors. For some, clerical feminization has been used as evidence to support arguments concerning the routinization and 'de-skilling' of clerical work more generally (Braverman, 1974). For others, the significance of feminization has been that it has rendered possible the preservation of the male career *out* of clerical work, thus the class location of the *male* clerk has been 'preserved'. That is, the promotion prospects of men who began their working lives as clerks have been demonstrated to be considerably better than those who began their careers as manual workers. The better life chances of the male clerk, therefore, justify the inclusion of male clerical work within an 'intermediate' class category (Goldthorpe, 1987).

It is certainly the case that, particularly during the 1960s and 1970s, the continuing influx of women into clerical jobs did effectively sustain the male clerks' career prospects. This vertical segregation by internal exclusion could usually rest upon formal criteria, as the women concerned were less well qualified than men, and were subject to employment breaks because of child-rearing responsibilities. The clearing banks and other financial institutions provide good examples of these practices. Breaking the clerical category down by industry, however, reveals that vertical segregation by recruitment is also extensive. For example, in 1961, 82 per cent of all railway clerks were men, and this percentage had only dropped to 74 per cent by 1981 – when, it will be remembered, over 70 per cent of all clerks were women. Conversely, 86 per cent of clerks in education were women in 1961, and this figure had risen to 93 per cent by 1981 (Crompton, 1988b). It would seem apparent, therefore, that within the clerical category as a *whole*, there are 'men's' clerical jobs and 'women's' clerical jobs, as well as the crowding of women into lower-level clerical occupations as a consequence of direct and indirect, formal and informal, exclusionary practices.

The presence of feminized 'niches' within an occupation (or intra-occupational segregation) has already been explored in the case of pharmacy. Such niches develop as a consequence of particular jobs within the occupation coming to be recognized as particularly 'suitable' as far as women are concerned. Suitability will depend in part upon the particularities of the domestic division of labour, as well as the cultural assumptions about femininity, which prevail as the occupation develops its gendered characteristics. Sex-typing is likely to take place as the sub-category within the occupation crystallizes, and, once established, its impact on the gender order as a whole will be such as to reinforce it. In the next section, it will be argued that intra-occupational segregation within the clerical category has been enhanced through the development of a largely female occupation throughout the 1970s – the cashier-clerk.

Building society cashier-clerks

Of employees in building society branches, the majority are clerks, and the majority of clerks are women. In the Cloister, for example, 85 per cent of field operation (that is, branch) employees are clerks (including part-time workers), and 97 per cent of these clerks are women. The rapid expansion of building society employment in the 1960s and 1970s coincided almost exactly with the accelerated re-entry of 'second phase' women (that is, women returning to work after a domestic break) into the labour force (Martin and Roberts, 1984). However, both the rate of branch expansion, and the technical change which facilitated it, meant that the work of a building society cashier-clerk from the 1960s through to the 1980s would have been very different from that in the 1940s and 1950s. In this earlier period, a cashier-clerk's job (and, of course, there were proportionately far fewer of them) provided an 'apprenticeship' training for a managerial position. Routinized work in branch offices, however, no longer performs this function.

A recent empirical study of the building society industry has concluded:

> Probably the major explanation of the feminisation of this occupation (cashiering) lies in the expansion of education which provided a supply of sufficiently well-educated women at the same time as opportunities for upward mobility made male labour scarce at the established level of wage rates (Craig, Garnsey and Rubery, 1984, p. 80).

This explanation is not incorrect; as we have seen (Chapter 3), girls' school-leaving qualifications were improving rapidly at this time. It is, however, rather misleading in its emphasis. The impression is given that women were recruited to fill jobs vacated by upwardly mobile men; the point being made here is that these jobs were not 'vacated'; they were *new* jobs. They were also *women's* jobs. As the review of the women's employment in the Abbey National commented: 'Counter work is traditionally seen as a woman's job, which is why so few men apply for clerical work.' (IR-RR, 1985,

p. 11). This 'tradition' may be of relatively recent creation, but nevertheless, clerical work in the branches *is* nearly 100 per cent female. Indeed, in the course of field-work in three different societies, we did not find a single example of a man on a clerical grade. The creation of 'feminized' cashiering may be contrasted with the situation in respect of management traineeships. Here, women *are* seeking to move into what have traditionally been 'men's' jobs. In the three societies in which we gathered information, the wages paid to female cashiers would not be sufficient to support a household; they were 'component wage' (Siltanen, 1986) jobs, ranging from £4,200 to just over £6,000 (1986–7 figures). Ashburner's (1987) research has emphasized the significance of technological developments in the feminization of building society cashiering. The routinization and mechanization of the job which has followed upon successive waves of computerization, she argues, has also facilitated the increase in part-time employment, as employees can now be trained very quickly for the de-skilled work tasks which were a consequence of mechaniza-tion. (One of the managers she interviewed suggested that cashiers could now be fully operational in two weeks, whereas previously it had taken between two and six months.) As a consequence:

> the greatly increased use of part-time staff . . . goes far beyond the requirements for staff flexibility . . . In some societies the increasing costs of technology and mergers has led directly to the decision to greatly increase the percentage of part-time staff in the branches as this is seen as the quickest way of cutting costs. (Ashburner, 1987, pp. 301–2)

Women's 'special' qualities have also been incorporated into the way in which the occupation is defined, and in its presentation to the customer – that is, cashiering has been culturally, as well as economically, 'gendered'. As noted earlier, much of the financial success of building societies has been founded upon the expansion of personal savings, particularly amongst the under-banked working classes. This proliferation of personal savings was both cause and effect of the expansion of the branch network. The building societies were uniquely well-placed to benefit from the increase in personal savings. They were familiar to many people because of their role in house purchase, they were mutual institutions, and they had strong local links. Market research evidence has suggested that working-class customers did not like entering the major clearing banks (Gough, 1982), and the building societies themselves do all they can to project their friendly image.[10] Publicity material issued by the Building Societies Association ('Understanding Building Societies',

BSA, 1986), for example, includes a photograph of a branch interior (with a small child amongst the customers) with the caption: 'A cross-section of investors! Easy to understand accounts plus open and friendly branches contribute to the universal appeal of building societies.'

The appeal of building societies, therefore, lies in large part in this 'friendliness', and it is here, it is being argued, that the gender of the building society cashier-clerk has been significant. Observation of building society offices confirms that much of the work of the cashier-clerks is taken up with interpersonal interactions; many, if not most, of the customers appeared to be known by name. A clerk in the Holyoake Permanent described the clientele as including 'quite a lot of older investors – they come in, they say "you're so friendly" – they won't change' (that is, societies). Another clerical supervisor in the Regional Plus said 'We make sure they [the customers] get nice treatment – either one of us will go out to the front or – if we know them well, we ask them back here [behind the counter] for a chat.'[11] The friendly, welcoming image is further projected in television advertising. What is being argued, therefore, is that *female* qualities of friendliness, helpfulness, being non-threatening but efficient have been taken up and developed in the projection of the image of the services offered by building societies. To reverse the previous quotation: 'So few men apply for clerical work' (see above) because it *is* a 'woman's job' in the building society industry, and is unlikely to attract many male applicants.

In building societies, therefore, it is more accurate to speak of the development and introduction of mass, feminized clerical-cashiering, rather than the 'substitution' of female for male cashier-clerks. This interpretation lends a rather different twist to the apparent penetration of the lower managerial grades by women. Data cited earlier suggested that women have been very successful in this respect – from 4 per cent to 60 per cent of assistant branch manager posts in the Abbey National between 1975 and 1985. However, in all three societies investigated, the job of assistant branch manager (or equivalent) was very different from that of branch manager, and it would have been unusual for an assistant branch manager to be promoted to a branch manager *unless* the assistant branch manager was also a management trainee.

The job of the assistant branch manager in the Cloister was described by the regional personnel officer as involving 'some responsibility for figures, day to day running of the branch, organizing staff if you've got people off. Spending a lot of time dealing with the customers.' The branch manager's job, it was emphasized, was quite different. 'Overall responsibility for the branch – costs and budget. Outside contacts – with builders, solicitors, companies. They are expected to bring business in. They will have quotas to lend on properties.' Branch managers do not get paid commission. In contrast, they will be expected to fulfil a business target. The job of an assistant branch manager, by comparison, was described as 'cosy' and undemanding. Most women in assistant branch manager posts, it was stressed, would not *want* to take on a branch manager's job with the outside contacts involved. In this account of the two jobs, the comparison between the gender division of labour within building societies and that between women and men more generally was quite suggestive. Women stay in the branch office/'home' ensuring that everything runs smoothly in the comfortable base, men go into the outside world/public sphere to bring in the business. This characterization and comparison places a lower relative value on the 'feminine' contribution in the branch offices. It is nevertheless entirely congruent with gender stereotypes.

A similar situation prevailed in both the Regional Plus and the Holyoake Permanent. In the Regional Plus, the 'branch managers' (although possessing this title, they were in reality office managers)[12] of the satellite offices had neither cars nor expense accounts, outside contacts were made by area managers with both. In the Holyoake Permanent, the assistant branch manager ('I used to be called Chief Clerk but Assistant Manager sounds better') 'couldn't see herself' as a branch manager. 'I might have to move out of the area, it would mean taking exams – I think I'm too old' (she was 28). 'Now the management trainee – *he'll* be a Branch Manager'. The presence of women in lower level management in the building society industry, therefore, is as female supervisors of an all-female labour force of cashier-clerks.

The gender/occupational structure of building society employment which has emerged over the last two decades has also had interesting consequences for the industry-specific qualifications offered by the Chartered Building Societies Institute. The associateship of the institute is a qualification pitched at a level similar to the qualifications offered by, say, the Institute of Bankers or the Chartered Insurance Institute, that is, a full professional qualification. Most management trainee schemes within the industry require that the trainee should register for the CBSI examinations. The number of women registered for and taking the CBSI examinations has been increasing, but by 1983 had only reached 14 per cent of the final pass rate, reflecting the relatively slow progress of women in the higher echelons of building societies.

In 1983 the CBSI launched a Cert.
Practice. No academic or age restrictions ɩ
to sit the certificate, and 'it was recognized
not have studied for some time'. Four subjects
a two-year registration period.[13] As we have set
relatively small minority of those passing the assoc
tions. In the case of the certificate, however, the sit.
exactly reversed. Of 187 gaining the final certificate in Jι
30 (16 per cent) were men. The certificate, it would
'woman's qualification'.

From discussions with the institute, it became apparent ...iat the
certificate is viewed as an ideal qualification for a clerical supervisor.
It is not surprising, therefore, that it should be predominantly women
who take it. Indeed, it was suggested that many women were taking
the qualification in anticipation of a career-break; it would render re-
entry into building society clerical work so much easier. Both the
Chartered Insurance Institute and the Institute of Banking have
recently developed similar, lower level, qualifications. These
developments in the area of formal qualifications, therefore, are
moulded to the contours of the gender/occupational structure which
has emerged within the building society industry (and the financial
sector more generally) over the last two decades.

Summary and conclusions

Since the end of the Second World War employment in the finance
sector has been gradually transformed from a pyramidal structure to
which access was obtained at the lower levels, followed by varying
progress through the hierarchy (the classic bureaucratic career), into
a segmented structure characterized by multi-portal entry. In this
restructuring the gender of the employees concerned has played an
important part. Women occupied the lowest positions within the
pyramidal structure and, to the extent that the segmented structures
are hierarchical, women are at the bottom of these as well. However
a change has taken place in that more women are gaining direct entry
into actual or potential managerial positions within the segmented
structure.

Under the pressure of liberal feminism, hierarchies which were
once all male are now being forced to admit women. The situation
may be compared with earlier campaigns of women to gain entry into
all-male professions. The initial impetus to change the gender
composition of building society management has come from

As the levels of qualifications and career competences amongst women have risen, so there has been increasing pressure, from educated women, for access to better jobs. It is the nature of the labour supply available, which is here the crucial variable, rather than the nature of the job. Jobs in accountancy, financial management and so on have been dominated by men, but by the 1980s a minority of women have gained entry to them. The gender composition of these occupations is being changed in the absence of a radical restructuring of the occupations in question, although there have been considerable changes in the normative and cultural context.

Rather different processes explain developments at the lower levels of financial sector employment. Here, the nature of demand was more important. Murgatroyd (1985) has suggested that occupations become defined as female if they are 'expanding at a time when the skills needed to do them were commonly held or easily learned, and when there was either a particularly high demand for labour or an especially large pool of women seeking work'. From the late 1960s, the occupation of cashier-clerk was effectively restructured as a consequence of extremely rapid technological innovation; simultaneously the demand for clerical labour increased rapidly as a consequence of branching. This demand was met from an increasing pool of relatively well-educated female labour, augmented by the return of 'second phase' women to the labour market. Cashier-clerking is now seen as a 'woman's job'. Although not particularly well paid, it does have other advantages associated with the development of firm labour markets. Jobs are secure, both in the sense of there being little likelihood of immediate job loss, and also in that jobs are easy to find, even after a career break, for the experienced financial clerk. (This was evident from the work histories of the women we interviewed.) For those women who stay with a single employer there will be the not inconsiderable benefit of a cheap mortgage: 'If you make use of the mortgage facility, it makes your job better paid' (Holyoake Permanent). Working conditions are pleasant, and the extent of contact with the public was often mentioned as a positive aspect of the job. Finally, there have developed short career ladders to the assistant branch manager level, complemented by a newly-introduced 'practitioner' qualification.

The job has also been culturally gendered. It is seen as requiring female qualities – warmth, friendliness, a caring attitude to the often elderly customers – and it is projected as a feminine job in the media image which the societies themselves create. In our interviews with cashier-clerks we found little evidence of dissatisfaction, except with pay. Managerial jobs were perceived as being in a different league altogether, requiring examinations and geographical mobility. This situation may be contrasted with that found in a major clearing bank during recent research (Crompton and Jones, 1984). In the bank many young women were bitterly resentful at being passed over for what they perceived were inefficient and inexperienced young male clerks. In the building societies we did not find evidence of this particular tension, which is not surprising as there *were* no male cashier-clerks. The feminization of the occupation, therefore, serves to *lower* the level of potential gender conflict relating to promotion prospects. The increased emphasis on marketing which, following recent legislation, is a characteristic of the finance sector at all levels has led to an emphasis on selling and customer care – and women are considered particularly appropriate as far as the latter activity is concerned.

In the financial sector, therefore, we find evidence of both continuity and change in the structuring of the occupations within it. The industry as a whole was once characterized by high-status clerical employment, with extensive job ladders facilitating both clerical and higher managerial careers. Technological and market changes have fragmented the occupational structure, and extended career ladders are being and have been replaced by the segmentation of jobs within the industry, combined with multi-tier entry (Rajan, 1987).

De facto segmentation within employment may take some time to be translated into recruitment practices (Crompton and Sanderson, forthcoming). In the building society industry, it would seem that multi-tier entry was achieved earlier than in the clearing banks. Building Society branch expansion occurred at a time when the technology available had removed the necessity for a cumbersome (and expensive) management structure in every branch. The distinction between 'clerks' and 'management trainees' was established as expansion was taking place. Thus the mass clerical labour force in building societies has been firmly established as female from the start. This must be seen as an important element of continuity in the structure of women's employment. At the same time, however, an important change has taken place in that women have been given access to the middle and upper tiers of employment in the finance sector. Indeed, having gained this access, the attitude of employers seems to have undergone something of a transformation. They now seem anxious to attract and retain qualified female labour, and 'career break' and 'returner' schemes are being devised in order to achieve this. This is sometimes represented in the media as the acquisition of equal rights by women as a consequence of wider material factors, such as the current shortage of young people following the demographic downturn in the 1970s and increased competition within the financial sector, rather than feminist pressures. However, this access has not been gained without a struggle, in which liberal feminist pressures have been important. The EOC investigation (1987) into Barclays Bank, for example, was a significant factor precipitating both the formalization of multi-tier entry in the clearing banks and the improved access of girl school leavers to the higher grades on recruitment. Another important point which should be emphasized is that this tapping of the pool of qualified female labour is dependent upon its being available, the fact that it is itself a consequence of more than two decades of change in the position and status of women in Britain.

Notes

1   This chapter draws upon a number of empirical and research sources including data provided by the Building Societies Association and the Chartered Building Societies Institute, who both allowed access to their records. Research was also carried out in three building societies: one very large – the 'Cloister'; one large – the 'Holyoake Permanent', and one small society – the 'Regional Plus' – which acquired 'medium' status through merger during the research period. The level of access allowed by the three societies varied. The 'Cloister' provided excellent documentation, and interviews with management, but did not allow branch interviews. The Holyoake Permanent allowed interviews in a single, large branch, but did not provide documentation. The Regional Plus allowed branch interviews and provided some documentation. Altogether, 8 managerial interviews, and 24 clerical and supervisory interviews, were carried out during the research. We would like to thank all of those who helped in the research.

2   Kanter's discussion, although exemplary in its treatment of gender, in fact reflects a fairly orthodox 'organization theory' approach to power in organizations, which emphasizes intra-organizational features rather than the significance of the wider social context. See, for example, chapter 5 of Handy (1984), *Understanding Organisations*.

3   A good example of this is to be found in the clearing banks. In response to pressures from the trade union (National Union of Bank Employees), the government (in the shape of the National Board for Prices and Incomes), and in anticipation of equal pay legislation, the clearing banks introduced in the 1960s and early 1970s a differentiated structure of clerical and managerial grades which replaced the earlier 'clerical career'. The new structure was gender neutral, and introduced under the banner of equal opportunities, but nevertheless embodied formal criteria, particularly those relating to qualifications, which indirectly excluded women. See Crompton (1989), Crompton and Sanderson (forthcoming).

4 Recent government policy, however, would appear to have brought it within the agenda of most universities. It is a sign of the times that, whereas in the 1960s, every university seemed anxious to possess a sociology department, in the 1980s, every university seems anxious to establish an MBA (Master of Business Administration).

5 Through the Manpower Services Commission, now the Training Commission.

6 This was the Pepperell Unit, a division of the Industrial Society. The Industrial Society was set up with the aim of promoting non-conflictual relationships within industry. Founded nearly seventy years ago, the society received its royal charter in 1984–5. Membership includes business organizations, public corporations, and trade unions. Only 6 per cent of the society's income derives from membership, 94 per cent is earned through courses, conferences and other similar activities.

7 We are grateful to the Pepperell Unit for allowing us to carry out this research. Simple questionnaires gathering basic personal information were distributed on a range of courses over a three-month period from September to December 1986. Usable replies were received from 219 women. We also were allowed to observe courses being taught, and carried out a number of interviews with staff of the unit.

8 Older women with a career break also had lower levels of formal qualifications.

9 See Chapter 1, also Blackburn (1967), Stewart, Prandy and Blackburn (1980), Crompton and Jones (1984), Goldthorpe (1987).

10 However, recently most bank branches appear to have undergone considerable physical restructuring in order to convert them from neo-classical Edwardian 'temples of finance' into lower middle-class living rooms.

11 Interviewing in the Regional Plus took place just before Christmas. Cards from the customers decorated the walls of the cosy, carpeted branch offices – complete with chromium and tweed armchairs and David Shepherd reproductions. In one particularly busy branch office, a pile of presents from customers to staff was visible, together with a (smaller) pile from staff awaiting distribution to customers.

12 In previous debates (Crompton, 1980; Goldthorpe, 1980), some scepticism has been levelled at the suggestion that variations in job titles might make occupational classifications difficult. During research, however, we found that the functionally equivalent job was described as branch manager, assistant branch manager, chief clerk, and office supervisor. To avoid confusion, however, these labelling differences have not been used in the text.

13 The academic level of the certificate is rather difficult to establish. It is claimed to represent 'about O level' standard, but other comments suggest the real level may be lower.

7   Women's work: cooking and serving

Introduction

All of the case studies of women's employment so far discussed have focused on relatively well-qualified women. This emphasis may be justified by the fact that the increase in the extent and levels of formal qualifications amongst women is one of the major changes to have affected the female labour supply since the 1970s. It should not, however, obscure the fact that a substantial minority of working women are in the lowest paid, least skilled manual occupations. If 'clerical' work, at 33 per cent, is the single most populous occupational group for women, then catering, cleaning, and hairdressing, at 23 per cent, is the next (1981 census data). Much employment in the area of cooking and cleaning is designated as unskilled, although the carrying out of such work may rely to a considerable extent on 'tacit' skills, or skills developed within the domestic or private sphere which are undervalued as far as paid employment is concerned.

As employment in manufacturing industry has declined in Britain, so employment in services has been rising. (Finance and the hotel and catering industry are key elements in the 'service economy'.) Even after the major collapse at the beginning of the decade, employment in manufacturing industry has continued to decline (from 23 per cent in 1981 to 21 per cent in 1984) and the numbers and proportions in services have risen. Industry division 6 (distribution, hotels, catering, repairs) increased from 19 to 20 per cent of total employment in this period.[1] The hotel and catering industry is one where the majority of those employed are women (over 70 per cent), and which is making an increasing contribution to total employment in Britain. Its importance therefore can hardly be doubted, but the industry presents a number of difficulties for empirical research.

These problems may be discussed under two broad headings: first, the nature of employment statuses within the industry, and second, the nature of the work itself. As far as the first aspect is concerned, a major difficulty for research is caused by the fact that the industry is characterized by unstable employment and 'non-standard' forms of working – casual, temporary and part-time work. This makes it extremely difficult to chart longitudinal trends, or even give precise estimates of the numbers of people involved in the industry. In respect of the second aspect, the proximity of many of the tasks in hotels and catering to what are often considered to be the domestic or 'private' sphere activities to do with food, comfort, and caring may give rise to considerable ambiguities as far as 'work' is concerned. 'Non-standard' employment relationships, together with the intimate and/or personal nature of much of the work, means that the hotel and catering industry is rich in examples of the kinds of ambiguities and problems relating to the definition of an occupation explored in Chapter 2, as neither employment practices nor employment statuses are particularly stable.

In this fluid and fast-moving industry, therefore, the research revealed a number of paradoxes as far as the gendered structuring of employment was concerned. Gender stereotypes abound (the glamorous barmaid, the fact that hotel housekeepers are almost invariably women) and sex segregation at both the industry and enterprise level is extensive. However, the highly competitive and changing nature of the industry also often renders it indifferent to the sex of the 'disadvantaged labour' upon which it depends.

This chapter cannot explore all of the aspects of this diverse industrial sector, but the case studies have been chosen with the aim of illustrating some of the range of employment and gender relationships within it. They include first, the school meals service and second, the hotel industry. The school meals service is a female enclave which has been, since 1979, under relentless pressure as a consequence of government policies. It offers both casual and permanent part-time employment, as well as short job hierarchies resembling firm labour markets (FLMs). The hotel industry offers yet another example of the use of the 'qualifications lever' in firm internal labour markets; as hotel management becomes professionalized, so more women are training for it. Both the school meals service and the hotel trade offer what was once considered archetypical women's work, described by Martin and Roberts in their classification of women's occupations as 'semi-skilled domestic work': waitress, barmaid, cleaner, kitchen worker, and so on. These kinds of jobs, which require no qualifications, are characteristic of the 'secondary' labour force or market (SLM). However, both non-standard employment relationships and non-standard work within the industry have been emphasized as being of particular significance, and these topics will be explored before the industry and case studies are examined further.

'Non-standard' employment

As the British economy has been restructured after the recession of
the late 1970s and 1980s, a feature which has received considerable
attention is the development of the so-called 'flexible' labour force.
'Flexibility' may describe both functional flexibility (that is, a reduced
demarcation between different categories of worker within the
workplace) and flexibility in employment. The latter is described by
Atkinson (1984) in his model of the 'flexible firm', where a core of
permanent employees is able to draw upon a range of services and
activities provided by a periphery of part-time, temporary and casual
workers. Both of these kinds of flexibility are much in evidence in the
hotel and catering trade, but it is flexibility in employment which
presents most difficulties for research. A debate has arisen as to
whether the development of such employment flexibility really does,
as some protagonists claim, reflect new and innovative strategies of
labour management, or whether it simply represents minor
variations in long-established patterns of labour use (Pollert, 1988).
These arguments raise issues somewhat outside the scope of this book
(we will be returning to them in the next chapter), although they are
clearly of significance to women's employment. In the particular case
of the hotel and catering industry, it may be noted that it has always
relied heavily on forms of non-standard employment and, therefore,
the sectoral shift in employment towards the industry will be a factor
underlying an overall increase in such flexibility. However government policy has been such as to increase the availability of these
flexible workers (especially young people), and the case studies
suggest an increase in this kind of working within the industry which
would augment any sectoral shift.

Another problem for research relates to the different categories of
non-standard or flexible workers – whether employed or self-
employed, part-time, contract, or casual. In this area, as an expert on
labour law has noted, 'The law has been left behind. The legal status
of many of the workers in so-called atypical employment is often
uncertain' (Wedderburn, 1986, p. 117). A growing number of
researchers have explored this complex topic and have attempted to
estimate the numbers of workers involved.[2] The major distinction
which concerns us here, however, is that between 'casual' and other
forms of non-standard employment. Casual workers are self-
employed, that is, they have no contract of service with their
employers. Important consequences follow from this legal status.
Such self-employed casuals have no legal rights under the Employment Protection Act, which relate to unfair dismissal, redundancy

compensation, trade union membership, maternity leave and so on; there is an 'absence of mutual obligation' between them and those for whom they are working. The fastest growing type of self-employment between 1981 and 1984 was that amongst people working no more than sixteen hours per week – and the majority of these are women (Casey and Creigh, 1988). A part-time contract of employment carries with it a number of legal rights which may be less extensive than for those in full-time work but are still, nevertheless, worth having. Self-employed, casual, part-timers, however, have no legal rights and are the potentially most exploitable elements of the 'secondary' labour force. Such casuals may on occasion work full-time hours, and recent evidence suggests that many individuals who would consider themselves to be dependent employees would be determined by the labour courts to be self-employed. In all of the establishments investigated during the research there had been a trend away from 'dependent employee' part-timers and towards self-employed casuals.

The nature of 'work'

All of the occupations examined in the previous chapters – pharmacy, accountancy, financial management, clerical work, and so on – are similar in that the activity or 'work' they involve has been clearly differentiated from 'private' or domestic sphere activity. (This would be the case even when the physical boundaries between the two overlap, in, for example, the self-employed accountant who works from home.) However in the case of much work within the hotel and catering industry, the boundaries between work and non-work are sometimes difficult to draw. This might seem paradoxical when the provision of food and shelter for travellers is one of the earliest forms of work on record – if 'work' is understood as labour for payment rather than directly for the household and/or self-subsistence (Medlik, 1972). However, although services offered within the hotel and catering industry are paid for, they are nevertheless an extension of 'household' activities. Indeed, this is suggested in the label, the 'hospitality industry', which is used to describe the industry. The hospitality industry, therefore, may be viewed as offering the amenities of the private or household sphere for sale in the public market, a situation which immediately presents boundary problems about what counts as work, as Finnegan (1985) has noted. (Indeed, in some cultures and contexts the very notion of a hospitality 'industry' might appear absurd.)

Very often this physical separation between household and market has not taken place, particularly in the case of women's work. Much of women's paid work has been carried out by offering domestic services within the home, for example, child-minding, or taking in laundry, or within the homes of others as full-time domestic servants. The latter was the single most numerous occupation for women until the 1930s. Taking in lodgers is an economic activity which exists on the very boundary of the public and private spheres. The Registrar General in 1851 described the lodging and boarding house as 'an intermediate form between the institution and the private family'. Davidoff (1979) has emphasized the very different connotation attaching to the word 'landlord' (one who owns property and collects rent) as compared to 'landlady' (one who, usually living on the premises, provides houseroom and services for cash). For keepers of lodging houses were and are usually women – reaching a pinnacle of perfection in the best examples of the Blackpool landlady (Walton, 1978).

Work in the hotel and catering industry, therefore, is characterized both by a lack of spatial separation between public and private spheres, and the intermingling of activities customarily found in one sphere or the other. Thus boundary problems are likely to occur, and the individual's sense of a separation of work from other areas of activity may be weakened. Another potential source of ambiguity lies in the nature of the material rewards offered by the industry. This is a low wage industry, but it is one which is also characterized by an almost infinite variety of payments in kind. These range from the perfectly legal provision of items such as meals, uniforms and residential accommodation, through tipping (which is legal but perhaps not always stated for tax purposes), to the frankly illegal 'fiddling' and 'knocking-off' which involves cheating customers and higher management together with the pilfering of quantities of food and equipment. Indeed, the extent of such marginal and illegal activity has led some to suggest that the apparent poor returns within the industry are something of a sham – at least as far as full-time, 'core' workers are concerned (Mars and Nicod, 1984). The extent of remuneration in kind will tend to blur employee status – indeed, Mars and Nicod have argued that an employee heavily dependent on tips and fiddles approaches more closely to an 'entrepreneurial' employment position.

A further factor, related to the issue of non-standard employment, is that the industry is a prime source of 'moonlighting', that is, working at two jobs but only declaring one for the purposes of taxation. How much of this work in the black economy takes place, and the importance of its contribution to the national income is, of course, widely disputed (Finnegan, 1985; Pahl, 1984). Paid work which is not declared as income may not be seen as 'real' work. If the employer is conscious of the presence of moonlighters this may be a source of potential power over the employees concerned, although turning a blind eye is much more likely. In any case, the origins of the industry in private service has resulted in the maintenance of what has been described as 'semi-feudal' (Chivers, 1973) traditions of employment in many areas, particularly in the larger hotels and more expensive restaurants. The presence of tips, fiddles, moonlighting, and so on, should not, however, be allowed to obscure the fact that probably the bulk of work in the hotel and catering industry is physically hard and poorly paid.

In a situation where the nature of the work is imprecise and ambiguous, as is the nature of employment and methods of payment, together with the often *ad hoc* and irregular working hours, it would be surprising if there existed a coherent work or industry culture, such as might be expected from say, professional groups such as pharmacists and accountants, or workers within a single industry such as building societies. Gabriel (1988) has argued that work in the hotel and catering trade is 'stigmatised' through its associations with personal servitude, and that a feeling of cultural inferiority adds to the multiple disadvantages of catering work. Although few of the catering workers in his study expressed a strong dislike for their work, Gabriel nevertheless described a situation where lower-level women and immigrant workers in a hospital canteen and local authority kitchen felt, for the most part, 'trapped' in their employment by their personal circumstances. In contrast, the young, single workers he studied in the fast food sector, who lacked domestic responsibilities, coped with their pressured and routinized work by regarding it as only temporary – which, in fact, it was.

Not all empirical studies of the hospitality industry conform to this rather grim picture. Marshall's (1986) account of the workplace culture of a licensed restaurant, for example, advances an explanation of worker attitudes which is almost the polar opposite to that of Gabriel. He argues that, despite poor pay and long hours of work, the restaurant workers were involved in and committed to their jobs because they experienced their work as leisure; that is, they socialized at work. In short, the boundary between work and leisure had been substantially obscured in the particular establishment he studied (a bar/restaurant complex on a Scottish housing estate).

This evidence suggests, therefore, that there are considerable ambiguities relating to both definitions of, and attitudes to, work in the hotel and catering industry. They are likely to be particularly relevant as far as women's work is concerned, given the close association of many of the tasks with women's conventional domestic roles. A particular example of this phenomenon is an occupation we shall examine in some depth: the school meals service (or 'dinner ladies') for whom work was very much an extension of their maternal, caring roles. In contrast, the attitudes of women working in the hotel trade were closer to those of the restaurant workers described by Marshall, for whom work was 'fun'. Before proceeding to these case studies, however, their background within this complex and heterogeneous industry will be briefly sketched.

The hotel and catering industry

As we have seen, the industry is a major employer of women, who are approximately 75 per cent of all employees. A distinction is often drawn between the 'commercial' (57 per cent of employment) and 'institutional' (43 per cent of employment) sides of the business. The commercial sector includes hotels and guest-houses, restaurants and snack-bars, pubs and clubs and contract catering. Institutional catering includes industrial and office catering (the works canteen), catering within education, the health services, public administration, and other catering in retail stores, tourist attractions, railways and so on. Until comparatively recently this division was reflected in the organization of the representative professional body, the Hotel Catering and Institutional Management Association (HCIMA). HCIMA was formed in 1971 by the amalgamation of the Hotel and Catering Institute (founded 1949, representing the commercial, private sector) and the Institutional Management Association (founded 1938, representing the public, institutional sector). The distinction between commercial and institutional catering is also reflected in gender distributions. Over 90 per cent of those working in institutional catering are women, as compared to 62 per cent of those working in commercial catering. These differences are reflected in the level of part-time working which is high in both areas; 62 per cent in institutional, and 55 per cent in commercial. The institutional sector is more likely to offer regular hours (given the 'captive' customers), as well as more opportunities for 'caring' work in hospitals, schools, etc. In contrast, the commercial sector has a more exciting, entrepreneurial image. Indeed, the rate of self-employment within the industry is high; over a third of all those listed as managers in 1985 were self-employed proprietors, and the number of self-employed grew by 26,000 between 1983 and 1984 (HCITB figures).

It is an industry, therefore, characterized by high levels of female and part-time employment, occupational mobility and changes in employment status, and low wages. In 1986, for example, 50 per cent of male manual workers in hotels and catering earned 260p an hour or less, as compared to only 11 per cent of all full-time manual males. Similarly, 47 per cent of women earned 220p or less, as compared to 26 per cent of all full-time manual females. Thirty-five per cent of part-time women workers earned 200p or less, as compared to 21 per cent of all part-time manual women (source: New Earnings Survey, 1986). However, both the official estimates of numbers employed, as well as wage rates, need, as we have seen, to be treated with some caution. As we have seen, the industry is well-known as a source of moonlighting, self- and casual employment, cash-in-hand and no questions asked, and therefore any estimate of the numbers working within it is likely to be approximate, and it is also an industry where tipping, 'perks' and 'fiddles' are widespread.

Table 7.1, therefore, should be interpreted with care. Besides the factors already mentioned, the very substantial 'managerial' category also requires some explanation. Well over a third of these 'managers' will be self-employed, owner-proprietors. The industry is also characterized by the youth of its 'managers' (1981 census data). For example, 28 per cent of male managers in hotels and catering are aged

Table 7.1 *Employment by gender and occupation in the hotel and catering industry (1981 census, 10% sample)*

Occupation	Men		Women		Total	
	nos	%	nos	%	nos	%
Professional	536	2	366	(★)	902	1
Managerial	13,826	47	9,693	15	23,519	25
Catering supervisors	1,143	4	1,832	3	2,975	3
Chefs, cooks	4,166	14	5,218	8	9,384	10
Waiting, bar staff	3,555	12	14,774	23	18,329	20
Counter and kitchen hands	1,154	4	14,205	22	15,359	17
Domestic staff	127	(★)	5,494	9	5.621	6
Porters, stewards	647	2	48	(★)	695	1
Caretakers, other cleaners	354	1	5,051	8	5,405	6
All other catering	366	1	685	1	1,051	1
All other occupations	3,350	12	6,461	10	9,811	10
Total	29,224	100	63,827	100	93,051	100

★ under 1 per cent.

between 25 and 34, in comparison to 24 per cent overall, and only 19 per cent are aged 45–54, as compared to 24 per cent of all managers. A newly-qualified HCIMA graduate, for example, can expect to move immediately into an assistant manager position on qualifying. It is not being denied that individuals in such jobs do 'manage' (in the sense that they will be responsible for organizing the workflow) but they will also be significant elements of the workforce. The banqueting manager (male) interviewed during the research, for example, was the senior member of a team that put up tables, counted and laid cutlery, carried food to the diners, and cleared away again. The pay of assistant managers within the hotel group studied ranged from the trainee grade of £4,500 up to £8,000 (1987 figures). As one of the (female) assistant managers interviewed put it, 'There aren't many jobs where you can get a manager's job straight from college – but you've got the status but no money.'

Nevertheless, the data in Table 7.1 suggests that approximately a third of the men and over 70 per cent of the women in the hotel and catering trade are employed as cleaners, kitchen hands, waitresses, bar staff, etc. These are jobs requiring no training or formal qualifications. Many of these workers are casuals, highly mobile and unprotected by formal legislation or trade union organization. An exception might be argued here for institutional catering in the public sector, where trade union organization is well established. However, as the evidence later in this chapter will demonstrate, the fact of union organization proved ineffective when faced with a sustained political attack on the school meals service. This, then, is the secondary labour market. Although all such secondary workers are disadvantaged employees, the secondary labour force is not homogeneous, but segmented by gender, race and age. These are all employees whose labour market position is weak, but the nature of their weakness varies.

Gender segmentation is immediately apparent from the gross data in Table 7.1. Women predominate amongst counter and kitchen hands, domestic staff and cleaners, men as porters and stewards. Segmentation is also very marked within different sections of the industry. One of the most visible and best documented examples of segmentation by age is found within the the fast food industry. The UK fast food industry is expanding by 15 per cent a year (Labour Research, 1986). The largest section of the market is still fish and chips; however, such establishments, together with Chinese, Indian and other ethnic takeaways, tend to be small-scale family concerns. The most rapid recent expansion has occurred amongst the fast food multi-nationals (or UK franchise operators): McDonalds, Wimpy,

Pizza Hut, and so on. These outlets employ a very high proportion of young people, many of whom are casual, part-time workers. McDonalds, for example, has 75 per cent of its work force under the age of 21; 80 per cent of its work force is part time and a 'typical' employee works 25 hours per week.

Gabriel's (1988) case study of 'Fun Foods' confirmed the youth of the labour force. Labour turnover was also high; 36 of the 48 people interviewed by Gabriel had been in their jobs for less than a year. He suggested that on average between 40 per cent and 70 per cent of new recruits leave within a month and more than 80 per cent within a year. It does not take very long, however, to train a new worker. Gabriel argued that workers in fast food render life bearable by regarding it as only temporary or casual; even the long-term staff (all managers, and all in their 20s) regarded their jobs as short-term. ('Long-term' was defined as up to five years' service, but only four of the fifteen managers he interviewed had over two years' service.) Age rather than race or gender segments the fast food workforce. Both functional and numerical flexibility is achieved through the use of this young, mobile workforce, lacking in specific skills, whose location in this particular sector is in any case likely to be only temporary.

If young people of both sexes are employed within fast food, the industry as a whole also includes jobs for which 'only women would apply'; that is, like cashier-clerking in the building society industry, the occupation has been sex-typed. The example investigated during the research was the school meals service, or 'dinner ladies', an occupation which has, as its popular title implies, from the first employed only women.

Dinner ladies

The occupational title also reflects the origins of the service in the inter-war years, at a time when to call a woman anything but a lady might have been seen as a term of abuse, and for consumers (state school children) for whom 'dinner' was a midday meal. Although the beginnings of school meals provision go back to the early years of this century, the service was fully established under the terms of the reforming Education Act of 1944. Education authorities had to provide a proper meal of a fixed minimum nutritional standard and at a fixed national price. Together with the provision of free school milk, the aim was to secure, through adequate nutrition, the health of the nation's children.

As general nutritional standards improved in the years of postwar affluence, the point was made increasingly that this universalist approach to children's feeding was anachronistic. However, it was an ideological shift in government policy that heralded the beginning of the end. The Conservative government elected in 1979 was committed to a roll-back of particular aspects of the Welfare State. The school meals service was vulnerable on a number of counts. As a universalistic benefit, it went against the principles of individual, or rather family, responsibility. (The introduction of school meals earlier in this century had been criticized on the grounds that it abrogated family responsibilities (Lewis, 1980)). As it was provided by employees of the local authority, the service fell into the same category as 'direct labour' – and the government was committed to the privatization of state and local authority services. In any case, given the pressures to reduce state expenditure which followed upon the worsening economic situation, school meals were portrayed as an expendable luxury item. These ideas culminated in the 1980 Education Act. It effectively removed central government controls, and local education authorities were now free to provide whatever service they wished, at whatever price. Nutritional standards were also abolished. The only requirement of LEAs was to provide food for pupils whose parents were receiving family income supplement or supplementary benefit. The 'freedom' of local authorities was, of course, severely constrained by the fact that central government policies, including rate-capping were systematically reducing local government funding. Nevertheless, there were still some local variations. Authorities such as Gateshead and the ILEA continued to give relatively generous support to the service, whereas authorities such as Essex, Merton in South London, and Norfolk took up the government's invitation to reduce the service with some enthusiasm.

The School Meals Service is an all-female enclave in the female-dominated sector of institutional catering. All kitchen assistants, cooks and cook supervisors, that is, those who directly provide the service, are women. The topmost level of the school meals service is organized by the National Association of School Meals Organisers, a professional body affiliated to HCIMA. NASMO has a membership of 500 out of a possible constituency of 800; of these, 21 (4 per cent) are men and none of these are actually described as 'school meals organisers' (1985 figures). It is, of course, hardly surprising that school catering should be dominated by women. The hours and holiday periods are tailor-made for women with young children at school and indeed, many women may have, or have had, children at the school in which they are employed. Cooking and/or serving food to children in schools is a 'public' sphere occupation virtually continuous with women's work in the private, domestic sphere. It is an occupation, therefore, which will reinforce female identity and particular aspects of cultural definitions of the feminine role. However, as with all such female hierarchies, there is a paradox. The concentration of women into women's jobs will tend to reinforce prevailing expectations and thus be a source of stability as far as gender relations are concerned. The hierarchy also offers opportunities for upward occupational mobility. In the service investigated during the course of the research,[3] there was a short hierarchy through the kitchen to cook-supervisor, from which it was possible to move through the positions of peripatetic organizer, and assistant organizer to school meals organiser. Women who had started in the School Meals Service with absolutely no formal qualifications had risen to this level (after twenty years or so), in the process gaining OND, HND and 'in house' qualifications.[4] (The two levels above organizer, with one person each, were occupied by younger women with HCIMA qualifications.) These short-range career hierarchies are similar to the FLMs which, as we have seen, have been established at the clerical level in the finance sector. Therefore, although the school meals service is badly paid, low-level 'women's work', it has offered some opportunities for upward occupational mobility for individual women.

The School Meals Service: the impact of the cuts

The authority investigated during fieldwork was one of the more enthusiastic respondents to the 1980 Education Act. Its immediate response had been to cut staffing levels (by 20 per cent), increase prices and adopt a trading account system of budgeting. Income from cash and the 'dinner discs' provided to children entitled to free school meals had to equal expenditure on wages, food and so on. Calculations are made on the basis of 'meal equivalents' rather than number of customers. Meal equivalents are calculated by dividing takings by 70p; staffing levels are calculated from this. Two children might spend 35p each in the new cafeteria system, but the staffing level will still be calculated as 'one meal equivalent'. Rising prices have led to a fall in the take-up of school meals, and only 25 per cent of children were entitled to free school meals, and thus were to some extent 'captive' customers, in 1986. Between 1984 and 1986 there had been a 4.8 per cent decline on 'meal equivalent' calculations, to a low level of 34 per cent of take up (calculated on the basis of all pupils). The actual decline, of course, is even greater, given that school rolls are falling. Since the Act, therefore, the service has suffered a relentless squeeze on staffing levels, combined with unending pressures towards enhanced profitability.

This process of attrition has been exacerbated for the women involved by direct cuts in their terms and conditions of employment. A number of changes were unilaterally imposed by the authority. These were contested by the union (NUPE), but nevertheless, by 1984 the women had lost their right to a free meal, the equivalent of the two bank holidays, and permanent staff had their retaining fee (paid during school holidays) cut from half to quarter pay. Progressive cuts in hours, harder work, and declining terms and conditions of service, therefore, has been the lot of the women employed by the authority. Privatization has been a threat but not put into practice, possibly because a private company would not be able to provide even an inferior service at current costs. A more serious prospect at the time of our investigation was the proposed introduction of Family Credits in 1988, when the benefit allocated via dinner discs (the only *guaranteed* source of income for the school meals service) would be paid in cash.

The number of staff employed by the authority in 1986 was 1,855: 60 per cent on permanent contracts, 30 per cent on short-term contracts, and 10 per cent casuals. With staffing levels calculated week by week on the basis of takings from school canteens, there have been considerable pressures to increase the proportion of short-term and self-employed casual staff. Permanent staff are paid a retainer and cannot have their hours cut to less than seven and a half a week; contract staff are employed by the term and are not paid a retainer; casual staff are employed when the hours are available. In September 1979 the comparable percentages were 75 per cent permanent, 20 per cent short-term contract, and 5 per cent casual; as can be seen, the proportion of permanent staff has declined and that of short-term and casual workers increased. In the school meals service, casuals may have long service – they are 'permanent casuals'. One of the more delicate aspect of the cook-supervisor's many tasks is to allocate the diminishing number of hours available amongst her permanent, short-contract and casual staff. Extra hours can be achieved by catering for non-school outlets, and the school kitchen studied also catered for a local museum and teachers' centre.

The rates of pay are not generous. In 1986 the weekly rate for a kitchen assistant was £88.62, for an assistant cook £91.92, and for a cook supervisor £99.32 (before deductions). Only the cook-supervisor, however, would actually receive a full wage as she was the only full-time employee. The maximum number of hours worked by other grades was 28.75, descending to 10 hours a week. From observation, the women worked extremely hard, and all of them complained of the shortage of hours and pressure of work.

There can be few occupational groups, therefore, to have suffered a greater deterioration in their working conditions or terms of service. Yet the women were not leaving the service. Six of the ten women in the kitchen studied had eight or more years' service, and one had been there for twenty-nine years. It has been argued that women are 'trapped' in such jobs by the convenient hours and lack of alternative employment. This emerged very strongly from Gabriel's study in which he drew a sharp contrast between married women and the young, highly mobile fast food employees. As one of his informants working in a local authority kitchen put it, 'It's the same boring job as you do at home, but at 46 it is hard to find another' (1988, p. 49).

The crucial difference between this particular local authority employee and those that we interviewed, however, was the greater extent of contact with the school children. All of the women complained – with justification – about the treatment they had received from their employers. However, their reaction has not been to engage in industrial action, or to leave the job, but rather, to increase their work intensity. The NUPE official explained that the 'loyalty of the meals staff has been traded on, the service continues on the backs of the ladies in the service. They're so loyal to the school and so proud of the service – they won't consider the traditional male response.' The cook-supervisor said that 'all the staff put their own time into the service – if they didn't, it wouldn't run so smoothly.' We were told several times of women who worked for nothing 'because they loved it so much'. We did not actually meet such a woman but, even if she is a myth, it is a powerful indicator of the prevailing work ideology amongst this group of women.

The focus of the dinner ladies is the children. Rather as a devoted mother will make sacrifices for her young, these women endured their declining conditions 'for the sake of the children'. The identification of the women interviewed in the school kitchen with domestic life was strong; all bar one had children of their own, and all had taken extended career breaks (including the woman with no children). 'Working with children' was seen by all as a very positive aspect of the job. Much emphasis was laid upon the need to give children a better choice of food, how much they (the children) enjoyed the cafeteria system, and so on. In fact, nutritional standards have declined since the introduction of the cafeteria system,[5] although efforts were made to improve matters by, for example, using wholemeal flour in pastry. In short, it is being suggested that the women remained dedicated and cheerful by defining their work as 'caring for children'.

When the boundaries between public and private sphere work are ill-defined it would seem that there is a corresponding increase in the women's capacity for *self* exploitation. This has been noted in other empirical studies of the School Meals Service (Cunnison, 1983), and Gabriel also notes of the dinner ladies in his sample who worked directly with children that 'their devotion to the children gave meaning to their work' (1988, p. 73).

Work in the School Meals Service could also be used to support arguments that skills socially defined as feminine, such as those in the school meals service, are likely to be downgraded (Craig, Tarling and Wilkinson, 1982). The work of the cook-supervisor would provide a particularly good example. She managed a kitchen cooking regularly for 600, together with an irregular amount of contract catering. She was responsible for devising the menus (in consultation) and ordering supplies, balancing the books each week and juggling with the hours and work rotas of ten to twelve staff week by week. She was also directly responsible for the day-to-day output and running of the kitchen. The pressure on staff hours meant that she could rarely stay in her office as her work was needed in the kitchen, and her book work had to be done at home. For this she received just over £99 a week, less deductions. In this unglamorous and impoverished niche within the hotel and catering trade, tips, perks and fiddles are largely absent. She carried out, therefore, skilled and demanding work, with unpaid overtime, for less than the average unskilled manual worker's wage. Now married with one child, she had begun her school meals career as a part-time kitchen assistant. After fourteen years, obtaining City and Guilds through a combination of night school and day release, she had obtained her present position. The material rewards were low, but she said, quite unprompted, 'I love my job'.

Women as a 'secondary' labour force in the hotel trade

The School Meals Service offers flexible working hours which are uniquely suited to the requirements of mothers of school-age children who have assumed the major burden of family responsibilities. It has been argued above that, as well as the convenient hours, there are also other aspects of this sex-typed occupation which serve to emphasize particular aspects of the female role. Other kinds of unskilled employment also offer convenient hours as far as women are concerned, but they do not emphasize the same kind of femininity and indeed, the employment in question may not have been firmly sex-typed.

An absence of firm sex-typing within the secondary or 'disadvantaged' labour force is suggested by the findings of a case study carried out within the hotel industry. Table 7.2 gives comparative data of staffing by gender and employment status for two hotels operated by 'Relax Partnerships', a regionally-based company trading in a medium-sized service centre. Both hotels were relatively new, substantial, up-market establishments. More than three-quarters of the women they employed were part-time or casual workers. The historical comparison indicates, as in the School Meals Service, a sharp increase in the proportion of casual workers employed over the period in question; from 39 per cent to 49 per cent.

The gender distributions by employment status are indicative of occupational segregation. In the 1979 figures, the men are overwhelmingly in full-time jobs, as porters, managers, waiters, chefs etc., and the women are working part time as waitresses and chambermaids. The 1987 figures, however, suggest that quite substantial changes have occurred. The proportion of full-time men has declined sharply (from 82 per cent to 61 per cent of male employees), whilst the proportion of full-time women has risen.

However, although the number of male casual workers has risen, this has been as a consequence of an increase in the employment of

Table 7.2 *Staffing levels by gender and employment status, Relax Partnerships Ltd (percentages by column)*

		October 1979			February 1987		
		M	F	Total	M	F	Total
part time (contract):	no.	6	76	82	4	65	69
	%	(8)	(34)	(27)	(5)	(25)	(20)
full time and salaried:	no.	65	36	101	51	57	108
	%	(82)	(16)	(34)	(61)	(22)	(31)
casual:	no.	8	110	118	29	140	169
	%	(10)	(50)	(39)	(35)	(53)	(49)
total nos:	no.	79	222	301	84	262	346
		(100)	(100)	(100)	(100)	(100)	(100)

Notes: Permanent part-time workers are employed for 16–29 hours per week. Casual workers are employed for less than 16 hours a week. There are regular casuals employed on a non-binding 'contract', and 'casual casuals', employed mainly at weekends.

1979–87 have been successful trading years for the company. This will have had an impact on staffing levels which it is not possible to calculate.

young casual workers, both male and female. The majority of these young people are still in full-time education; students from the hotel school, local sixth formers, and so on. The casual, secondary labour force in the hotel trade, therefore, has been augmented by another of its components, young people. These may, of course, only be temporary residents in the secondary labour market.

This kind of evidence suggests that lower level work in the hotel trade has not been firmly sex-typed. In this highly competitive industry it is necessary that labour should be cheap, rather than it should be of one sex or another. Thus, despite evidence of what may appear to be quite extensive segregation by gender, the realities are more complex. An 'inverse statistical discrimination' operates. Female labour is used because it is both cheap and available at the right time of day and season. If another source of cheap labour becomes available, it will be used as well. The economic recession, in combination with central government policies, has made young people such a source. Unemployment rates are particularly high amongst the younger age groups, and the system of benefits has been structured so as to make it more likely that they will accept poorly-paid work.[6] More young people are staying on into the sixth form, and/or going into further education. The declining value of student grants and pressures on parental incomes has further increased the necessity for part-time work of some kind. As we have seen, a whole section of the industry – fast food – operates with such labour, and it would seem to be increasingly utilised in the hotel trade.[7] As Rubery and Tarling have noted:

> It is . . . the case that women are being increasingly forced into competition with other disadvantaged groups in their traditional (i.e. low-paid) employment areas, particularly from young people and the long-term unemployed of both sexes . . . Thus women could lose their dubious advantage of being the most important source of disadvantaged labour supply to British employers. (1988, p. 126).

The increase in part-time working in the 'hospitality industry' shown in Table 7.2 has been well-documented by others (Robinson and Wallace, 1983). Their discussion, however, does not discriminate between contracted part-time and casual employment, and the increase in the latter was a noticeable development in staffing in the School Meals Service, Relax Partnerships, and a major hotel chain which was also investigated. Relax Partnerships, locally considered to be very good employers, provided their casual workforce with a booklet describing their 'terms of engagement' which began: 'You have agreed to join the company as a casual worker and to render your services from time to time as requested by the Hotel Management.' The casuals were not eligible for staff benefits such as holiday pay, pension, or Christmas bonus, and, the text continued: 'As you will appreciate, since the terms of engagement of your services do not require you to make yourself available at all times to provide services for the company, you will be entitled to seek employment or offer services to other hotels.'

Precise details of the proportion of casuals employed by the major hotel chain investigated were not made available, but it may be stated with confidence that it would be well over the 49 per cent found at Relax Partnerships.[8] The company is well known in the trade for running an extremely tight ship and the personnel manager of one of their hotels described the situation as follows:

> We used to have more full-timers and permanents (i.e. part-timers) but as the need to make more profit becomes the greater you have to find a way of making your workforce work for you rather than keeping it on all year. The computer can forecast trends more accurately, you can control your workforce by using casuals. Casuals can now work as much as full-timers.

The hotel manager working for this company would find himself/ herself in a very similar situation to that of the school meals supervisor as far as staffing levels were concerned. She/he would be given a wage budget, calculated by means of the costs of wages relative to sales week by week. Wage costs are not allowed to increase beyond a certain percentage, which is determined by central management. Each week, therefore, the manager has to juggle with his/her quota of staffing hours for the week, and declining sales will automatically result in fewer staff.

Casual workers, as we have seen, are the most unprotected in the secondary labour force. The potential for exploitation is extremely great, although there are doubtless a large number of casuals who find the arrangement highly convenient. Amongst the employees of Relax Partnerships, for example, there were few complaints amongst any of the staff we interviewed, at all levels. (Labour turnover in Relax Partnerships, in all grades, is low for the industry. For example, the highest quarter's turnover in 1986 was 19 per cent.) Figure 7.1 describes the work history of a banqueting waitress who had been with the company for ten years as a casual worker. Her employment had not been continuous, but she perceived herself as having been an employee of the hotel for a decade.

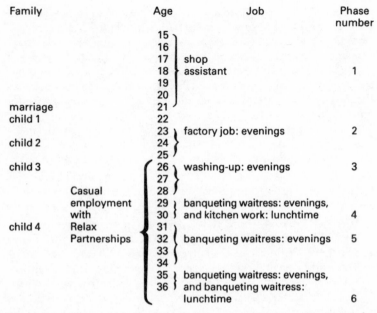

Figure 7.1   *The work history of Valerie, banqueting waitress, age 36, married, four children*

Figure 7.1 has been presented not because it shows a work/life pattern which is in any way exceptional, but rather because it describes a typical employment 'career' amongst unskilled women (Yeandle, 1984). The 'two-phase' work profile, it would seem, is being supplemented by a pattern in which women enter and leave the paid labour force with some frequency (Dex, 1984). In strictly-defined terms, only work phase 1 (Figure 7.1) would count as full-time employment, the rest being part time. However, casual employment allows considerable flexibility in working hours. In work phases 4 and 6, for example, Valerie was working what amounted to split shifts. In busy periods, she would be employed full time as a casual worker. This work flexibility has enabled Valerie to tailor her work around the arrival and ages of her children: evening work when the children are young, lunchtime work combined with evening work as they progress to school. Although rates of pay will obviously be very different, Valerie's employment career is similar to that of the pharmacists described in Chapter 4.

The work histories of the other women working as waitresses, bar staff and room maids suggested that, like the school dinner ladies, they had structured their working lives around the demands of their families. There were a number of other similarities between these hotel workers and those working in the School Meals Service. The hotel, like the school, was situated near to the ring road of a medium-sized city, in close proximity to a large local authority housing estate. Most of the women lived near to their place of work. However, whereas the School Meals Service had been relentlessly squeezed, Relax Partnerships was a successful business, and we heard no complaints about the lack of hours available.

This last factor, however, cannot entirely account for the fact that whereas the women working in the School Meals Service saw their work as 'caring for children', not a few of those working for Relax Partnerships saw their work as 'fun'. It is not being suggested that either group of workers would be doing their jobs unless they were paid, but a highly 'instrumental' (Goldthorpe *et al.*, 1968) attitude was remarkable for its absence in both cases, albeit for different reasons. These variations in attitude offer an interesting sidelight upon debates about the origins of 'attitudes to work' (ibid). The women working for the School Meals Service and for Relax Partnerships were from very similar, working-class backgrounds and localities, and of similar age, life cycle stage, and educational attainments (usually minimum school leaving age). Yet the significance they gave to their employment were very different. It would seem that the *experience* of work has produced rather different attitudes.

There can be little doubt that many people working in the hotel trade do regard themselves as special. A woman assistant manager said:

> We're a breed of our own. Specific types of people work in hotels, [you need] dedication, commitment – servicing other people's needs – you need to be naturally outgoing – your work becomes your social life. If you like a social life – forget it – you have to cope with the pressure as management – there's no room for anything else.

Those who embark on a hotel training may justify the description 'special breed', as they have selected themselves for this kind of employment. For the women at the lower levels, however, the nature of their occupation appears to have been largely contingent; a particular hotel was built at a particular time and drew many of its part-time and casual workers from a particular local authority estate. Nevertheless, they, too, have been influenced by the apparent glamour and excitement of hotel work.

Women and management in the hotel trade

The examination of lower level employment within the hotel and
catering industry suggests that, although gender segregation is
apparent, it is not always exclusively linked to particular occupations
(as in, for example, the shoe industry). An established female enclave
within the industry (the School Meals Service), is gradually being
eroded as a consequence of political pressures, and in commercial
catering, new developments such as the fast food industry, new
working practices associated with 're-skilling' and flexibility and the
greater availability of young people (of both sexes) as casual,
temporary employees has tended to reduce gender segregation in
employment. (Young men, as well as women now make hotel beds
at the weekends in Relax Partnerships hotels; they did not in the
1970s.) At the higher levels of employment, as well, there are
indications that gender segregation is being eroded. In comparison
with other industries, the proportion of women in what are deemed
to be managerial positions within the hotel trade is relatively high –
although not, as Table 7.1 has shown, in proportion to their
representation in the industry as a whole. However, the proportion
of women managers reflects not only the historical legacy of female
entrepreneurship within the industry, but also the predominance of
female managers in institutional catering. In commercial catering,
particularly the larger hotels, women are under-represented. There
are women's specialities within hotel management: housekeeping
and personnel. There are few women, however, in general management.

   The difficulties women face in progressing into the higher levels of
hotel management have been described as a particular case of both
formal and informal indirect male exclusionary practices (Guerrier,
1986). Formal indirect practices relate to the presumed requirements
of the occupation. The job demands long hours and extensive
geographical mobility as the neophyte acquires the necessary
experience. If women have domestic responsibilities, then long hours
and mobility are both difficult. More particularly, however, Guerrier
argues that informal indirect exclusion, or an 'old boy network'
operates in hotel management as far as the best jobs are concerned.
This is particularly marked in food and beverages, a high-status area
where it is essential to gain experience if a top-level management job
is to be achieved. However, by tradition, kitchens in top-quality
hotels have been predominantly male, from the *plongeur* to the chef.
Chefs are renowned in the industry for their bad tempers and
autocratic behaviour. This can result in a virtual immunity from

managerial sanctions coupled with a tyrannical treatment of sub-ordinates. Although the situation is supposed to be changing, the point was often made that hotel kitchens had been, historically, improper places for women, who would not have been able to tolerate the bad language, heavy weights, and so on. Similarly, the top restaurant manager and wine waiter jobs are usually held by men. These male networks, therefore, have operated so as to exclude women from the traditional 'craft route' to hotel management which involved a process of working through the various craft positions in the hotel trade.

It is interesting, therefore, that as the 'qualifications route' has been developed in the hotel industry, women are increasingly taking advantage of it. In 1982/83, women were 70 per cent of students enrolled on higher-level catering courses (that is, HNC/HND courses giving part qualification for the Hotel, Catering and Institutional Management Association qualification (HCIMA). Source: Technical Education Council Report and Accounts, 1983) As Table 7.3 demonstrates, women are also a clear majority of the younger members of HCIMA. It can also be seen that, as with accountancy, HCIMA members are predominantly young; over 70 per cent are under 40 years of age.

The youth of the HCIMA membership will also be in part a consequence of membership loss amongst young women as they move into the domestic phase of their life cycle. In any case, the qualification itself is of relatively recent origin. Catering is only slowly acquiring graduate-level status, and, of nineteen institutions offering degree-level qualifications meeting HCIMA's educational requirements, only four are universities. However, a process of professionalization is apparently under way and, in 1986, the Association petitioned for a royal charter.

It might be argued that, even if the attrition rate proved not to be too great, this evidence of rising levels of qualifications amongst young women in the hotel and catering industry is not particularly significant. This is because only approximately 5 per cent of those at management level within the industry are professionally qualified (HCITB, 1984). However, as 25 per cent of those working within the industry are on managerial grades this category clearly incorporates a fairly wide spread of occupations, and thus the low level of qualifications within the group need not necessarily be indicative of an underqualified management in the sense in which the term is usually employed. In the hotel sector in particular, much emphasis is laid upon managerial qualifications. None of the six assistant managers interviewed during the research lacked qualifications, and

Table 7.3 *Membership of the Hotel, Catering and Institutional Management Association, 1986, by gender, age and level of membership (percentages)*

Membership grade		under 20	over 20–30 yrs	over 30–40 yrs	over 40–50 yrs	over 50–60 yrs	60 yrs plus	Total nos	%
Student:	M	27	40	63	51	*	*	2,430	42
	F	73	60	37	49	*	*	3,341	58
Intermediate:	M	*	45	56	30	*	*	585	47
	F	*	55	44	70	*	*	668	53
Licentiate:	M	0	31	66	76	*	*	2,327	44
	F	*	69	34	24	*	*	3,014	56
Member:	M	0	44	57	55	59	65	4,864	56
	F	0	56	43	45	41	35	3,881	44
Fellow:	M	0	0	85	80	81	79	1,374	80
	F	0	0	15	20	19	20	336	20
Total:†	no.	1.008	9,334	6,016	3,208	2,147	1,217	22,930	
	%	4	41	26	14	9	5	100	

Notes: Data supplied by HCIMA. * = cell frequency less than 3% of row total. Zero = empty cell.
† Totals include 110 affiliate members, graduates with non-catering qualifications working within the industry. Levels of membership have been arranged in order from student to Fellow. Intermediate level includes possessors of part qualifications. Licentiates have either (a) acquired the full academic qualification, but have yet to complete their work-related qualification (77%) or (b) acquiring work experience and qualifications on a points system (23%). Fellowship is acquired after ten years' experience in the industry.

neither the international chain nor the local business group to whom we had research access would accept recruits to junior managerial posts without formal qualifications. In order to survive in a competitive market, it was argued, management had to be of a status and calibre acceptable to the bank managers, solicitors and so on who were the origins of much of their business, and qualifications were regarded as an indicator of these qualities.

In summary, it would seem that an increasing stress on formal qualifications within the hotel industry has facilitated the use of the 'qualifications lever' by the young women who are, in increasing numbers, gaining qualifications within the industry. As with the accountants and the building society management trainees, it is as yet too early to predict how the careers of these young women will finally develop. What is apparent, however, is that, even in this very different industry the numbers of young women signalling a career intention by the acquisition of formal, work-related qualifications shows no sign of slackening.

Summary and conclusions

The hotel and catering industry, like building societies, is female dominated, and women predominate at the lower levels of employment. However, the occupations studied differ somewhat from the others investigated in this book. Pharmacy, accountancy, and work within the building society industry are characterized by clear boundaries, and the distinction between 'work' and 'non-work' (in the sense of employment) is not problematic. The industries and occupations concerned have been relatively protected from competitive pressures, and employment is secure. In contrast, the hotel and catering industry is an extremely heterogeneous, competitive, low wage industry. The boundaries between work and non-work, full and part time, casual and contract employment are all fluid. The unstable and somewhat turbulent nature of the industry is also reflected in the mobility of labour – both in and out of the industry, between different employers, and different sectors within the industry (HCITB, 1984). Nevertheless, many of the processes documented in other industries and occupations can also be discerned within hotels and catering.

The industry is apparently characterized by extensive job segregation by gender. At the more senior levels, women predominate in housekeeping and personnel, as managers within institutional catering and as proprietors of small establishments. At the lower levels, women are employed as counter and kitchen hands, waitresses, chambermaids, etc., the majority working part time. In part, the concentration of women in these occupations is a reflection of the fact that they offer suitable hours and/or work career paths that can be combined with women's domestic roles. However, in the more expensive and exclusive reaches of the hotel and restaurant trade, the lack of women at managerial levels is also a consequence of a history of male exclusion which is frankly acknowledged within the industry. Women have lacked the sponsorship for the best jobs, and those women who do find their way into male preserves are made conscious of their anomalous presence (Guerrier, 1986).

However, in this highly idiosyncratic, individualistic industry, things are changing. Efforts are being made to raise the status of the work via professionalization. Within the hotel trade in particular it was constantly stressed that progress through management without an HCIMA qualification would be extremely difficult. The rationalization of entry requirements and career paths, however, renders hotel management liable to the 'qualifications lever' as far as women are concerned. Women are a substantial majority of students in the hotel schools, and there is considerable competition, from the major employers, for the products of the more highly-rated establishments. However, the high-calibre labour force which they desire is increasingly feminine. The young women assistant managers interviewed spoke of their difficulties in getting taken seriously as potential management trainees by the major hotel chains: 'When we [that is, women] were interviewed by the big chains – hotel chains, you had to justify yourself – the same old questions – "are you planning to get married?" and so on'; nevertheless they had obtained assistant manager positions, in relatively prestigious hotels.[9]

At the lower levels of employment, competitive and other pressures have led to an increase in flexible employment and work patterns which employ an increasing quantity of casual labour. Casual labour does not have a permanent contract of employment, does not work fixed hours, is not eligible for overtime, holiday pay or bonus schemes, and is not protected by legislation. Such labour has always been used in the hotel and restaurant trade, but there is ample evidence that its use is increasing in all areas – in fast food, in the School Meals Service, and in the large hotels. In the hotel industry, a majority of workers employed are probably casuals. In the major chain, for example, the total wage costs of casuals' labour was higher than that of full-time employees. When the differential hourly rates are taken into account, it will be appreciated that a very substantial proportion of the workforce will be casual workers.

These pressures toward flexible working, however, seem to have had the effect of eroding some of the manifestations of gender segregation in employment. As young labour, both male and female, has become available it has been used in jobs which have been previously occupied by women. For example, Table 7.1 records that 92 per cent of counter and kitchen hands were women in 1981. In one rapidly expanding sector of the industry – fast food – the proportion today will be very different. Pressures towards flexibility whilst at work (that is, 'functional flexibility') will also break down the boundaries between occupations, as male and female workers become interchangeable at the task level (for example, 'getting the hall porter to work in the coffee shop'; 'getting the housekeeper to chop a few onions' – two examples of 'multi-skilling' cited by the major hotel chain). Thus, although aggregate level data might suggest extensive occupational segregation by sex, the situation 'on the ground' in this fast-moving industry might be quite different.

The growth of flexible employment and working patterns in hotel and catering is a consequence of a number of factors. First, much of the labour employed is disadvantaged in some way or other and therefore unlikely to produce sufficiently strong resistance at the level of the work place; Gabriel's (1988) recent account provides extensive evidence of this. Collective organization is often difficult because of the fragmented and turbulent nature of the industry. There are, however, some compensations (which should not be exaggerated): freedom to come and go, perks and fiddles in some cases, and the personal satisfaction and interest which seems to go with many of the jobs. However, as suggested earlier, the nature of the work itself presents boundary problems which, it may be argued, makes flexible working easier to impose. As the history of trade unionism and professional organizations has demonstrated, craft and professional exclusion can only be practised when the territory to be defended has been clearly marked out. It may also be suggested that such demarcation has often been accompanied, historically, by sex-typing. Rapidly changing technologies and patterns of ownership, as well as the nature of the work itself, makes boundary maintenance difficult in the hotel and catering industry.

It is not being argued that sex-typing in the hotel and catering trade is non-existent. As we have seen, working in the School Meals Service develops and accentuates the caring and maternal aspects of the feminine role. It is being suggested, however, that the stability of segregation may be not as great in some sectors and establishments as might at first appear. Bielby and Baron have concluded, from their detailed empirical research on sex segregation at the enterprise level, that 'large and systematic reductions in gender segregation seem unlikely to occur in the absence of fundamental shocks to the social system' (1984, p. 52). However, where the situation is permanently in flux, and where neither workers nor managers appear free to exercise their preferences (as would seem to be the case in this highly competitive industry) this would not seem to be so. This argument is not being presented as evidence of some sort of victory for gender equality. However, as long as women remain as disadvantaged workers, they will be crowded into the secondary labour force, where they are liable to be undercut by those at an even greater disadvantage.

Notes

1 Figures calculated from *Employment Gazette*, January 1987, Table 2: 1984 Census of Employment and revised employment estimates.
2 See: Dale and Bamford, 1988; Hakim, 1987; Casey, 1987; Casey and Creigh, 1988.
3 Fieldwork was carried out within a single education authority. Interviews were carried out with the head of the service, two school meals organizers, and the trade union (NUPE) representative. We were also able to interview all women working in the kitchen of a large comprehensive school. Brief life history details were collected, and longer, unstructured interviews were carried out with the cook and cook–supervisor.
4 The decline of the service means that this route will almost certainly cease.
5 A popular meal in a large comprehensive in the authority concerned used to consist of double chips, a doughnut, and a 'tizer float' (a fizzy drink with a scoop of ice cream). This came to the sum of a dinner disc. Children with 67p dinner discs would sell them for 50p, which was then spent in the chip shop. The School Meals Service has reason to be afraid of this particular entrepreneurial section of the fast food industry.
6 Young people living at home do not receive housing benefit. Young people refusing youth (or 'employment') training placements (on 'pocket money' wages) are liable to have benefit removed, thus increasing the likelihood they will accept work at rates which, although poor, are nevertheless more than those offered by the Training Commission.
7 The cheapest labour of all is that of the very young. In 1986, the Unlicensed Place of Refreshment Wages Council set minimum hourly rates at £1.22 for workers under 17, £1.41 at 17 and £1.88 for 18 years and over (Labour Research, 1986). Casual workers are not guaranteed any fixed number of hours per week. A casual could work as many, or more, hours as a full-timer, or as little as five hours a week. Casuals work on demand; they can, of course, refuse an offer of work. In the fast food trade, it is widely suspected, amongst these young, casual workers, that the number of hours offered declines as the casual employee becomes older and therefore more expensive. Thus employment which offered some-

thing approaching a living wage at the age of 16 or 17 gives progressively less as hours are reduced.

8 Considerable frustrations attached to the negotiation of access in the hotel industry. The major conglomerate and the successful local business each had hotels of similar size and style located at diametrically opposite points of the ring road encircling a reasonably prosperous, medium-sized city. Much of their short-term and casual labour was drawn from two different local authority estates which also encircled, in classic 'Chicago School' fashion, the free-standing service centre. There were thus many points of comparison but the management style of the two companies could not be more different. The conglomerate was famous in the trade for its exceptionally tough attitude towards its staff (its chairman is an outspoken supporter of the present government and the 'new entrepreneurialism'), which no doubt went some way towards explaining its successful market position. In contrast, the local business stresses friendliness, a family atmosphere and a paternalistic attitude in the treatment of its staff. A comparison of the two establishments was therefore an initial objective, but the conglomerate refused to allow any interviews with lower-level staff. However, it should be reported that the conglomerate is apparently able to rely on considerable loyalty and hard work from its managerial staff.

Two explicit strategies described the conglomerate's labour management, in an extremely competititive environment. First, there was a policy of acquiring the 'multi-purpose employee' ('you train the lady that's always done housekeeping to chop a few onions'). The multi-purpose employee was often a casual worker, thus combining numerical with functional flexibility. 'Multi-skilling' (*sic*) has in fact been achieved via technological deskilling and the breaking down of craft-like barriers between different categories of work. Second, as previous experience is no longer as important in the recruitment of staff, the emphasis has switched to the *socially* skilled employee. The low status of hotel work is seen as creating a barrier between staff and client, so the aim is to remove the 'bad faith' via the social skills of the staff and render hotels friendly, welcoming places.

9 At the Norwich Hotel School, women outnumber men by approximately 5:1 (1986/7). Commenting on this fact, a female assistant manager speculated that perhaps wages in the hotel trade were just too low to attract men.

8 Conclusions and comparisons

Occupational structuring and women's employment in Britain

The suggestion has often been made that new concepts and theories are required in order to comprehend the complex structuring of gender and employment (for example, Allen 1982; Beechey and Perkins, 1987, p. 182). This is perhaps because the theoretical and empirical questions raised by the subject of gender relations remained for so long neglected in the social sciences. However, in the first chapter of this book we have seen how the understanding of the relationship between gender and class theory required not so much a radical transformation of class concepts, as in the first place, a recognition of the limitations of existing concepts and, in the second, a willingness to adapt and modify empirical measures in the light of a changing empirical reality.

In this final chapter, we will first review the implications of the empirical evidence presented in the previous four chapters for theories of both occupational segregation, and women's employment more generally. Again, it will be argued that what is required are not radically new theories and concepts, but rather, a careful appreciation of both the limitations of the old ones as well as their appropriateness in particular situations and contexts. Economic, political and ideological factors are interrelated in the creation of the empirical reality of both gender and employment relations; and it is not a particularly useful exercise to attempt to establish causal primacy in respect of a single one of these as far as explanations and interpretations of the whole are concerned. However, at the level of the occupation, it may be reasonable to assert a degree of causal primacy. Evidence in support of the various theories (reviewed in Chapter 2) which have been developed to explain occupational segregation (sex role theory, human capital theory, labour market segmentation, patriarchal exclusion, and so on) could be found in each of the case study chapters. However, in particular instances, some explanations are clearly more appropriate than others.

Pharmacy is an occupation which bestows equivalent 'human capital' upon those individuals who qualify to practise it. However the historical record of the employment careers of male and female pharmacists demonstrates quite clearly that the majority of women pharmacists have followed conventional practices relating to sex roles, and have assumed the primary responsibility for the care of their children. Legal requirements relating to pharmacy practice ensures a constant supply of flexible, part-time work at a professional (practitioner) level. It would probably be reasonable to assert in this case that it is the 'moral despotism' of motherhood, rather than systematic male exclusionary practices, which is the most important in explanations of the pattern of female employment within the occupation.

In contrast, direct and indirect male exclusionary practices have been of historic importance in keeping women out of accountancy, and appear to be still of considerable significance in firm internal labour markets. Although, therefore, some women may have not thought it worthwhile (as human capital theorists might argue) to obtain expensive and time-consuming qualifications such as in accountancy in anticipation of some future domestic division of labour, male exclusionary practices are and have probably been of equal, if not more, importance. However, women's employment patterns in both pharmacy and accountancy are also being changed as a consequence of developments in the wider context of the 'gender order' at the societal level.

Male exclusionary practices have also been very important in keeping women out of the upper levels of management in the finance sector. A literature documenting these practices is already available for important industries such as banking (Crompton and Jones, 1984), and further evidence relating to building societies was discussed in Chapter 6. However, employer strategies (rather than 'men' as a category) have also played an important part in segmenting the labour force by gender. The building society industry also provided an example of the development of a feminized clerical occupation – the cashier-clerk – as a consequence of the interaction of technological developments, changes in the nature of the demand for clerical labour, and changes in the female labour force available (Crompton and Sanderson, forthcoming).

The strategies of employers (and associated theories of labour market segmentation) are of considerable relevance to the understanding of labour use in the hotel trade. Women have long been a source of cheap and convenient labour in this highly competitive industry. At the level of the enterprise there are doubtless still many individual examples of gender segregation, but the ease with which even cheaper and more convenient forms of labour (for example, young people) have been substituted for part-time female labour suggests that, despite outward appearances, lower-level jobs in the hotel industry have not been firmly sex-typed. This is not the case, however, as far as a closely related occupation within the hotel and catering industry – the School Meals Service – is concerned. These are 'women's jobs', heavily imbued with the maternal and caring elements of the stereotypical female role. Both recruitment to the occupation, and the behaviour of the women within it (for example, in response to the deterioration in their terms and conditions of employment), can only be understood in these terms.

The evidence reviewed above of the effect of the pressure of normative expectations, male exclusionary practices, and employer strategies would tend to work against human capital explanations of gender segregation, which emphasize the effect of individual and domestic unit choices on the nature of the female labour supply. Nevertheless, such explanations should not be rejected out of hand. In the case of accountancy and hotel and catering management (and indirectly, building society management as well), we have examples of individual women seeking, through improvements in their 'human capital' (that is, by gaining qualifications) to increase the returns on their labour. Many women with interrupted careers, or in part-time jobs, may have 'chosen' these alternatives and feel little sense of constraint. However, there is obvious room for considerable argument about the extent to which these options have, in fact, been freely chosen.[1] It is necessary to continue to emphasize the problematic status of this 'choice'; it is unlikely that the matter could ever be conclusively resolved empirically. (See, for example, Dex's (1988) efforts, discussed in Chapter 4 above, to resolve the question of whether traditional attitudes amongst women were 'caused' by part-time work or vice versa, which arrived at no firm conclusions one way or the other.)

A variety of theories, therefore, explain the different patterns of female (and male) employment in the range of occupations studied in this book. The case studies were theoretically developed (on the basis of the arguments in Chapter Two) in order to illustrate the major trends in, and underlying processes structuring women's employment in postwar Britain. Such processes, it was argued, are not always discernible at the aggregate level and, indeed, in some circumstances aggregate level indices might be positively misleading. The case study approach was also preferred on the grounds that it facilitated theoretical, rather than enumerative or 'statistical' inference and reasoning. Thus, as summarized above, it has been possible to assess the relative merits of different theories in respect of particular occupations, as well as to illustrate the dialectical relationship between the development of particular occupations and their changing context.

However, despite the strengths of case study research, it is nevertheless important that work at the 'micro' occupational level should be contextualized in respect of aggregate 'macro' indicators. An indication of these macro changes is given in Table 8.1. It compares, for the census years 1971 and 1981, the distribution of male and female employment in Britain by socio-economic groups (SEGs). The SEG classification, which was introduced in 1951, 'aims to bring together people with jobs of similar social and economic status' (*Classification of Occupations*, 1980, p. xi). It has remained the same between 1971 and 1981, although some changes in the allocation of individual occupations has taken place as a result of the revision of the *Classification of Occupations*. It should be stressed that these data are being used for comparative purposes, rather than as a robust example of an occupational hierarchy. Anomalies are evident both in the ordering of the hierarchy as well as the location of particular occupations within it. For example, SEG 5 (ancillary workers and artists) includes all of the medical and paramedical professions, as well as systems analysts and computer programmers. Despite these problems, however, the data confirm, at the aggregate level, the changing trends which have emerged from the case study evidence. Elements of continuity, as well as change in the distribution of occupations by gender should be stressed. The gross SEG figures (not included in Table 8.1), show that men were over 80 per cent of employers, managers and professionals in both both 1971 and 1981, although the proportion of women did increase from 16 per cent to 19 per cent. The most populous occupation for men in 1971 and 1981 was skilled manual work, although it has declined from 30 per cent to 26.3 per cent of all male employment. For women, the most populous SEG in both 1971 and 1981 was, as would be expected, junior, non-manual employment. Although the numbers of women in clerical work increased, the proportion of women in clerical employment has remained the same (at 37.3 per cent) over the decade. However, the upward trend of women's employment overall has continued, and has increased from 37 per cent to 39 per cent of the total 'economically active'.

In Table 8.1, SEG categories have been aggregated in order to simplify presentation. Full SEG descriptions have been retained, however, as a guide to the combined categories. The first section of

Table 8.1 *Changes in the proportions of men and women in socio-economic groups, 1971–81. Great Britain, economically active*

SEG no.	Description	(1) Percentage change 1971–81			(2) Percentage distribution of total (men and women) by column	
		Men	Women	Total	1971	1981
1, 2, 3, 4	Employers, managers, etc., in industry and commerce: large establishments; Employers, managers, etc., in industry and commerce: small establishments; Professional workers, self-employed; Professional workers, employees	+16%	+45%	+20%	12.5	14.8
5	Ancillary workers, artists; foremen & supervisors – non-manual	+28%	+41%	+35%	7.6	10.1
6	Junior – non-manual workers	−32%	8%	−3%	21.2	20.3
7	Personal service workers	+12%	+5%	+6%	5.2	5.4
8, 9, 10, 11	Foremen and supervisors – manual; Skilled manual workers; Semi-skilled manual workers; Unskilled manual workers	−11%	−11%	−11%	44.0	38.6
12	Own account workers (other than professional)	+17%	+3%	+14%	3.5	4.0
13, 14, 15	Farmers – employers and managers; Farmers – own account; Agricultural workers	−19%	+18%	+19%	2.4	1.9
16	Members of armed forces	+1%	+50%	+4%	1.0	1.0
17	Inadequately described and not stated occupations	★	★	★	2.6	3.8
	nos.				100% 2,503,143	100% 2,540,559

Source: census data.

the table calculates the percentage change, for men and women separately, in the numbers in the SEG categories between 1971 and 1981. In the second part, percentage SEG distributions (total by column) for 1971 and 1981 have been given to indicate the overall significance of the different SEG groupings within the occupational structure. Thus, in the first part of the table, a large percentage change in respect of a relatively small grouping (for example, SEG 16: members of armed forces, or SEG 13-15: workers in agriculture), will be of relatively less significance than a smaller change affecting a larger grouping.

The most striking change is in the rate of increase of women in professional and managerial occupations (SEG 1–4), a change which would have been anticipated on the evidence of both the case studies and the rising levels of qualification amongst young women as a whole. A similar high rate of increase (as compared to men) is also evident in SEG 5, which as we have seen is a rather anomalous grouping that includes most medical, and many financial and technical occupations. The major decrease for men has been in junior non-manual occupations (although the proportion of economically active men in this SEG in 1971 was only 11.9 per cent). It may be suggested that, with the rationalization and segmentation of clerical grade structures which has been in process, a relatively lower proportion of men will have been recruited into lower clerical grades with a view to working their way up through the organizational hierarchy. Although the change is small, the pattern of increase in SEG 7 (personal service workers) suggests that more men, possibly disadvantaged workers, are entering this female-dominated enclave which includes domestic helpers, waiters and waitresses, counter hands, hairdressers, cooks, etc.

On the evidence of the case studies, the trends indicated by the table will continue. The decline in manual occupations, and the intensification of competition between different types of disadvantaged labour at the lower levels of service employment, might be expected to result in a decline in sex-typed occupations in the structure as a whole. Sex-typing in manufacturing has a tendency to be associated with established, traditional industries and processes. (These are, of course, also the bastions of culturally 'male' employment such as steelworking, shipbuilding and so on.) As such industries decline, so do the traditionally gendered jobs associated with them. Unskilled or disadvantaged female labour may be deliberately recruited by new industries and services (Pearson, 1988, also Thompson and Bannon, 1985), but the present socio-political climate renders overt discrimination problematic in Britain and encourages the use of disadvantaged labour of both sexes. This does not mean, of course, that the occupational structure will cease to reflect the impact of gender, nor that particular occupations will cease to be regarded as more suitable for women. Of particular interest here are developments in clerical work, where, as we have seen, the restructuring of white-collar hierarchies has resulted in the consolidation of women's specialities in addition to those already long established in typing and secretarial work. These specialities are associated with a particular kind of femininity and men, although not barred from such occupations, are likely to remain a minority in them.

Although women's 'equality of advantage' in higher-level occupations might not match a growing 'equality of disadvantage' at the lower levels, the highly educated and qualified working woman is likely to be one of the most enduring phenomena carrying over into the twenty-first century. Such women, however, are still a minority as compared to men at the same level, and will continue to be for the next decade or more. The impact of their presence upon the overall structure of material advantage and disadvantage, however, may be of greater significance than their numerical representation in the working population.

Occupational class advantages, and disadvantages, are transmitted through families (that is, households). The tendency for individuals with similar levels of education and employment to establish households through marriage is well known (Prandy, 1986). Thus we might expect that an increasing number of households will contain two 'service class' individuals. (The term 'service class' has been widely employed to describe the upper levels of the occupational structure (Goldthorpe, 1982).) The increase in the number of service class individuals, and thus the size of the service class, therefore, might be greater than the actual increase in service-class households. If we assume that experience of a service class household advantages those members, such as children, who are not themselves in paid employment, then the phenomenon of the dual service-class household implies that the benefits of service-class expansion will be enjoyed by fewer household members than the actual rate of service-class expansion would seem to imply.[2] It is paradoxical, therefore, that the expansion of opportunities for women may have the effect of widening the gulf between the most materially advantaged and disadvantaged households in Britain.

This examination of occupational segregation, therefore, has revealed both continuities and change. Gender differentiation will be a persisting feature within work and employment; indeed, such differentiation is a significant feature of the gender order as a whole.

However, the gender order may be more or less oppressive and inegalitarian, and there is room for cautious optimism as far as the division of labour between men and women in the public sphere is concerned. Changes and developments in respect of occupational segregation, however, could have taken place even in the absence of the growth of women's paid employment which has occurred over the last quarter of a century. This increase has been accompanied by a rise in non-standard forms of employment more generally, and it is to the implications of this that we now turn.

A description of part-time working amongst women has been given in Chapter 3. (Over 40 per cent of all women in Britain, and 50 per cent of married women, work part time.) Problems with the measurement of the extent of such non-standard forms of employment were also discussed briefly in Chapter 7; in particular, the difficulties of establishing whether part-time workers had some kind of contract with their employer, and therefore some minimum of employment rights, or whether part-timers are casual workers, with an 'absence of mutual obligation' between themselves and their employers. These are important questions which require further research, as the nature of an employee's status is of considerable significance as far as the employer's use of labour is concerned. Employment status, therefore, has important implications for the debate on flexibility. In the following discussion, however, 'part-time work' will be used as a general label to include both casual and contractual part-time employment.

Britain has one of the highest rates of part-time working amongst women in Europe. (The subject has recently been explored in depth by Beechey and Perkins, 1987, chapter 1.) Some forms of work, for example, seasonal work in agriculture, home-working, and work in parts of the service sector such as catering have always been organized on a part-time basis. Part-time work in manufacturing industry in Britain was introduced and developed during the Second World War, and persisted in the years of postwar boom when part-time employment was regarded as a necessary concession in order to attract women into the labour force. With the advent of the recession in the 1970s part-time jobs in manufacturing declined rapidly, but part-time working as a whole continued to rise as jobs were created in the service sector. The most recent evidence shows no substantial decline in either women's economic activity or part-time working, but does suggest that a plateau may have been reached as the proportion of married women working part time has fallen slightly but there has been no increase in part-time working amongst single women.[3]

It is not, however, the precise level of part-time working that concerns us here, but rather, its implications. It has been argued that part-time work is a specifically *female* form of employment. For example, Beechey and Perkins assert that part-time work is a 'new' form of work (1987, p.6) and: 'It is a central argument. . . that gender enters into the construction of part-time jobs and that the division between full-time and part-time work is one crucial contemporary manifestation of gender within the sphere of production' (ibid., p. 7). A parallel argument is developed by Walby, who has argued that there is no harmonious fit between patriarchal and capitalist interests, and that the development of part-time work represents an historic resolution of the conflict between capital and 'patriarchs' over the use of women's labour: 'Part-time work for married women since the Second World War is . . . a result of a compromise between patriarchal and capitalist demands for women's labour, arrived at during the war' (1986, p. 247).

As we have seen, part-time workers lack the job security and other occupational advantages of full-time workers (for example, in the finance sector, part-timers are not usually eligible for employment benefits such as cheap mortgages); and part-timers in the upper levels of the occupational structure will not be considered eligible for promotion or linear career development. Beechey and Perkins argue (1987, p. 25) that the 'least desirable' kinds of work have from the first been associated with part-time working. The theoretical implications of the arguments summarized above may be briefly stated: do the low status and poor returns of part-time work stem from the fact that it is specifically *women's* work which has been constructed in this manner? Dex, however, has suggested: 'It has not been possible to distinguish the extent to which it is women workers who are being demanded, or part-timers, who just happen to be women' (1988, p. 117).

Nevertheless, the sheer weight of empirical evidence makes it impossible to contradict the broad assertion that many, if not the majority of part-time jobs have been constructed for women as such. This was particularly noticeable during the period when these employment conditions were seen as a necessary concession in order to lure women back in to the paid labour force, and when part-time employment was structured in a way that was compatible with 'women's two roles' (for example, the 'twilight shift') (Myrdal and Klein, 1956). However, although part-time jobs may be women's jobs, it does not follow that the task in question is necessarily sex-typed as 'feminine', as may be seen from the evidence of the case studies in this book.[4]

Part-time employment was a feature of all of the industries and occupations studied. In two instances in particular – pharmacy and the hotel and catering industry – it was a long-established type of employment, deriving from the nature of the industry/occupation in question. In the case of building societies, part-time work was a more recent development.[5] In pharmacy women are the overwhelming majority of part-time workers. However, part-time working is also common amongst older men, suggesting that part-time work has not necessarily been sex-typed (22 per cent of male pharmacists aged 60–4; 58 per cent aged 65–9; and 78 per cent over 70 work part-time. See Chapter 4, p. 80). In the hotel trade, the industry has always relied to a considerable extent on part-time, short-term, casual employment. Women have been widely used as a consequence, given their status as disadvantaged workers. However, recent government policies in respect of employment, in particular those directed at young people, have been such as to increase the available pool of cheap, short-term labour. More young people, male and female, have been employed in the industry as a consequence.

Building societies are a rather different case. Although a specific study was not made of the topic, it would appear that, across the finance sector as a whole, increasing use is being made of part-time employees. It may be suggested that this is a consequence of both 'supply' and 'demand' factors. As far as the nature of demand for labour in the finance sector is concerned, there has been a substantial transformation over the last twenty-five years, stemming from the impact of computerization. It was once necessary for a clerk-cashier to be able to recognize the signature of every single customer, to have the mental facility to balance the books, and so on. Smart, competent machine operators and sales persons are what are required today. They are increasingly available, and on a part-time basis, as more mature women who already have experience of the finance sector look for convenient employment to combine with their domestic (usually child-rearing) responsibilities. The increased supply of such labour is itself a consequence of the increase in the employment of these women as young, non-career workers in the finance sector in the 1960s and 1970s. Trained as full-timers then, they are now available as part-timers in the 1980s. (The Regional Plus, which relied heavily on part-time workers, had a preference for ex-clearing bank employees as they were likely to be *au fait* with computerized systems.)

Thus part-time work in building societies is being constructed as a woman's job; part-timers are used to cover for peak periods, and/or two part-timers may be employed instead of one full-timer, but with an overlap during the busy lunch-time period. The increased use of this kind of part-time employment may lead to a diminution of the extent of the recorded decline in occupational status which has been noted as taking place when women return to work. (Elias and Main, 1982. Much of the occupational decline they detected was from clerical to unskilled service work. See also Dex and Shaw, 1986.) However, as the quality of female labour is further enhanced (through qualifications, work experience, and so on) there might be continuing pressure from women to maintain not only their occupational status on a return to work (this has always been the case in respect of 'practitioner' roles in the professions), but also their investment in a professional or occupational linear career. Evidence that this might be a growing problem was suggested by the attitudes of young women accountants. As women move into occupations where a degree of upward mobility is considered normal, pressures for the removal of the 'part-time penalty' might increase.

It is true, therefore, that part-time work is 'women's work', but this should not obscure the fact that (i) the manner of its construction, and the kinds of jobs on offer, will vary according to the type of female labour available, and (ii) although women are, and are likely to remain, a majority of part-time workers, other groups of workers at a relative disadvantage or requiring only 'component' wages (Siltanen, 1986) may also take on these jobs. These could include, for example, young people still in full-time education or other forms of training, and older men who have taken retirement or early retirement. Proportionately, both of these categories have been growing in recent years.

As we have seen in previous chapters, the prevalence of part-time working amongst women has been linked to arguments suggesting that economic restructuring (that is, the recession and its aftermath) has been associated with the growth of the 'flexible firm'. These are described as organizations characterized by a relatively small group of full-time 'core' employees, and a 'periphery' of full and part-time, short-term and contract workers (Atkinson, 1984). Pollert has argued that the 'flexible firm' is not a novel development, but rather a consequence of sectoral restructuring (or the shift to the service sector) combined with public sector privatization, and the enhanced capacity for exploitation of a labour force weakened by recession and the impact of government policies. Such flexibility, she argues, is not so much new, as a 'repackaging of well-worn employment patterns and practices' (1988, p. 310). In a similar vein, part-time work *for women* might be argued to be not so much new, as a repackaging of old practices, and indeed, its gender specificity might be in decline. It is interesting that, in anticipation of a short-term shortage of particular kinds of labour as a consequence of the decline in the birth rate in the 1970s, older men are being targeted as a possible labour reserve. In pharmacy (and indeed, in all professions characterized by a universal qualification), this practice has been common for many years.

Cross-national comparisons[6]

A major theme of this book has been that gender is and has been significant in the structuring of individual occupations, and thus, the occupational order as a whole. However, 'gender' cannot be reduced to the status of a single variable, as might be implied by this statement. Rather, gender is a multi-faceted phenomenon manifest through a net of social and institutional relationships linked across different areas of social life. This pervasiveness of gender has informed recent attempts to theorize the concept; as, for example, in Connell's (1985) description of the gender order as inter-related structures of labour, power and cathexis; and in J. Scott's (1986) definition of gender as incorporating first, interrelated elements of perceived difference in social relationships between the sexes, and second, as a primary way of signifying relationships of power. She lists these interrelated elements as: cultural symbols; normative prescriptions; social institutions (kinship, economy, and society); and subjective identity. Given that gender as a whole is composed of these different aspects, the precise manner of their combination will vary. We should, therefore, expect gender relations to be different in different societies (or nation states). There is no universal logic in the patterning of gender relations; rather, they are socially and historically constructed (A. Scott, 1986).

Nevertheless, broad-brush statistics do suggest similarities in the overall trends of women's work in different societies. Since the Second World War women's paid employment has been increasing in all of the OECD countries, and did not decline during the recent recession (Table 8.2). (A decline might have been anticipated if women's labour had been used as merely a flexible reserve, to be taken on during peaks of demand such as the postwar economic boom.) Part-time working has also been on the increase, although there are still very substantial cross-national variations in its extent. In all countries women's employment is concentrated in services, and in lower-level occupations, and, therefore, their full-time earnings are lower than those of men in all sectors (Bakker, 1988; OECD, 1985). Beyond these very broad generalizations, however, there are

Table 8.2   *Women's employment: cross-national comparisons*

	Female share of the labour force (percentages) 1950	Female share of the labour force (percentages) 1982	Ratio of part-time working 1981
Canada	21.3	40.9	31.8
France	35.9	38.6	15.9
Germany	35.1	38.2	25.7
Italy	25.4	33.8	5.8
Sweden	26.3	46.2	46.4
United Kingdom	30.7	39.1	37.1
United States	28.9	42.8	23.7

Source: Derived from OECD (1985), Tables I.2, I.3.
Note: This table has been included to illustrate broad trends. Where more recent data are available, they are cited in the text.

considerable methodological difficulties associated with cross-national comparisons. For example, as Rubery (1988) has argued, the pay and opportunities associated with particular occupations may have been standardized in countries such as Italy and France, where there are industry-wide agreements which will result in broad comparability within the formal sector. However, in countries such as Britain and the USA, where there is more emphasis on plant- and company-based structures, and only weak controls in small establishments, the same occupation may be associated with very different life-chances. Drawing on the work of the LEST group,[7] she also points out that the same job may have a very different meaning (and therefore status and rewards) within the organizational context of different countries, deriving from differences in the educational system, cultural values, and social expectations in the societies in question. Particular social, political and cultural factors shape not only the division of labour between men and women, but also the rewards and statuses associated with these divisions. (There are obvious parallels between these arguments and the extended discussion of occupational comparability in Chapter 2 above.)

An interesting example of the dangers of making universalistic assumptions as far as the gender division of labour is concerned is given in Jenson's (1986) critique of Marxist feminist analyses of the relationship between the organization of the family, the labour process and the state in capitalist society. McIntosh (1978) had argued that the actions of the capitalist state supported a particular form of household; that is, one in which the man was the main breadwinner, dependent upon domestic (rather than commodified) 'servicing', whilst women, as well as reproducing the working class from day to day and over the generations, also served as a reserve army of labour. However, argues Jenson, McIntosh is generalizing from the history of a specific capitalist state – Britain, – at a specific moment of historical development – the nineteenth century and earlier part of the twentieth century. Jenson organizes her discussion of state policies in respect of women and the family around the state's need for a continuing supply of healthy subjects – in short, babies. Both the British and French states were concerned to formulate strategies in respect of maternity to ensure the production of healthy infants, but whereas state policy in Britain sought to protect the health of children by stopping mothers from going out to work, in France, paid maternity leave was the preferred option. Therefore, she argues,

> little was heard from those who wanted to discourage or forbid women to engage in paid labour in order that they might bear more and healthier children. In this way, state policy-makers in France indicated their acceptance of women's employment as a fact of life, and selected policy from a range of alternatives delineated by that given (1986, p. 19).

In Britain, in contrast, state policies have been organized around the concept of the 'family wage' (as described by McIntosh), and on the assumption that mothers will be economically dependent on the fathers of their children.[8]

One consequence of the difference in the policies of the British and French states towards maternity and women's employment was that, as married women in Britain began to re-enter the labour force, the level of part-time work amongst them was much higher than in France. The female share of the labour force in Britain and France is exactly the same at 39 per cent (1982) and participation rates are not too dissimilar (55 percent France, 60 per cent UK in 1985: Bakker, 1988), but whereas 42 per cent of British women worked part-time in 1983, only 20 per cent of French women did so (Dale and Glover, 1987). Motherhood as such would not seem to have much of an impact upon the level of part-time working amongst women in France. A direct comparison of the 1980 Department of Employment Women and Employment Survey data with that of a similar French survey found that 35 per cent of British mothers were employed part-time, as compared to 9 per cent of French mothers (Dex and Walters, forthcoming).

Dex and Walters lay considerable emphasis on the policies of the French state in their explanation of the variations in employment status between French and British women. (See also Bouillaguet-

Bernard and Gauvin, 1988b.) The long history of paid maternity leave in France has already been briefly discussed, and the French state, in contrast to the British, also provides high quality and heavily subsidized child-care services, which include the pre-school years. These provisions facilitate continuous, full-time working amongst women; it has also been encouraged by the system of personal taxation; married French women working full-time retain more of their income than do British women. Finally, the relatively protected employment position of part-time workers in France has not made these kinds of jobs particularly attractive to employers, whereas in Britain employers have been exempt from paying National Insurance contributions for low earning and/or short hours part-timers who are, as a consequence, cheaper to employ. In France, therefore, there is a greater tendency for women to work full time or not at all, and the number of children, rather than a woman's age, has the greatest impact on employment continuity. This factor is also related to state policy, which has always been strongly pro-natalist. The French system of family allowances is such as greatly to enhance the level of benefit to families with more than two children, to rates which appear to act as a disincentive to mothers' employment. There is also a 'bringing-up allowance', introduced in 1985, which makes direct payments to a parent who stops work in order to bring up a third child (Bouillaguet-Bernard and Gauvin, 1988b). Whereas in Britain, therefore, women's labour force participation curve still resembles the 'M' form, as women characteristically take breaks in employment with the arrival of children, and then re-enter the labour force part time, that of France resembles an inverted 'U' (Paukert, 1984).

In recent years, however, the situation has been changing in that the incidence of part-time working among women in France has increased (Jenson, 1988; Bouillaguet-Bernard and Gauvin, 1988a). Here again, however, the actions of the French state have been crucial. The recent economic crisis has led to a shift towards more competitive forms of the 'rapport salarial' (loosely translated, this term describes the 'employment relationship'), and flexible working, including part-time and contract employment, has been encouraged as a consequence. Women's employment, it is argued, is spearheading the development of this flexible, marginalized labour force, much as women were once drafted into the unskilled jobs in manufacturing characteristic of the previous, 'Fordist', 'accumulation regime' in the West during the postwar boom.

The French state is well-known to be *dirigiste*; it is not surprising, therefore, to find that its policies have had a marked impact on women's work and family lives. However, a relative absence of interventionist state policies – even, indeed, an attempt to roll them back – may have a negative impact which is just as substantial in its effects. This is suggested by the example of the United States. The USA has a high level of female employment (64 per cent in 1985; Bakker, 1988), but a relatively low level of part-time working amongst women: 24 per cent in 1984 (Dale and Glover, 1987; see also OECD, 1985). Part-time employment rates amongst women in the USA, therefore, are closer to those of France, than to Britain. In the previous discussion of the French case emphasis was given to state provision of child care, and the protection of part-time workers' employment rights, in the explanation of the relatively low level of part-time work amongst French women. In the USA, however, there is little in the way of state child care, or state welfare provision more generally. However, part of the expenses of private child care are tax deductible, which is not the case in Britain. In addition, whereas full-time employees in the USA will usually have health insurance paid by their employer, part-time employees will not. In the absence of a general network of state services, the likelihood of health insurance must provide a powerful incentive to work full-time (Dex and Shaw, 1986).

These cross-national comparisons show, therefore, that whereas the overall growth in women's paid employment in western industrial countries is an international phenomenon, women's employment status (that is, their propensity to work full or part time), which is an important aspect of their location in the occupational structure, shows considerable cross-national variation. It would appear that state policies, particularly those relating to motherhood and child care, have had a considerable impact in this regard. Although, therefore, part-time work appears to be an increasing category of (mainly) female employment, there are still enormous variations in its extent; in Italy, for example, the level of part-time working amongst women was only 6 per cent in 1981 (Table 8.2).

That part-time work can have an important effect on the structure of women's eployment is suggested by the findings of Dex and Shaw (1986) who, on the basis of a comparison of the work-life histories of British and American women, concluded that the higher level of upward occupational mobility amongst women in the USA was in significant part a consequence of the fact that women there were more likely to work full-time, rather than to return to part-time work after childbirth, as is common amongst women in Britain. (As in the case of France, the employment curve amongst women in the USA resembles an inverted 'U' rather than the British 'M'.) Relatively *laissez-faire* state policies in respect of child care and welfare have been suggested as factors underlying the higher level of full-time work amongst American women. But one respect in which the USA has, in the last two decades, been more interventionist than Britain is in the area of equal opportunities. Equal opportunities legislation was not only introduced earlier in the USA than in Britain (equal pay was introduced in 1963, and sex discrimination legislation in 1964, as Title VII of the Civil Rights Act), but also, since the late 1960s, legislation has been explicitly linked with affirmative action, administered by the Office of Federal Contract Compliance (OFCC).[9] The principle of equal pay for work of equal worth, established in Britain only in 1984 following EEC rulings, has been current in the USA since the 1970s (Steinberg, 1988).

In their investigation of the impact of Equal Opportunities in Britain and the USA, however, Dex and Shaw (1986) concluded that it was the greater propensity for British women to work part-time which explained their generally low occupational mobility in comparison to American women, rather than differences in the extent and timing of equal opportunities legislation in the two countries. They did suggest, however, that 'there might well be an environmental effect from the more aggressive pursuit of equal opportunities for American women. This environmental effect appears to have opened up more opportunities to American women and it has raised their overall status in the eyes of employers' (1986, p. 128). The proportion of (and increase in) women in the USA in 'administrative and managerial' occupations is a notable feature of women's employment there. OECD data suggest that 1.5 per cent of French women, 0.9 per cent of British women, but 5.9 per cent of women in the United States were in administrative and managerial occupations in the early 1980s (OECD, 1985, Table 1.5)[10] (See also Reskin and Hartmann, 1986.)

The increasing proportion of women in professional and managerial jobs in the USA (a trend also associated with women's employment in Britain), has been argued by some observers to presage an incipient polarization of the female labour force (Power, 1988). She demonstrates that, between 1972 and 1982, women increased their representation amongst professional and technical workers in the USA by just over 57 per cent, and amongst managers and administrators by 52 per cent. However, during the same period, there had been swingeing cuts in state welfare programmes following the coming to power of the Reagan administration. As a consequence, she argues:

> there was a developing polarization between a newly-emerging female elite and an expanding (though not new) group of

marginalized women on the bottom of the economic scale. This polarization is racial as well, as women entering the elite occupations are disproportionately white, while women (and men) in poverty are disproportionately black. (Power, 1988, pp. 145–6).

As argued in the first part of this chapter, this polarization might be further exacerbated if households, rather than individuals, are taken as the unit of analysis, due to the fact that high-earning, well-educated women will be likely to enter into relationships with high earning, well-educated men. However, Steinberg suggests that the increase in the proportion of women in higher-level positions in the USA has been of considerable benefit as far as the interests of women as a whole are concerned. She argues: 'Having entered the political arena – as elected officials, as appointed high-level administrators, and as leaders of mobilized interest groups – political elite women are using their new leverage to achieve their reforms'. (1988, p. 205). Their activities, Steinberg argues, made it impossible for the Reagan administration to amend Title VII legislation, to stop the movement of comparable worth procedures at the state and local level, or to dismantle job training programmes aimed at women.

It would seem, therefore, that legislation for sex equality can have an independent effect upon the structure of women's employment, although the impact is not likely to be immediate. Affirmative or some other sort of positive action is also required, however, as in some instances, the principle of equality has been used as a deliberate strategy (by trade unions, for example) in order to avoid the substitution of male by cheaper female labour. At a national level, something akin to this process can be discerned in the 'official' sector of the Italian economy (del Boca, 1988; Bettio, 1988a). Within this sector, the trade unions have pursued a policy of equal pay for women, which has been legally established in the formal sector since the early 1960s.[11] Further developments in industrial relations consolidated gains for all workers during the early 1970s, particularly in limiting the ability of employers to lay off workers in medium and large firms. The Cassa Integratzione, instituted in 1945 but of most importance from the 1970s onwards, gives out-of-work employees of a restructuring firm continuing employee status and 80 per cent of their wages. As a consequence of these developments women within the formal sector enjoy considerable protection, but their participation rate is low. At 41 per cent in 1985 it is the lowest of the OECD countries, and was actually in decline during the 1960s and early 1970s, when participation rates were rising in the other OECD countries (Bakker, 1988; see also note 11).

Straightforward explanations of the pattern of women's employment in Italy are difficult to achieve, not least because of the very rapid growth of the informal sector (small firms, home-working, and so on) since the 1970s. It has been estimated that at the end of the 1970s there were about 3,745,000 workers in underground manufacturing, of whom 60 per cent were women, in contrast to the low rates in the formal economy (del Boca 1988, p. 124). It is obvious that, by its very nature, reliable data on informal employment are lacking. There does seem to be general agreement that the growth of the informal sector in Italy is a consequence of the institutional rigidities which developed in the formal sector, and that flexible work practices, in which women predominate, are largely confined to the informal sector. (It will be remembered that official rates of part-time working in Italy are very low, but home-workers in the informal sector are likely to work part time; and that job security in the formal sector is protected, but (i) such regulations do not apply to small firms and (ii) voluntary labour turnover amongst women is presumed to be high.) In summary, therefore, the very distinctive characteristics of the Italian economy have clearly resulted in a structure of employment for women which is in important respects different from that of many other OECD states.[12]

However, despite these differences in the nature and structure of women's employment in different western countries, there are also, as we have seen, important similarities. One common feature is that, although the nature and extent of flexible and/or non-standard employment might vary between different nation states, it is usually women who predominate as far as such practices are concerned. As discussed in the first section of this chapter, economic restructuring (following the recession of the late 1970s and 1980s) and flexible labour use are seen as going hand-in-hand. Thus the growth in women's employment has been explicitly linked with economic restructuring.

Hagen and Jenson (1988) have described the way in which women's paid employment has been articulated with the two major phases of western economic development (or 'economic regimes') discernible since the end of the Second World War. During the first, or 'Fordist' phase, western economies were dominated by Keynsian economic policies and consensus-style social democratic politics which, through regulating demand, controlling exchange rates, and so on, encouraged the growth of mass production for mass markets. Keynsian economic policies were associated with a deliberate increase in the level of state expenditure on welfare and the social services, that is, the growth of the welfare state; this, as we have seen in Chapter 3, Marshall (1951) considered central to the development of social citizenship. These policies had obvious benefits for women. They have gained from the extension of educational and employment opportunities, and the expansion of social services meant that less private 'caring' was required for women, who found jobs in the expanding public sector. However, economic policies were mainly oriented towards the male, mass production, manufacturing worker. (In Britain, as we have seen in Chapter 3, social welfare policies were consciously constructed around the 'male bread-winner' model.) As a consequence, segregation in employment persisted, and was enhanced by the recruitment of women into 'caring' jobs in the service sector and de-skilled, mass production jobs in manufacturing.

From the 1970s onwards, however (and after global shocks such as the oil price rises), these policies have become less and less effective, and the link between mass production and stable demand has collapsed. As national economies restructured themselves out of recession, there was an increase in competition as employers cut costs and shortened product cycles, and unemployment rose. (The political growth of neo-liberal ideologies was one factor which 'allowed' massive rises in unemployment.) However, as we have seen, women's economic activity continued to increase. Hagen and Jenson suggest that with the fragmentation of demand and other economic changes came the need for an increasingly flexible workforce, for which women are eminently suitable:

> Women have emerged as very desirable employees in these circumstances because their relationship to the labour market has traditionally displayed the characteristics of flexibility . . . Individual women have had a less continuous relationship to the labour market . . . women have been willing to work part-time and take jobs which lack the full social protections . . . women have traditionally had lower rates of unionization than men, employers have seen them as more docile employees (Hagen and Jenson, 1988, p. 10).

There is certainly a neatness of fit between Hagen and Jenson's argument and the overall trajectory of women's employment in the West over the last twenty-five years. However, in criticism it may be argued, in a similar vein to Pollert's (1988) critique of the theory of the 'flexible firm', that state and employer strategies towards increased competitiveness, reliance on market forces, are not new, but rather, a late twentieth-century manifestation of an orthodox capitalist restructuring, through an increase in the rate of exploitation of the labour force. However, whatever the merits of the different arguments, it cannot be denied that the growth in women's paid employment reflects a qualitative difference from previous 'economic regimes'. One problem with this account, however, is that there is a tendency within it to treat women as a reactive category, rather than as active agents. There is no reason to assume (to borrow a phrase from Giddens) that women have an inherently greater capacity to behave as structural and cultural 'dopes' than men, although the kinds of pressures on them will be different. Although, therefore, Hagen and Jenson's broad interpretation of developments in women's employment is extremely insightful, it needs to be modified through an emphasis upon the actively-constructed nature of both employment and the economic relationships between men and women more generally.[13]

Gender and stratification

In conclusion, we will briefly consider the implications of these cross-national comparisons for the debate on gender and stratification. It was argued in earlier chapters that theoretical attempts to operationalize the class structure through the structure of employment have been seriously compromised by the growth of women's employment in the public sphere, as gender appears to be at least as important as class in structuring this division of labour. However (and in contrast to both Marxist and Weberian accounts of class theory), gender relationships, although universal, do not assume a universal form. Thus, in the discussion of particular occupations and industries in the previous chapters, considerable emphasis has been given to the active structuring of gender relationships with them.

The cross-national evidence demonstrates that, at the nation state level, there are similarities which may be observed between them in respect of the employment of women, which are associated with the long-term development of capitalism as a mode of production. (There are, of course, debates about the nature of this development, and indeed, about the concept of capitalism, but they cannot be considered here.)[14] More women have been drawn into the paid labour force with the increasing commodification of all aspects of human production, and more women are employed in flexible, low-level jobs than men. However, we have also seen that there are very substantial differences in the structure of women's paid employment between different countries, relating to both the extent of flexible working by women (this term is used in its very broadest sense), and their individual distribution within the occupational hierarchy. These variations have been related to the multi-faceted and socially constructed nature of gender relations, and they suggest that, as the impact of women's employment on the occupational structure is changing and dynamic, some caution should be exercised as far as the identification of systematic or fixed relationships between women and the occupational structure is concerned. This feature suggests that the 'gender problem' in occupational class analysis can not be conclusively resolved. A flexible approach to the topic, dependent upon both context and circumstance, will continue to be necessary.

This argument may be illustrated through an examination of a recent discussion of the relationship between changes in female employment and developments in the occupational class structure which, despite its many insights, has not been completely successful. Mann (1986) develops a historical account of the relationship between gender and stratification. In agrarian societies, he argues, there was an almost total division between the public and private spheres. Patriarchs ruled in public, and women, when they had any power in the public sphere, held it as 'honorary patriarchs'. Over the eighteenth and nineteenth centuries, both women and economic life were gradually transferred into the public realm as the power of the lineage weakened. However male domination ensured that women were allocated a subordinate role in the public sphere, and a structure of 'neo-patriarchy' emerged to govern male-female relationships. Around the end of the nineteenth century, classes were coming to be significant collective actors in the public sphere: 'A conscious, organized capitalist class was in place in Britain by about 1880, a middle class slightly later, a working class by about 1914' (Mann, 1986, p. 46).[15] Employment is now both public and waged: 'Wage hierarchies are institutionalized, and the large corporations and state departments are organized with charts showing integrated hierarchies. Perhaps these would undermine the particularism of patriarchy and generate a single hierarchy . . . including both men and women?' (ibid.). That is, as a structure of (supposedly) gender-neutral 'places' developed, he asks whether gender (or, more precisely, the impact of neo-patriarchy) will lose its relevance as a property intersecting with orthodox (class) categories (ibid., p. 40).

Mann then argues emphatically that it has not. The continuing presence of occupational segregation is central to his argument. Men's and women's occupations, he asserts, cannot be combined on a single scale. 'Few jobs are occupied interchangeably by men and women and their career patterns differ. Their jobs are just "different"' (ibid., p. 40). Women are clustered into particular occupations, and:

A kind of compromise between patriarchy and a more gendered stratification hierarchy has emerged. Women in the economy now form a number of quasi-class fractions. In each main case they occupy a 'buffer zone' between the men of their own class grouping and the men of the next class grouping down the hierarchy. (Mann, 1986, p. 47).

Women in part-time and unskilled manual employment 'buffer' skilled manual workers (there is an obvious resonance between this point and the argument that unskilled women were recruited to manufacturing during the 'Fordist' era); women in clerical and sales occupations 'buffer' male manual and non-manual workers. Finally, women in lower-level professional jobs (the 'semi-professions'), often in educational and 'caring' occupations, buffer 'an important educational divide within the middle class' (ibid., p. 47).[16] Thus the occupational order comprises gendered, as well as technically and socially defined aggregations within it. Once women have moved into the public sphere, gender becomes a segregating mechanism; economic stratification has become gendered.

Whilst it would not be possible to disagree with the broad conclusions which Mann derives from his analysis, that is, that economic stratification and so the occupational order, is, indeed, gendered, the specificities of his argument cannot be sustained. This is because of the fluid and changing nature of both the occupational order and patterns of occupational segregation. If occupations could be classified into separate 'male' and 'female' hierarchies, as Mann implies, then the problems which gender has presented for stratification theory (and approaches which attempt theoretically to derive the class structure from the occupational structure (see Chapter 1)) would indeed be resolved. However, they cannot be (Crompton, 1988b). There are considerable overlaps between men and women within occupations and occupational categories; occupational segregation is far from complete. Mann's description of 'buffered stratification' corresponds, very roughly, to the occupational divisions that had emerged between men and women in Britain by the end of the 1970s; that is, it has a tendency to be historically and culturally specific. As we have seen, considerable changes have taken place since then, and even more are likely in the future. Many of these changes will be associated with the use of the 'qualifications lever' and other liberal feminist strategies – a feature Mann himself might have been expected to emphasize given his discussion of the emergence of women as independent persons with the development of 'liberal citizenship'.

It may be suggested that one reason why Mann has described what will in all probability be a relatively short-term gendered structuring of occupations as if it were a permanent set of stratification arrangements is that, like Hagen and Jenson's description of the close association of women's employment patterns with first 'Keynsian' and subsequently 'post-Fordist' stages of economic development, his account tends to underplay the role of women as active agents, and the multi-faceted and changing nature of the gender order. The role of liberal feminists in gaining citizenship rights for women, and building the institutions of the British Welfare State is fully acknowledged by Mann. However, his insights in this respect need to be further developed through a more thorough appreciation of the role of the contemporary women's movement (which has brought an emphasis upon 'equal value' and affirmative action rather than equality alone), as well as the structuring of gender identities by individual men and women in a context which is more and more in a state of flux.

One consequence of these developments is that occupational class differences between women appear to be widening at the moment, as women seek to consolidate and improve their labour market positions in competition with men (Rubery, 1988, p. 278). This is not particularly surprising, as there will inevitably be a learning period associated with a change in behaviour on the part of any social group. Given the long-established male dominance within the occupational sphere, it might have been expected that women hoping to succeed within it would follow male patterns to a considerable extent. As long as women remained a minority, and in relatively segregated occupations and/or niches (such as practitioner jobs in pharmacy, the School Meals Service, low level clerical work, and so on), then the dominance of the male pattern might be expected to persist. However, with women's increasing tendency towards long-term, permanent labour force participation, it is likely that this will no longer be the case. It could be argued that part-time work will become the new female pattern, thus perpetuating the male employment model. However, the level of part-time employment amongst women tends to be lower amongst the better qualified. In any case, as we have seen, there are wide variations in the extent of part-time working, and in respect of particular occupations (see the examples of pharmacy and the hotel industry), gender ratios can change. The occupational order will always bear the imprint of gender, but in the present situation, some kind of convergence between male and female patterns is probably more likely in Western industrial societies than the restructuring of a highly segregated occupational matrix.

Notes

1 An interesting sidelight on rational choice theory is that, according to Banton, its application to social relations rests upon the principle of 'prescriptive altruism': 'a rule requiring recognition of binding mutual inter-dependence and a willingness to forego selfish gratification. The capacity for prescriptive altruism is generated in the relationship of mother and child' (1987, pp. 123–4). Thus we find that this version of rational choice theory rests upon stereotypical assumptions relating to the nature of male and female roles, as do the neo-classical theories of 'human capital' and 'new family economics' which it so closely resembles.

2 This discussion does not address the difficult question of the definition of the service class and the allocation of particular occupations to this category. The process of occupational restructuring means that some occupations which have been technically 'de-skilled' will nevertheless still be allocated to service-class categories (Crompton and Jones, 1984).

3 See *Employment Gazette*, March 1988, '1987 Labour force survey – preliminary results', pp. 144–58.

4 Beechey and Perkins argue that 'there is nothing *inherent* in the nature of particular jobs which makes them full-time or part-time. They have been constructed as such, and such constructions are closely related to gender' (1987, pp. 145–6). It may be argued that this argument has a tendency to elide the meanings of 'job' and 'task'. 'Tasks' are performed by people who then have 'jobs' as a consequence. Their discussion cited above refers to the nature of the task, rather than the job.

5 Part-time work is also available in accountancy, but detailed empirical evidence relating to its current nature and extent is lacking.

6 The discussion which follows is not comprehensive. In particular, it does not include any discussion of the structure of women's employment in 'less developed' or Third World countries, or of ethnic minority women in the 'First World'. See Scott (1986) and Mitter (1986).

7 LEST refers to the Laboratoire d'Economie et de Sociologie du Travail, Aix-en-Provence. See Maurice, Sellier and Silvestre (1986).

8 Jenson explains these differences in state policies with reference to the different rates of industrial development, and the nature of trade union movements, in Britain and France. She argues that by the late nineteenth/ early twentieth century women's employment in Britain was already highly concentrated, and the craft unions organized to prevent its spread into new areas. British unions were also protectionist, rather than aggressively class conscious, in their ideology. In contrast, more French women were employed in manufacturing industry, as the lack of a craft base had allowed their penetration as a consequence of de-skilling. French trade unions, in contrast to the British, were revolutionary syndicalist and egalitarian in their ideology. It should be noted that there would not be complete consensus on Jenson's interpretation of the policies of the French state. See Bouillaguet-Bernard and Gauvin, 1988b.

9 The OFCC requires that plans relating to affirmative action should be instituted by all firms obtaining federal contracts.

10 Dale and Glover discuss the considerable difficulties in achieving cross-national comparability in respect of the 'managerial' category, which means that these figures should be used with care. In particular, French coding procedures will result in a considerable under-recording of the 'managerial' category. Their data record that in 1983/4, 11 per cent of women in the USA, compared to 2.4 per cent of women in the UK and 0.2 per cent in France were in 'administrative and managerial' occupations (Dale and Glover, 1987).

11 Del Boca (1988, p. 122) argues that the introduction of equal pay in the 1960s was responsible for the decrease in women's employment throughout the decade that followed. Bettio (1988a), on the other hand, argues that the decline was a consequence of the loss of sex-typed women's jobs.

12 The slower entry of Italy into the full market economy, and the persistence of agriculture, are associated with a particular family structure which has also affected women's employment (See Bettio, 1988b).

13 As in most, if not all, attempts to summarize complex arguments, there has been some misrepresentation of Hagen and Jenson's position. Elsewhere in their discussion they are careful to emphasize that there is no one-way relationship of cause and effect to be specified in explaining the pattern of women's employment (Hagen and Jenson, 1988, p. 5), and that the final outcome, as far as women are concerned, 'will be the product of choices made by all the actors involved, including women themselves' (ibid., p. 11).

14 See Piore and Sabel, 1984; Lash and Urry, 1987.

15 Mann is not entirely precise in his conceptualization of class. Given that he describes women as becoming 'members of such classes' (1986, p. 46) it may be taken to refer to individuals in employment, that is, occupational groupings. However, to describe an 'organized capitalist class' suggests that the term is also being used to describe a more abstract collectivity. For the difficulties in linking 'occupational' and 'abstract' conceptualizations of class, see the discussion in Chapters 1 and 2.

16 Mann also identifies 'passive rentier widows, spinsters and divorced women, and the "sleeping-partner" wives and daughters' (1986, p. 47) as a 'buffer' between capital and labour.

Appendix
Women in professional occupations

The research sponsored by the Joseph Rowntree Memorial Trust was 'Women professionals and part-time work'. It included 36 extended interviews with professionally qualified women in pharmacy, accountancy and banking (interviews in banking have not been used in this book). The interviews were unstructured, and most were carried out by Kay Sanderson. As the research population was small, the sample was not randomly selected but recruited via the network of contacts established during the research. Our background knowledge of the occupations, however, was used to achieve a reasonable mix of women in the various sub-categories within the occupations. The interviews were tape recorded, and transcribed verbatim. Extracts from some of the interviews have been used in Chapters 4 and 5; further details of the interviewees are given below.

Pharmacists
Frances Law (FL): d.o.b. 1940. Married, doctor (consultant). Two children, born 1969, 1970. Present employment: job-share in a hospital pharmacy.
Jennifer Payne (JP): d.o.b. 1962. Married, pharmacist (NHS). No children. Present employment: full-time hospital pharmacy.
Sheila McKay (SMc): d.o.b. 1946, Married, pharmacist (community). Two children, born 1970, 1972. Present employment: full-time community pharmacy.
Susan Green (SG): d.o.b. 1960. Married, pharmacist (community). No children. Present employment: full-time community pharmacy.
Nina Bowyer (NB): d.o.b. 1941. Married, pharmacist (community). Two children, born 1969, 1971. Present employment: community, flexible rising full-time.
Vera Jenkins (VJ): d.o.b. 1933. Married, insurance manager (retired). No children. Present employment: Senior Manager, pharmaceutical industry.
Gina Smith (GS): d.o.b. 1949. Married, BT engineer. Two children, born 1975, 1977. Present employment: full-time hospital pharmacy.

Accountants

Anne Tibble (AT): d.o.b. 1943. CIPFA. Married, Local Authority Officer (Planner). Two children, born 1976, 1981. Not working.

Lucy Smith (LS): d.o.b. 1961. ICAEW. Married, tax consultant. No children. Present employment: full-time finance sector.

Miriam Brown (MB): d.o.b. 1952. ACCA. Married, self-employed businessman. One child, born 1986. Present employment: full-time finance sector.

Janet Colgate (JC): d.o.b. 1958. ICAEW. Married, graduate engineer. No children. Present employment: full-time finance sector.

Nicola Jones (NJ): d.o.b. 1965. ACCA (trainee). Living with partner. No children. Present employment: full-time finance sector.

Sarah Emerson (SE): d.o.b. 1968. ACCA (trainee). Not married. No children. Present employment: full-time finance sector.

Bibliography

Allen, I. (1988), *Any Room at the Top?: a study of doctors and their careers* (London: Policy Studies Institute).

Allen, S. (1982), 'Gender inequality and class formation', in A. Giddens and G. Mackenzie, op. cit.

Althauser, R. P. and Kalleberg, A. L. (1981), 'Firms, occupations, and the structure of labor markets', in I. Berg (ed.), *Sociological Perspectives on Labor Markets* (New York: Academic Press).

Anderson, G. (1976), *Victorian Clerks* (Manchester: Manchester University Press).

Angrist, S. and Almquist, E. M. (1975), *Careers and Contingencies* (New York and London: Dunellen).

Armstrong, P. (1985), 'Changing management control strategies: the role of competition between accountancy and other organisational professions', *Accounting, Organisations and Society*, vol. 10, no. 2, pp. 129–48.

Armstrong, P. (1987), 'The rise of accounting controls in British capitalist enterprises', *Accounting, Organisations and Society*, vol. 12, no. 5, pp. 415–36.

Ashburner, L. (1987), 'The effects of new technology on employment structures in the service sector', PhD thesis, University of Aston in Birmingham.

Atkinson, J. (1984), 'Manpower strategies for flexible organisations', *Personnel Management*, August.

Bagguley, P. (1987), 'Flexibility, restructuring and gender: changing employment in Britain's hotels', Lancaster Regionalism Group Working Paper 24, University of Lancaster, Lancaster.

Bakker, I. (1988), 'Women's employment in comparative perspective', in Jenson, Hagen and Reddy, op. cit.

Banton, M. (1983), *Racial and Ethnic Competition* (Cambridge: Cambridge University Press).

Banton, M. (1987), *Racial Theories* (Cambridge: Cambridge University Press).

Barnes, P. (1984), *The Myth of Mutuality* (London: Pluto).

Barrett, M. (1980), *Women's Oppression Today* (London: Verso).

Barron, R. D. and Norris, G. M. (1976), 'Sexual divisions and the dual labour market', in D. L. Barker and S. Allen (eds), *Feminism and Materialism* (London: Routledge).

Becker, G. (1981), *A Treatise on the Family* (Cambridge, Mass.: Harvard University Press).

Beechey, V. (1979), 'On Patriarchy', *Feminist Review* Part 3, pp. 66–82.

Beechey, V. (1986), 'Women and employment in contemporary Britain', in V. Beechey (ed.), *Women in Britain Today* (Oxford: Oxford University Press).

Beechey, V. and Perkins, T. (1987), *A Matter of Hours: Women, Part-time Work, and the Labour Market* (Cambridge: Polity).

Bernstein, B. (1971), *Class, Codes and Control* (London: Routledge).

Bertaux, D. and Bertaux-Wiame, I. (1981), 'Artisanal bakers in France: how they live and why they survive', in F. Bechhofer and B. Elliott (eds), *The Petite Bourgeoisie: Comparative Studies of an Uneasy Stratum* (London: Macmillan).

Bettio, F. (1988a), 'Sex-typing of occupations, the cycle and restructuring in Italy', in J. Rubery, op. cit.

Bettio, F. (1988b), 'Women, the State and the family in Italy: problems of female participation in historical perspective', in J. Rubery, op. cit.

Bielby, W. T. and Baron, J. N. (1984), 'A woman's place is with other women: sex segregation within organisations', in B. F. Reskin (ed.), *Sex Segregation in the Workplace* (Washington: National Academy Press).

Blackburn, R. H. (1967), *Union Character and Social Class* (London: Batsford).

del Boca, D. (1988), 'Women in a changing workplace: the case of Italy', in Jenson, Hagen and Reddy, op. cit.

Boléat, M. (1986), *The Building Society Industry* (2nd edn) (London: George Allen & Unwin).

Bone, A. (1980), *The Effect on Women's Opportunities of Teacher Training Cuts* (Manchester: Equal Opportunities Commission).

Bouchier, D. (1983), *The Feminist Challenge* (London: Macmillan).

Bouillaguet-Bernard, P. and Gauvin, A. (1988a), 'Female labour reserves and the restructuring of employment in booms and slumps in France', in J. Rubery (ed.) *Women and Recession* (London: Routledge).

Bouillaguet-Bernard, P. and Gauvin, A. (1988b), 'Women, the State and the family in France: contradictions of State policy for women's employment', in J. Rubery (ed.) *Women and Recession* (London: Routledge).

Bowlby, J. (1953), *Child Care and the Growth of Love* (Harmondsworth: Penguin).

Braverman, H. (1974), *Labor and Monopoly Capital* (New York: Monthly Review Press).

Brenner, J. and Ramas, M. (1984), 'Rethinking women's oppression', *New Left Review*, no. 144, pp. 33–71.

Burrell, G. (1984), 'Sexual organisational analysis', *Organizational Studies*, vol. 5, no. 2, pp. 97–118.

Burrell, G. (1987), 'No accounting for sexuality', *Accounting, Organisations and Society*, vol. 12, no. 1, pp. 89–101.

Byrne, E. M. (1978), *Women and Education* (London: Tavistock).

Caplow, T. (1966), *The Sociology of Work* (Originally published in 1954, University of Minnesota Press) (New York: McGraw-Hill, 1966).

Carter, M. J. and Carter, S. B. (1981), 'Women's recent progress in the professions or, women get a ticket to ride after the gravy train has left the station', *Feminist Studies*, vol. 7, no. 3, pp. 477–504.

Casey, B. and Creigh, S. (1988), 'Self-employment in Great Britain: its definition in the Labour Force Survey, in Tax and Social Security Law and in Labour Law', *Work Employment and Society*, vol. 2, no. 3, pp. 381–91.

Chiplin, B. and Sloane, P. J. (1982), *Tackling Discrimination at the Workplace* (Cambridge: Cambridge University Press).

Chivers, T. S. (1973), 'The proletarianisation of a service worker', *Sociological Review*, vol. 21, pp. 633–56.

Chodorow, N. (1978), *The Reproduction of Mothering* (Los Angeles: University of California Press).

Civil Service National Whitley Council Committee (1946), *Marriage Bar in the Civil Service*, Cmnd. 6886, 31 March (London: HMSO).

Cockburn, C. (1986), 'The relations of technology', in R. Crompton and M. Mann, op. cit.

Cohn, S. (1986), *The Process of Occupational Sex-Typing* (Philadelphia: Temple).

Collins, R. (1979), *The Credential Society* (Orlando, Florida: Academic Press).

Collinson, D. and Knights, D. (1986), ' "Men only": theories and practices of job segregation in insurance', in D. Knights and D. Collinson (eds), *Gender and the Labour Process* (Aldershot: Gower).

Connell, R. W. (1985), 'Theorising Gender', *Sociology*, vol. 19, no. 2, pp. 260–72.

Connell, R. W. (1987), *Gender and Power* (Cambridge: Polity).

Coyle, A. (1982), 'Sex and skill in the organisation of the clothing industry', in J. West (ed.), *Women, Work and the Labour Market* (London: Routledge).

Craig, C., Tarling, R. and Wilkinson, F. (1982), *Labour Market Structure, Industrial Organisation and the Low Pay* (Cambridge: Cambridge University Press).

Craig, C., Garnsey, E. and Rubery, J. (1985), *Payment structures and smaller firms: women's employment in segmented labour markets*, Research Paper no. 48 (London: Department of Employment).

Crompton, R. (1980), 'Class mobility in modern Britain' (critical note), *Sociology*, vol. 14, no. 1, pp. 117–19.

Crompton, R. (1987), 'Gender, status, and professionalism', *Sociology*, vol. 21, no. 3, pp. 413–28.

Crompton, R. (1988a), 'Occupational segregation', Working Paper 2: the economic and social research council: the Social Change and Economic Life Initiative, ESRC, Swindon.

Crompton, R. (1988b), 'The feminisation of clerical work since the Second World War', in G. Anderson (ed.), *The White Blouse Revolution* (Manchester: Manchester University Press).

Crompton, R. (1989), 'Women in banking', *Work, Employment and Society*, vol. 3, no. 2, pp. 141–56.

Crompton, R. and Jones, G. (1984), *White-collar proletariat: de-skilling and gender in the clerical labour process* (London: Macmillan).

Crompton, R. and Jones, G. (1988), 'Doing research in white-collar organisations', in A. Bryman (ed.), *Doing Research in Organizations* (London: Routledge).

Crompton, R. and Mann, M. (eds) (1986), *Gender and Stratification* (Cambridge: Polity).

Crompton, R. and Sanderson, K. (1986), 'Credentials and careers: some implications of the increase in professional qualifications amongst women', *Sociology*, vol. 20, no. 1, pp. 25–42.

Crompton, R. and Sanderson, K. (1987), 'Where did all the bright girls go?', *Quarterly Journal of Social Affairs*, April, pp. 135–47.

Crompton, R. and Sanderson, K. (forthcoming), 'The gendered restructuring of employment in the finance sector'.

Cunnison, S. (1983), 'Participation in local union organisation: school meals staff, a case study', in E. Gamarnikow, D. Morgan, J. Purvis and D. Taylorson (eds), *Gender Class and Work* (London: Heinemann).

Dale, A. (1987), 'Occupational inequality, gender and life-cycle', *Work, Employment & Society*, vol. 1, no. 3, pp. 326–51.

Dale, A. and Bamford, C. (1988), 'Temporary workers: cause for concern or complacency?', *Work, Employment & Society*, vol. 2, no. 2, pp. 191–209.

Dale, A. and Glover, J. (1987), 'A comparative analysis of women's employment patterns in the UK, France and USA', Department of Sociology, University of Surrey, Guildford.

Davidoff, L. (1979), 'The separation of home and work? Landladies and lodgers in nineteenth and twentieth century England', in S. Burman (ed.), *Fit Work for Women* (London: Croom Helm).

Davies, G. (1981), *Building Societies and their Branches – A Regional Economic Survey* (London: Franey).

Davis, K. and Moore, W. E. (1964), 'Some principles of stratification', reprinted in L. A. Coser and B. Rosenberg (eds), *Sociological Theory* (London: Collier-Macmillan).

Deem, R. (1978), *Women and Schooling* (London: Routledge & Kegan Paul).

Delphy, C. (1977), *The Main Enemy: a materialist analysis of women's oppression*, Explorations in Feminism No. 3 (London: Women's Research and Resources Centre).

Delphy, C. and Leonard, D. (1986), 'Class analysis, gender analysis, and the family', in R. Crompton and M. Mann, op. cit.

Dex, S. (1984), 'Women's work histories: an analysis of the women and employment survey', Research Paper No. 46 (London: Department of Employment).

Dex, S. (1985), *The Sexual Division of Work* (Sussex: Wheatsheaf).

Dex, S. (1988), *Women's Attitudes towards Work* (Basingstoke: Macmillan).

Dex, S. and Shaw, L. B. (1986), *British and American Women at Work* (Basingstoke: Macmillan).

Dex, S. and Walters, P. (forthcoming), 'Women's working experience in France and Britain', in S. MacRae (ed.), *Keeping Women In* (London: Policy Studies Institute).

Dingwall, R. (1983), 'In the beginning was the work . . . reflections on the genesis of occupations', *Sociological Review*, vol. 31, pp. 605–24.

Dore, R. P. (1976), *The Diploma Disease* (London: Allen & Unwin).

Duke, V. and Edgell, S. (1987), 'The operationalisation of class in British sociology: theoretical and empirical considerations', *The British Journal of Sociology*, vol. XXXVIII, no. 4, pp. 445–63.

Dworkin, A. (1981), *Pornography: Men Possessing Women* (London: The Women's Press).

Eisenstein, Z. (1981), *The Radical Future of Liberal Feminism* (New York: Longman).

Elias, P. and Main, B. (1982), *Women's Working Lives*, IER Research Report (Coventry: University of Warwick).

Engels, F. (1940), *The Origin of the Family, Private Property and the State* (London: Lawrence and Wishart).

Equal Opportunities Commission (EOC) (1985), *Formal Investigation Report: Leeds Permanent Building Society* (Manchester: EOC).

Equal Opportunities Commission (1987), *Interim Report of the Commission's agreement with Barclay's Bank PLC* (Manchester: EOC).

Esland, G. M. (1976), 'Professions and professionalism', Unit 12 of DE351 *People and Work* (Milton Keynes: Open University Press).

Etzioni, A. (1969), *The Semi-Professions and their Organisation* (New York: Free Press).

Finnegan, R. (1985), 'Working outside formal employment', in R. Deem and G. Salaman (eds), *Work Culture and Society* (Milton Keynes: Open University Press).

Freear, J. (1984), 'An historical perspective', in B. Carsberg and T. Hope (eds), *Current Issues in Accounting* (2nd edn) (Oxford: Philip Allan).

Friedan, B. (1975), *The Feminine Mystique* (Harmondsworth: Penguin).

Gabriel, Y. (1988), *Working Lives in Catering* (London: Routledge & Kegan Paul).

Game, A. and Pringle, R. (1984), *Gender at Work* (London: Pluto Press).

Garnsey, E. (1978), 'Women's work and theories of class and stratification', *Sociology*, vol. 12, no. 2, pp. 223–43.

Gellner, E. (1985), 'Positivism against Hegelianism', in E. Gellner, *Relativism and the Social Sciences* (Cambridge: Cambridge University Press).

Gerth, H. H. and Mills, C. W. (eds) (1948), *From Max Weber: Essays in Sociology* (London: Routledge & Kegan Paul).

Giddens, A. (1973), *The Class Structure of the Advanced Societies* (London: Hutchinson).

Giddens, A. (1984), *The Constitution of Society* (Cambridge: Polity Press).

Giddens, A. and Mackenzie, G. (eds) (1982), *Social Class and the Division of Labour* (Cambridge: Cambridge University Press).

Goldthorpe, J. H. (1966), 'Attitudes and behaviour of car assembly workers: a deviant case and a theoretical critique', *British Journal of Sociology*, vol. XVII, no. 3, pp. 227–44.

Goldthorpe, J. H. (1980), 'Reply to Crompton', *Sociology*, vol. 14, no. 1, pp. 121–3.

Goldthorpe, J. H. (1982), 'On the service class, its formation and future', in A. Giddens and G. Mackenzie, op. cit.

Goldthorpe, J. H. (1983), 'Women and class analysis: in defence of the conventional view', *Sociology*, vol. 17, no. 4, pp. 465–88.

Goldthorpe, J. H. (1984), 'Women and class analysis: a reply to the replies', *Sociology*, vol. 18, no. 4, pp. 491–9.

Goldthorpe, J. H. (with C. Llewellyn and C. Payne) (1987), *Social Mobility and Class Structure in Modern Britain* (2nd edn) (Oxford: Clarendon Press).

Goldthorpe, J. H. (1988), 'Employment, class and mobility: a critique of liberal and Marxist theories of long-term change', in H. Haferkamp and N. Smelser (eds), *Theories of Long-Term Social Change* (University of California Press).

Goldthorpe, J. H., Lockwood, D., Bechhofer, F. and Platt, J. (1968), *The Affluent Worker: Industrial Attitudes and Behaviour* (Cambridge: Cambridge University Press).

Gough, T. J. (1982), *The Economics of Building Societies* (London and Basingstoke: Macmillan).

Granovetter, M. (1985), 'Economic action and social structure: the problem of embeddedness', *American Journal of Sociology*, vol. 91, no. 3, pp. 481–510.

Guerrier, Y. (1986), 'Hotel manager – an unsuitable job for a woman?', *Service Industries Journal*, pp. 227–40.

Hagen, E. and Jenson, J. (1988), 'Paradoxes and promises: work and politics in the post-war years', in J. Jenson, E. Hagen and C. Reddy (eds), op. cit.

Hakim, C. (1979), 'Occupational segregation', Research Paper No. 9, November (London: Department of Employment).

Hakim, C. (1981), 'Job segregation: trends in the 1970s', *Employment Gazette*, December, pp. 521–9.

Hakim, C. (1987), 'Trends in the flexible workforce', *Employment Gazette*, November, pp. 549–60.

Handy, C. (1984), *Understanding Organisations* (Harmondsworth: Penguin).

Hartmann, H. (1979), 'Capitalism, patriarchy and job segregation by sex', in Z. Eisenstein (ed.), *Capitalist Patriarchy and the case for Socialist Feminism* (New York: Monthly Review Press).

Hartmann, H. I. (1981), 'The unhappy marriage of Marxism and feminism: towards a more progressive union', in L. Sargent (ed.) *Women and Revolution* (Boston: South End Press).

Hearn, J. (1982), 'Notes on patriarchy, professionalization and the semi-professions', *Sociology*, vol. 16, no. 2, pp. 184–202.

Hearn, J. and Parkin, W. (1987), *'Sex' at 'Work': The Power and Paradox of Organisational Sexuality* (Sussex: Wheatsheaf).

Heath, A. and Britten, N. (1984), 'Women's jobs do make a difference', *Sociology*, vol. 18, no. 4, pp. 475–90.

Heath, A., Jowell, R. and Curtice, J. (1985), *How Britain Votes* (Oxford: Pergamon).

Hencke, D. (1978), *Colleges in Crisis* (Harmondsworth: Penguin).

Heritage, J. (1983), 'Feminisation and Unionisation: a case-study from banking', in E. Gamarnikow, D. Morgan, J. Purvis and D. Taylorson, op. cit.

Hindess, B. (1987), *Politics and Class Analysis* (Oxford: Blackwell).

Hirsch, F. and Goldthorpe, J. H. (eds) (1978), *The Political Economy of Inflation* (London: Martin Robertson).

Holmwood, J. and Stewart, A. (1983), 'The role of contradictions in modern theories of social stratification', *Sociology*, vol. 17, no. 2, pp. 234–54.

Industrial Relations Review and Report (IR-RR) No. 356 (1985), November pp. 9–11.

Jenson, J. (1986), 'Gender and reproduction: or babies and the state', *Studies in Political Economy*, vol. 20, pp. 9–46.

Jenson, J. (1988), 'The limits of 'and the' discourse: French women as marginal workers', in J. Jenson, E. Hagen and C. Reddy, op. cit.

Jenson, J., Hagen, E., and Reddy, C. (eds) (1988), *Feminization of the Labour Force: Paradoxes and Promises* (New York: Oxford University Press).

Johnson, T. J. (1972), *Professions and Power* (London: Macmillan).

Johnson, T. J. (1980), 'Work and power', in G. Esland and G. Salaman (eds), *The Politics of Work and Occupations* (Milton Keynes: Open University Press).

Kanter, R. (1976), *Men and Women of the Corporation* (New York: Basic Books).

Keat, R. and Urry, J. (1975), *Social Theory as Science* (London: Routledge).

Kreckel, R. (1980), 'Unequal opportunity structure and labour market segmentation', *Sociology*, vol. 14, pp. 525–50.

Kreckel, R. (1988), 'Class and gender: some reflections on the theoretical implications of gender-blindness' (unpublished).

Labour Research (1986), 'The fast food profits race', vol. 75, June, no. 6, pp. 10–13.

Land, H. (1983), Poverty and gender: the distribution of resources within the family', in M. Brown (ed.) *The Structure of Disadvantage* (London: Heinemann).

Lash, S. and Urry, J. (1987), *The End of Organized Capitalism* (Cambridge: Polity).

Lee, D. (1981), 'Skill, craft and class', *Sociology*, vol. 15, no. 1, pp. 56–78.

Lewis, J. (1980), *The Politics of Motherhood: Child and Maternal Welfare in England 1900–1939* (London: Croom Helm).

Lewis, J. (1984), *Women in England 1870–1950: Sexual Divisions and Social Change* (Sussex: Wheatsheaf).

Llewellyn, C. (1981), 'Occupational mobility and the use of the comparative method', in H. Roberts (ed.), *Doing Feminist Research* (London: Routledge).

Lockwood, D. (1964), 'Social integration and system integration', in G. K. Zollschan and W. Hirsch (eds), *Explorations in Social Change* (Boston: Houghton Mifflin).

Lockwood, D. (1966), 'Sources of variation in working class images of society', *Sociological Review*, vol. 14, no. 3, pp. 244–67.

Lockwood, D. (1982), 'Fatalism: Durkheim's hidden theory of order', in A. Giddens and D. Mackenzie, op. cit.

Lockwood, D. (1986), 'Class, status and gender', in R. Crompton and M. Mann, op. cit.

Loveridge, R. (1987), 'Stigma: the manufacture of disadvantage', in G. Lee and R. Loveridge (eds), *The Manufacture of Disadvantage* (Milton Keynes: Open University Press).

Lowe, G. S. (1987), *The Feminization of Clerical Work: Women and the Administrative Revolution in Canada, 1901–31* (Cambridge: Polity).

Lown, J. (1983), 'Not so much a factory, more a form of patriarchy: gender and class during industrialisation', in E. Gamarnikow, D. Morgan, J. Purvis and D. Taylorson, op. cit.

MacCormack, C. and Strathern, M. (eds) (1980), *Nature, Culture and Gender* (Cambridge: Cambridge University Press).

S. MacRae (ed.) *Keeping Women In*, Policy Studies Institute (London, forthcoming).

Mallier, A. T. and Rosser, M. J. (1985), 'Changes in occupational segregation in Britain, 1971–1981', *Equal Opportunities International*, vol. 4, part 2, pp. 34–9.

Mann, M. (1970), 'The social cohesion of liberal democracy', *American Sociological Review*, vol. 35, pp. 423–39.

Mann, M. (1979), 'Idealism and materialism in sociological theory', in J. W. Freiberg (ed.), *Critical Sociology* (Boston: Halstead Press).

Mann, M. (1986), 'A Crisis in stratification theory?', in R. Crompton and M. Mann, op. cit.

Mars, G. and Nicod, M. (1984), *The World of Waiters* (London: Allen & Unwin).

Marshall, G. (1986), 'The workplace culture of a licensed restaurant', *Theory, Culture and Society*, vol. 3, no. 1, pp. 33–47.

Marshall, G., Newby, H., Rose, D. and Vogler, C. (1988), *Social Class in Modern Britain* (London: Hutchinson).

Marshall, T. H. (1951), 'Citizenship and social class', in T. H. Marshall, *Sociology at the Crossroads* (London: Tavistock).

Martin, J. and Roberts, C. (1984), *Women and Employment: a Lifetime Perspective* (London: HMSO).

Marx, K. (1962), 'The eighteenth Brumaire of Louis Bonaparte', in K. Marx and F. Engels, *Selected Works*, Vol. 1 (Moscow: Foreign Languages Publishing House).

Marx, K. and Engels, F. (1962), 'Manifesto of the Communist Party', in K. Marx and F. Engels, *Selected Works*, Vol. 1 (London: Lawrence & Wishart).

Matthaei, J. (1982), *An Economic History of Women in America* (Brighton: Harvester).

Maurice, M., Sellier, F. and Silvestre, J.-J. (1986), *The Social Foundations of Industrial Power* (trans. A. Goldhammer) (Mass.: MIT Press).

McIntosh, M. (1978), 'The State and the oppression of women', in A. Kuhn and A. Wolpe (eds), *Feminism and Materialism* (London: Routledge).

Medlik, S. (1972), *A Profile of the Hotel and Catering Industry* (London: Heinemann).

Merton, R. K. (1965a), 'Manifest and latent functions', in R. K. Merton, *Social Theory and Social Structure* (New York: Free Press).

Merton, R. K. (1965b), 'Social structure and anomie', in R. K. Merton, *Social Theory and Social Structure* (New York: Free Press).

Milkman, R. (1983), 'Female factory labour and industrial structure: control and conflict over "women's place" in auto and electrical manufacturing', *Politics and Society*, pp. 159–203.

Mincer, J. and Polachek, S. (1974), 'Family investments in human capital: earnings of women', *Journal of Political Economy*, no. 82, pp. 76–108.

Mitchell, J. (1975), *Psychoanalysis and Feminism* (Harmondsworth: Penguin).

Mitchell, J. C. (1983), 'Case and situation analysis', *Sociological Review*, vol. 31, pp. 187–211.

Mitter, S. (1986), *Common Fate, Common Bond* (London: Pluto).

Murgatroyd, L. (1982), 'Gender and occupational stratification', *Sociological Review*, vol. 30, no. 4, pp. 574–602.

Murgatroyd, L. (1985), 'Occupational stratification and gender', in *Localities, Class and Gender* Lancaster Regionalism Group (London: Pion).

Myrdal, A. and Klein, V. (1956), *Women's Two Roles* (London: Routledge & Kegan Paul).

Newson, J. and Newson, E. (1963), *Patterns of Infant Care in an Urban Community* (Harmondsworth: Penguin).

Oakley, A. (1972), *Sex, Gender and Society* (London: Temple Smith).

Oakley, A. (1981), *Subject Women* (Oxford: Martin Robertson).

OECD (1985), *The Integration of Women into the Economy* (Paris: OECD).

O'Neill, J. (1987), 'The disciplinary society: from Weber to Foucault', *The British Journal of Sociology*, vol. XXXVII, no. 1, pp. 42–60.

Ouchi, W. S. (1981), *Theory Z* (Massachusetts: Addison-Wesley).

Owen, S. J. (1987), 'Household production and economic efficiency: arguments for and against domestic specialisation', *Work, Employment and Society*, vol. 1, no. 2, pp. 157–78.

Oxenham, J. (ed.) (1984), *Education versus Qualifications? A Study of Relationships between Education, Selection for Employment and the Productivity of Labour* (London: George Allen & Unwin).

Pahl, R. (1984), *Divisions of Labour* (Oxford: Blackwell).

Pahl, R. E. and Wallace, C. D. (1988), 'Neither angels in marble nor rebels in red: privatization and working-class consciousness', in D. Rose (ed.), *Social Stratification and Economic Change* (London: Hutchinson).

Parkin, F. (ed.) (1974), *The Social Analysis of Class Structure* (London: Tavistock).

Paukert, L. (1984), 'The employment and unemployment of women in OECD countries' (Paris: OECD).

Pearson, R. (1988), 'Female workers in the First and Third World: the greening of woman's labour', in R. E. Pahl (ed.), *On Work* (Oxford: Blackwell).

Perrow, C. (1972), *Complex Organisations: A Critical Essay* (Glenview, Ill.: Scott, Foresman & Co.).

Peters, T. J. and Waterman, R. H. (1982), *In Search of Excellence* (New York: Harper & Row).

Phillips, A. and Taylor, B. (1980), 'Sex and skill: notes towards a feminist economics', *Feminist Review*, no. 6, pp. 79–88.

Piore, M. J. and Sabel, E. (1984), *The Second Industrial Divide* (New York: Basic Books).

Polanyi, K. (1957), *The Great Transformation* (Boston: Beacon Press).

Pollert, A. (1981), *Girls, Wives, Factory Lives* (London and Basingstoke: Macmillan).

Pollert, A. (1988), 'The "Flexible Firm": fixation or fact?', *Work, Employment and Society*, vol. 2, no. 3, pp. 281–316.

Popper, K. (1972), *Objective Knowledge* (Oxford: Oxford University Press).

Power, M. (1988), 'Women, the State and the family in the US: Reaganomics and the experience of women', in J. Rubery, op. cit.

Purcell, K. G. (1986), 'Gender and experience at work: an ethnographic study of work and social interaction in a manufacturing workshop', PhD thesis, University of Manchester.

Prandy, K. (1986), 'Similarities of lifestyle and occupations of women', in R. Crompton and M. Mann, op. cit.

Rajan, A. (1987), *Services – The Second Industrial Revolution?* (London: Butterworth).

Renshall, M. (1977), 'A short survey of the accounting profession', in B. Carsberg and T. Hope (eds), *Current Issues in Accounting* (1st edn) (Oxford: Philip Allan).

Reskin, B. F. (ed.) (1984), *Sex Segregation in the Workplace* (Washington, DC: National Academy Press).

Reskin, B. F. and Hartmann, H. I. (1986), *Women's Work, Men's Work* (Washington, DC: National Academy Press).

Rex, J. (1983), *Race Relations in Sociological Theory* (revised ed.) (London: Routledge & Kegan Paul).

Riley, D. (1983), *War in the Nursery: Theories of the Child and Mother* (London: Virago).

Robbins Report (1963), *The Demand for Places in Higher Education* (London: HMSO).

Roberts, B., Finnegan, R. and Gallie, D. (eds) (1985), *New Approaches to Economic Life* (Manchester: Manchester University Press).

Robinson, E. (1968), *The New Polytechnics* (Harmondsworth: Penguin).

Robinson, O. and Wallace, J. (1983), 'Employment trends in the hotel and catering industry in Great Britain', *Service Industries Journal*, pp. 260–78.

Royal Commission on Equal Pay (1946), Cmnd. 6937 (London: HMSO).

Rubery, J. (1978), 'Structured labour markets, worker organisation and low pay', *Cambridge Journal of Economics*, vol. 2, pp. 17–36.

Rubery, J. (ed.) (1988), *Women and Recession* (London: Routledge & Kegan Paul).

Rubery, J. and Tarling, R. (1988), 'Women's employment in declining Britain', in J. Rubery (ed.), *Women and Recession* (London: Routledge & Kegan Paul).

Rueschemeyer, D. (1986), *Power and the Division of Labour* (Cambridge: Polity).

Scott, A. (1986a), 'Industrialization, gender segregation, and stratification theory', in R. Crompton and M. Mann, op. cit.

Scott, J. W. (1986b), 'Gender: a useful category of historical analysis', *The American Historical Review*, vol. 91, no. 5, pp. 1053–75.

Seccombe, W. (1974), 'The housewife and her labour under capitalism', *New Left Review*, no. 83, pp. 3–24.

Siltanen, J. (1986), 'Domestic responsibilities and the structuring of employment', in R. Crompton and M. Mann, op. cit.

Silverstone, R. (1980), 'Accountancy', in R. Silverstone and A. Ward (eds), *Careers of Professional Women* (London: Croom Helm).

Simpson, R. L. and Simpson, I. H. (1969), 'Women and bureaucracy in the semi-professions', in A. Etzioni (ed.), *The Semi-Professions and their Organization* (New York: Free Press).

Solomons, D. and Berridge, T. M. (1974), (Solomons Report), 'Prospectus for a profession: the report of the long range enquiry into the education and training for the accountancy profession', (London: Advisory Board for Accounting Education).

Stacey, M. (1981), 'The division of labour revisited or overcoming the two Adams', in P. Abrams, R. Deem, J. Finch and P. Rock (eds), *Practice and Progress: British Sociology 1950–1980* (London: George Allen & Unwin).

Stanworth, M. (1984), 'Women and class analysis: a reply to Goldthorpe', *Sociology*, vol. 18, no. 2, pp. 159–70.

Steinberg, R. (1988), 'The unsubtle revolution: women, the State, and equal employment', in J. Jenson, E. Hagen and C. Reddy, op. cit.

Stewart, A., Prandy, K. and Blackburn, R. M. (1980), *Social Stratification and Occupations* (London and Basingstoke: Macmillan).

Strober, M. (1984), 'Toward a general theory of occupational sex segregation: the case of public school teaching', in B. F. Reskin, op. cit.

Summerfield, P. (1984), *Women Workers in the Second World War* (London: Croom Helm).

Supple, B. (1970), *The Royal Exchange Assurance: A History of British Assurance 1720–1970* (Cambridge: Cambridge University Press).

Thompson, P. and Bannon, E. (1985), *Working the System: the Shop Floor and New Technology* (London: Pluto Press).

Tinker, A. M. (1980), 'Towards a political economy of accounting', *Accounting, Organizations & Society*, pp. 147–60.

Walby, S. (1986), *Patriarchy at Work* (Cambridge: Polity).

Walby, S. (1988), 'Gender politics and social theory', *Sociology*, vol. 22, no. 2, pp. 215–32.

Walton, J. K. (1978), *The Blackpool Landlady* (Manchester: Manchester University Press).

Watts, R. L. and Zimmerman, J. L. (1983), 'Agency problems, auditing and the theory of the firm', *Journal of Law and Economics*, vol. 26, no. 3, pp. 613–34.

Weber, M. (1948), 'Bureaucracy' in H. Gerth and C. W. Mills (eds), *From Max Weber* (London: Routledge & Kegan Paul).

Wedderburn, Lord (1986), *The Worker and the Law* (Harmondsworth: Penguin).

Wickham, A. (1986), *Women and Training* (Milton Keynes: Open University Press).

Wilson, E. (1977), *Women and the Welfare State* (London: Tavistock).

Wood, E. M. (1986), *The Retreat from Class* (London: Verso).

Wood, E. M. (1988), 'Capitalism and human emancipation', *New Left Review*, vol. 167, pp. 3–20.

Wright, E. O. (1980), 'Class and occupation', *Theory and Society*, vol. 9, pp. 177–214.

Wright, E. O. (1985), *Classes* (London: Verso).

Wright, E. O. and Martin, B. (1987), 'The transformation of the American class structure, 1960–1980', *American Journal of Sociology*, vol. 93, no. 1, pp. 1–29.

Wright, E. O. (1989), 'Women in the Class Structure', *Politics and Society*, vol. 17, no. 1, pp. 35–66.

Wrong, D. (1966), 'The oversocialized conception of man in modern sociology', reprinted in L. A. Coser and B. Rosenberg (eds), *Sociological Theory* (London: Collier-Macmillan).

Yeandle, S. (1984), *Women's Working Lives: Patterns and Strategies* (London: Tavistock).

Index